To: Sue   *Christmas 2011*

BettyCrocker

cooking
basics

Recipes and Tips to Cook with Confidence

Love, Keith, Dianne.
Whimsy, Wylie + Moxie

WILEY

Wiley Publishing, Inc.

General Mills

Betty Crocker Kitchens

Publisher, Cookbooks: Maggie Gilbert/ Lynn Vettel

Manager and Editor, Cookbooks: Lois Tlusty

Food Editor: Jann Atkins

Recipe Development and Testing: Betty Crocker Kitchens

Photography: General Mills Photography Studios and Image Library

Photographers: Chuck Nields and Scott Anderson

Food Stylists: Nancy Johnson, Sharon Harding and Amy Peterson

Wiley Publishing, Inc.

Publisher: Natalie Chapman

Executive Editor: Anne Ficklen

Editor: Adam Kowit

Production Editor: Alda Trabucchi

Cover Design: Suzanne Sunwoo

Art Director: Tai Blanche

Photography Art Direction: Judy Meyer and Mary Johnson

Interior Design and Layout: Tai Blanche and Holly Wittenberg

Manufacturing Manager: Kevin Watt

Prop Stylist: Veronica Smith

FIND MORE GREAT IDEAS AND SHOP
FOR NAME-BRAND HOUSEWARES AT

Betty Crocker.com

Published by Wiley Publishing, Inc., Hoboken, New Jersey

Published simultaneously in Canada

Library of Congress Cataloging-in-Publication Data:

Crocker, Betty.
  [Cooking basics]
  Betty Crocker cooking basics : recipes and tips to cook with confidence / Betty Crocker editors.
    p. cm.
  Rev. ed.: New York : Macmillan, c1998.
  Includes index.
  ISBN 978-0-470-11135-2 (cloth)
  1. Cookery. I. Title. II. Title: Cooking basics.
  TX714.C7617 2008
  641.5—dc22

                    2007039336

Printed in China

10 9 8 7 6 5 4 3 2 1

Dear Friends,

Maybe, as you were growing up, you picked up some cooking skills here and there, but you still want someone to walk you through a recipe. Or perhaps you've got three or four recipes mastered but you're tired of eating the same things and want to broaden your horizons. Whatever the reason, you need to feed yourself—and possibly others—and you're looking to increase your confidence in the kitchen. You've come to the right place.

Betty Crocker Cooking Basics is here to help you every step of the way. The recipes are simple to follow, the ingredients easy to find and the flavors will keep you coming back again and again. The helpful Cook's Tips and how-to photos will assist you through each recipe.

In addition to recipes, we've included the low-down on essential equipment, a glossary of cooking terms and techniques, goof-proof menus for get-togethers (including the often-intimidating Thanksgiving) and helpful food safety information.

If you've ever found yourself wondering what the difference is between dicing and mincing, how many teaspoons in a table-spoon or whether the fork goes on the left or right of your plate this cookbook is the resource for you.

So, come on, what are you waiting for? Roll up your sleeves and let's get cooking!

Happy Cooking,

Betty Crocker

CONTENTS

The BASICS of GETTING STARTED

Understanding the Recipe

First things first: Read all the way through the recipe before you do anything else. It sounds like a no-brainer, but when you're eager to get cooking, it's easy to jump in before you realize you don't have an ingredient you need.

Before you start, ask yourself:

- Do I have all the ingredients to make the recipe?
- Do I have all the tools and equipment to make the recipe?
- Do I understand the directions within the recipe?
- Do I have the time it takes to make the recipe?

When you can answer "yes" to these questions, go ahead and start the recipe. For recipes that require baking, check your oven and make sure the racks are where you need them. This usually means the rack should be near the middle.

The first time you make a recipe, it's a good idea to follow the directions and ingredients exactly. Once you taste the results, you're in a better position to tinker with the ingredients. Don't be afraid to make notes on the page as you go. Want to up the garlic level next time? Write it down. The more you cook, the more you'll learn about ingredients and how to make changes that suit your taste.

Lastly, while no one looks forward to cleanup, you'll find it's a lot easier to wash utensils or rinse and put them in the dishwasher as you use them. That way, when you get to the end of the recipe, you can focus on the fantastic food you've just prepared and not the mess you left in the kitchen.

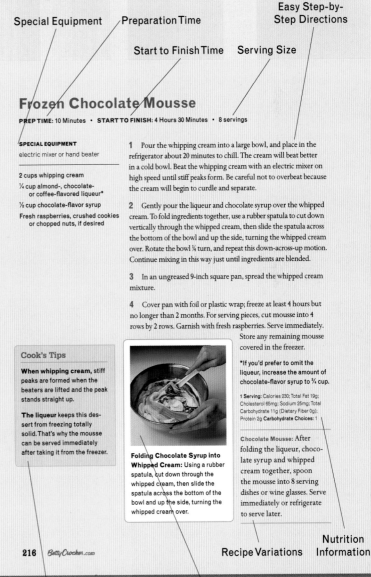

Special Equipment   Preparation Time   Easy Step-by-Step Directions

Start to Finish Time   Serving Size

Frozen Chocolate Mousse

PREP TIME: 10 Minutes • START TO FINISH: 4 Hours 30 Minutes • 8 servings

SPECIAL EQUIPMENT
electric mixer or hand beater

2 cups whipping cream
¼ cup almond-, chocolate- or coffee-flavored liqueur*
½ cup chocolate-flavor syrup
Fresh raspberries, crushed cookies or chopped nuts, if desired

1 Pour the whipping cream into a large bowl, and place in the refrigerator about 20 minutes to chill. The cream will beat better in a cold bowl. Beat the whipping cream with an electric mixer on high speed until stiff peaks form. Be careful not to overbeat because the cream will begin to curdle and separate.

2 Gently pour the liqueur and chocolate syrup over the whipped cream. To fold ingredients together, use a rubber spatula to cut down vertically through the whipped cream, then slide the spatula across the bottom of the bowl and up the side, turning the whipped cream over. Rotate the bowl ¼ turn, and repeat this down-across-up motion. Continue mixing in this way just until ingredients are blended.

3 In an ungreased 9-inch square pan, spread the whipped cream mixture.

4 Cover pan with foil or plastic wrap; freeze at least 4 hours but no longer than 2 months. For serving pieces, cut mousse into 4 rows by 2 rows. Garnish with fresh raspberries. Serve immediately. Store any remaining mousse covered in the freezer.

*If you'd prefer to omit the liqueur, increase the amount of chocolate-flavor syrup to ¾ cup.

1 Serving: Calories 230; Total Fat 19g; Cholesterol 65mg; Sodium 25mg; Total Carbohydrate 11g (Dietary Fiber 0g); Protein 2g Carbohydrate Choices: 1

Chocolate Mousse: After folding the liqueur, chocolate syrup and whipped cream together, spoon the mousse into 8 serving dishes or wine glasses. Serve immediately or refrigerate to serve later.

Cook's Tips

When whipping cream, stiff peaks are formed when the beaters are lifted and the peak stands straight up.

The liqueur keeps this dessert from freezing totally solid. That's why the mousse can be served immediately after taking it from the freezer.

Folding Chocolate Syrup into Whipped Cream: Using a rubber spatula, cut down through the whipped cream, then slide the spatula across the bottom of the bowl and up the side, turning the whipped cream over.

216 *BettyCrocker.com*

Tips and Useful Information   Helpful How-To Photographs   Recipe Variations   Nutrition Information

Measuring Ingredients

Measuring correctly is the first step to cooking success. Not all ingredients are measured the same way or with the same type of measuring cups or measuring spoons. Here are some tips for using the correct measuring utensil and method when measuring ingredients.

Liquid Measuring Cups: usually glass or clear plastic. They have a spout for pouring and space above the top measuring line to avoid spills. Look for measuring cups with an angled rim inside that let you read the measurement from above rather than eye level. They come in 1-, 2-, 4- and 8-cup sizes.

Measuring Spoons: often come as a set that includes ¼-, ½- and 1-teaspoon sizes plus a 1-tablespoon size. Some sets may have a ⅛-teaspoon size and a "dash." These special spoons are designed for measuring and should be used instead of spoons intended for eating. They are used for both liquid and dry ingredients.

Dry Measuring Cups: to measure dry ingredients, such as sugar, and solid ingredients, such as butter. These cups are made to hold an exact amount when filled to the top. They usually come as a set of cups that contains ¼-, ⅓-, ½- and 1-cup sizes. Some sets also may have a ⅛-cup (2 tablespoons) and/or a 2-cup size.

Measuring Liquids: place the cup on a level surface, then bend down to check the amount at eye level. If using an angled cup, you can check the amount from above. To measure sticky liquids such as honey, molasses and corn syrup, lightly spray the cup with cooking spray or lightly oil first, so the liquid will be easier to remove.

Measuring Dry Ingredients: gently fill a dry measuring cup to heaping, using a large spoon. While holding the cup over the canister or storage container to catch the excess of the ingredient, level the cup off, using something with a straight edge, such as a knife or the handle of a wooden spoon.

Measuring Brown Sugar or Solid Fats: fill a dry measuring cup, using a spoon or rubber spatula. Pack down the ingredient, and level off, if necessary, so it is even with the top of the cup.

Measuring Chopped Nuts, Shredded Cheese or Cereal: fill a dry measuring cup lightly without packing down the ingredient, and level off so it is even with the top of the cup.

Measuring Butter or Margarine Sticks: cut off the amount needed, following guideline marks on the wrapper, using a sharp knife. A whole ¼-pound stick equals ½ cup, half a stick is ¼ cup, an eighth of a stick is 1 tablespoon.

Measuring Salt, Pepper, Herbs and Spices: fill measuring spoon with salt, pepper or a ground spice such as cinnamon; level off. For fresh chopped or dried herbs, lightly fill the spoon to the top.

MEASURING GUIDE

What's different, yet exactly the same? All these measurements! The recipes in this cookbook use the larger measurement, such as ¼ cup rather than 4 tablespoons, because it is quicker to measure and reduces the risk of making a mistake. The equivalency below will help you when measuring ingredients in the kitchen.

Dash or pinch	=	less than ⅛ teaspoon		
1 tablespoon	=	3 teaspoons		
¼ cup	=	4 tablespoons		
⅓ cup	=	5 tablespoons + 1 teaspoon		
½ cup	=	8 tablespoons		
¾ cup	=	12 tablespoons		
1 cup	=	16 tablespoons	=	8 fluid ounces
2 cups	=	1 pint	=	16 fluid ounces
4 cups	=	1 quart	=	32 fluid ounces
4 quarts	=	1 gallon	=	128 fluid ounces
¼ pound	=	4 ounces		
½ pound	=	8 ounces		
1 pound	=	16 ounces		

COMMON ABBREVIATIONS

Abbreviations used in this cookbook in the ingredient list are "oz" for ounce and "lb" for pound. The reason is many food labels use "oz" and "lb" rather than spelling out the word. Other recipe sources may use abbreviations, so here are some common ones you may see in recipes.

t	=	teaspoon
tsp	=	teaspoon
T	=	tablespoon
Tbsp	=	tablespoon
c	=	cup
oz	=	ounce
pt	=	pint
qt	=	quart
gal	=	gallon
lb	=	pound
in	=	inch
"	=	inch
Pkg	=	package
doz	=	dozen
°	=	degree
F	=	Fahrenheit

Basic Preparation Techniques

Chop: Cut into fine, medium or coarse irregular size pieces using a chef's knife.

Crush: Press with side of chef's knife blade, or use a mallet, rolling pin or bottom of heavy saucepan to smash food into small pieces.

Cube or Dice: Cut food into ½-inch or wider strips for cube or ½-inch or narrower strips for dice. Then cut across strips to make uniform size cubes.

Cut Up: Cut into small irregular size pieces using kitchen shears or scissors or a knife.

Grate: Cut into tiny particles by rubbing food across the small rough holes of a grater.

Julienne: Cut into 2 × ¼-inch slices. Stack the slices and cut lengthwise into matchlike sticks about ⅛ to ¼ inch wide.

Peel: Cut off outer covering with a knife or vegetable peeler, or strip off outer covering with fingers.

Shred: Cut into long thin pieces by rubbing food across the large holes of a shredder. For finely shred, rub food across the smaller holes of a shredder. To shred cabbage or lettuce, see page 255. To shred cooked meat, see page 256.

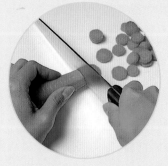

Slice: Cut into flat, usually thin, pieces of the same width from a larger piece

Basic Kitchen Gadgets and Equipment

The Bare Essentials

Your kitchen is equipped with just a few gadgets and a couple of pots and pan. No problem because you can still learn to cook with just the bare essentials. Here are some you may want to have in your kitchen to get started.

KITCHEN GADGETS

Can Opener: Purchase one that fits comfortably in your hand and is easy to wash after each use.

Cutting Boards: Hard plastic or glass cutting boards are best for cutting raw poultry, meat, fish and seafood. Wooden cutting boards are best for cutting fruits, vegetables and breads. The thin, flexible silicone cutting boards and disposable cutting sheets are also good.

Knife, Chef's: The workhorse of the kitchen knives because it is so versatile. It can be used for chopping and cutting large pieces of food or chopping tender herbs. The wide blade with its curved cutting edge is perfect for the rocking motion used for chopping. Available in 8- to 10-inch blades.

Knife, Paring: A short blade used for peeling vegetables and fruits and cutting small amounts of food. Available in 3- to 4-inch blades.

Measuring Cups, Dry: Look for these nests of metal or plastic cups, which usually increase in size from ¼ cup to 1 cup. Fill the cup to the top and level off the ingredient with a straight-edge knife or metal spatula.

Measuring Cups, Liquid: These glass or plastic cups have a pour spout with conventional and metric markings on the side. There is space above the top measuring mark so the liquid doesn't spill.

Measuring Spoons: Look for sets of metal or plastic spoons that range in size from ¼ teaspoon to 1 tablespoon. Some sets contain ⅛ teaspoon and ¾ teaspoon. Spoons are used to measure either dry or liquid ingredients.

Mixing Bowls: Choose two or three deep bowls in different sizes. A large mixing bowl can double as a salad bowl.

Pot Holders/Trivets: Use pot holders to lift or move hot pans. Place hot pans or serving plates on pot holders or trivets to protect the counter or table.

Spatula, Rubber: For scraping the side of mixing bowl, blender or food processor and for scraping out measuring cups and jars.

Spoons, Wooden: For all-purpose mixing and especially good for stirring hot foods because the handle will stay cool. Do not use for stirring raw meat, poultry, fish or seafood.

Strainer, Wire Mesh: For draining the liquid off cooked foods, draining liquid from canned fruits and vegetables and draining fruits or vegetables after washing.

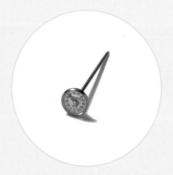

Thermometer, Dial Instant-Read: Not designed to stay in food during cooking. Can be used to test internal temperature of roasts, poultry, casseroles and stuffing.

Timer: To ensure that your foods are cooked to perfection. If the recipe gives a range of time, set the timer for the minimum time to check for doneness.

Tongs: Especially good to use when grilling foods, but can also be used to lift or turn food without piercing it. Cooking tongs should be made of metal, in contrast to salad tongs, which might be wooden or plastic and usually have a larger end for tossing a salad.

Turner: Also referred to as a pancake turner, it is available in metal or, for nonstick pans, heat-proof plastic. Used to turn foods over during cooking as well as for serving lasagna or pizza.

Wire Whisk: Use for mixing sauces, dressing, gravy and beating eggs as well as for all-purpose mixing.

POTS AND PANS

Saucepan, 2-Quart: Used for cooking vegetables and small amounts of food. A tight-fitting lid is needed to keep the moisture in during cooking.

Skillet, 10-inch: Used for sautéing vegetables, stir-frying and pan frying meats, chicken and fish.

Baking Pan, 8-inch Square: Use for lasagna, main dishes, meat loaf, roasting small pieces of meat as well as for desserts and bars.

A Few More Essentials

Now that you have been cooking with the bare essentials, you may want to consider adding some more basic gadgets and equipment to your kitchen. Having the right equipment makes cooking easier and more fun.

KITCHEN GADGETS

Grater, Box: A box grater has different size openings on each side for shredding and grating and a slot for slicing. Use the larger holes for shredding and the small holes for grating.

Knife, Carving: A long, thin blade used for carving meat and poultry. Available with 10-inch blade.

Spoons, Metal: Use the regular spoon to stir mixtures and to spoon juices over meats or poultry as they roast, and to lift large pieces of meat from the cooking pan to the serving plate. Use the slotted spoon to lift solid foods out of cooking liquids.

Thermometer, Meat: An easy way to be sure meats, poultry and fish are cooked to the proper doneness. This thermometer is ovenproof so it can be inserted in meat during cooking.

Vegetable Brush: Use to clean vegetables such as potatoes, carrots and celery.

Vegetable Peeler: Use to remove a thin peel from apples, potatoes and carrots.

POTS AND PANS

Dutch Oven (4-Quart or Larger): A large pot used most often on top of the range to prepare a large batch of soup, stew, chili or pasta. It should have a tight-fitting lid. Many Dutch ovens are ovenproof and can be used for cooking pot roast or stew in the oven.

Saucepan, 1-Quart: Use for heating small amounts of food.

Saucepan, 3-Quart: Good for cooking large amounts of vegetables, smaller amounts of pasta, soups and stews.

Baking Pan, 13 × 9-inch Rectangle: A popular pan size used for making larger amounts of lasagna, casseroles and roasting vegetables and meats. It is also used for baking cakes, brownies and bars.

Setting the Table

Even the most basic meal can look elegant when you serve it at a table that's been set correctly. Not sure what goes where? Follow the guidelines below.

- Arrange flatware so that the utensils used first are placed farthest from the plate. Forks are typically on the left, and the knife (with the blade toward the plate) and the spoons on the right.

- If you are using a butter plate, place it above the forks.

- If you're serving salad as a main course, place the salad plate to the left of the forks. The salad fork may be placed at either side of the dinner fork.

- Arrange glasses above the knife. The water glass is usually at the tip of the knife, with the beverage and wine glasses to the right of the water glass.

- If you plan to serve coffee or tea at the table, put the cup slightly above and to the right of the spoons.

- The napkin can go either in the center of the dinner plate or to the left of the forks at each place setting.

- Before you offer dessert, clear the table of all serving dishes, plates, salt and pepper shakers and any unnecessary flatware.

Casual Setting

Formal Setting

A Great Cup of Coffee

1 Choose the correct grind for your coffeemaker:

- Automatic drip coffeemaker: medium grind
- Espresso maker: fine grind
- Percolator: coarse grind
- Plunger or French press pot: coarse grind

2 Use fresh cold water for best flavor.

3 Serve hot coffee as soon as it's done brewing or within 15 minutes. The longer coffee stays in contact with heat, the more harsh and bitter it becomes. If you aren't going to drink it right away, pour it into an insulated container.

COFFEE BREWING CHART
COFFEE BREWING STRENGTH (PER SERVING)*

Strength of Brew	Ground Coffee	Water
Regular	1 level tablespoon	¾ cup (6 ounces)
Strong	2 level tablespoons	¾ cup (6 ounces)

Best general recommendation

Decaffeinated Coffee

Caffeine is a stimulant found in regular coffee that makes many people jittery and shaky. Decaffeinated coffee comes to the rescue!

Caffeine is removed by either a water or solvent process, both causing the loss of some aroma and flavor. The solvent process is faster, less expensive and leaves more flavor. But if you're concerned about solvent residues, choose water-processed decaf.

A Perfect Pot of Tea

Enjoying a cup of tea is steeped in tradition, from the afternoon tea of the English to the tea ceremony of the Japanese. Next to water, tea is the most commonly consumed beverage in the world.

There are three main types of tea:

- Black tea's color and aroma develop as the leaves ferment or oxidize during processing. Black tea contains the most caffeine, about 50 to 65 percent of the amount in coffee. Some familiar varieties are Darjeeling, Assam and Ceylon orange pekoe.

- Green tea is pale green in color with a light, fresh flavor. Gunpowder, so named because it's rolled in little balls that "explode" when they come in contact with water, and Lung Ching are two popular green teas.

- Oolong tea is partially fermented, a cross between green and black teas. You'll also recognize it as "Chinese restaurant tea." Imperial oolong is prized for its honey flavor, while Formosa oolong tastes a little like peaches.

Black, green and oolong teas are just the processing methods. There are literally thousands of varieties of teas, including:

- Blended tea: A combination of teas such as English Breakfast and Earl Grey.
- Decaffeinated tea: Almost all the caffeine is removed during processing.
- Herb tea: Really not a tea because it doesn't contain tea leaves. It is a blend of dried fruits, herbs, flowers and spices in many flavors such as lemon, orange and peppermint.

Brewing Black or Oolong Tea

1 Start with a spotlessly clean teapot. Warm the pot by filling it with very hot water; drain just before adding the tea.

2 Bring fresh, cold water to a full boil in your teakettle.

3 Add tea to the warm teapot, about 1 teaspoon of loose tea or 1 tea bag for each ¾ cup of water. Pour the boiling water over the tea, and let it steep for 3 to 5 minutes to bring out the full flavor. Instead of color, judge the strength of the tea by tasting it. Stir the tea once to blend evenly. Remove the tea bags or infuser, or strain the tea as you pour. If you prefer weaker tea, add hot water after brewing the tea. Serve tea with milk, sugar and lemon if you like.

Brewing Green Tea

Green tea is brewed differently than other types of tea. Brew green tea using very hot water, about 170°F to 190°F, not boiling water. If you've already boiled the water, let it stand about 3 minutes before brewing green tea. Stir once to blend evenly.

Iced Tea

For clear iced tea, follow these guidelines:

1 Brew a pot of tea, using double the amount of tea.

2 Remove the tea bags or strain the tea while pouring it into ice-filled glasses or a pitcher.

3 If you're making tea in advance, let it cool to room temperature before putting it in the refrigerator so it doesn't get cloudy.

Because bacteria can multiply during brewing, making sun tea isn't recommended.

1 MAIN DISH SALADS, SANDWICHES and SOUPS

Lemon-Basil Chicken-Pasta Salad

PREP TIME: 25 Minutes • **START TO FINISH:** 1 Hour 25 Minutes • 4 servings

½ teaspoon salt (for cooking pasta), if desired

2 cups uncooked rotini or rotelle (spiral) pasta (6 oz)

10 asparagus stalks (about 8 oz)

1 clove garlic or ⅛ teaspoon garlic powder

5 oz cooked chicken or turkey

½ cup fresh basil leaves

½ cup shredded Parmesan cheese (2 oz)

¼ cup olive or vegetable oil

1 tablespoon grated lemon peel

1 Fill a 4-quart Dutch oven about half full of water. Add ½ teaspoon salt if desired. Cover with lid; heat over high heat until water is boiling rapidly. Add the pasta. Heat to boiling again. Boil uncovered 9 to 11 minutes, stirring frequently, until tender but not mushy. While water is heating and pasta is cooking, continue with recipe.

2 Break off and discard the tough ends of the asparagus stalks where they snap easily; wash asparagus. Cut asparagus into 1-inch pieces to measure 2 cups. Add asparagus to the pasta during the last 2 to 3 minutes of cooking.

3 Peel and finely chop the garlic. Cut the chicken into ½-inch cubes to measure about 2 cups. Tear the basil leaves lengthwise into narrow strips.

4 Place a strainer or colander in the sink. Pour pasta and asparagus in the strainer to drain. Rinse with cold water; drain.

5 In a large glass or plastic bowl, toss pasta, asparagus and chicken. Stir in garlic, basil, cheese, oil and lemon peel. Cover with plastic wrap; refrigerate 1 to 2 hours or until chilled.

1 Serving: Calories 440; Total Fat 21g; Cholesterol 45mg; Sodium 250mg; Total Carbohydrate 39g (Dietary Fiber 3g); Protein 24g **Carbohydrate Choices:** 2½

Lemon-Basil Ham-Pasta Salad: Substitute ham for the chicken and shredded Swiss cheese for the Parmesan cheese.

Cook's Tip

Cut edges of basil leaves turn black very quickly, which is fine when adding to a sauce or mixture. Carefully tear the basil leaves just before adding to this salad to prevent the edges from darkening as quickly.

Grating Lemon Peel: Rub the lemon peel over the small holes of a grater. Grate only the yellow peel because the white part (pith) is bitter.

Tearing Basil Leaves: Carefully tear the basil leaves lengthwise into narrow strips.

Turkey Salad with Fruit

PREP TIME: 20 Minutes • **START TO FINISH:** 2 Hours 20 Minutes • 4 servings

4 cups mixed salad greens

10 oz cooked turkey or chicken

2 medium stalks celery

1 medium green onion with top

1 can (11 oz) mandarin orange
  segments

1 can (8 oz) sliced water chestnuts

1 container (6 oz) peach, orange or
  lemon yogurt (⅔ cup)

¼ teaspoon ground ginger

1 cup seedless green grapes

1 Wash the salad greens, let drain and refrigerate.

2 Cut the turkey into ½-inch pieces to measure 2 cups. Thinly slice the celery to measure 1 cup. Peel and cut the green onion into ⅛-inch slices. Drain the orange segments and water chestnuts in a strainer.

3 In a large bowl, mix the yogurt and ginger. Stir in the turkey, celery, onion, orange segments, water chestnuts and grapes. Cover with plastic wrap; refrigerate at least 2 hours.

4 On 4 plates, arrange the salad greens. Top greens with turkey salad.

1 Serving: Calories 270; Total Fat 6g; Cholesterol 65mg; Sodium 135mg; Total Carbohydrate 29g (Dietary Fiber 4g); Protein 25g **Carbohydrate Choices:** 2

Ham Salad with Fruit: Substitute 2 cups cut-up cooked ham for the turkey.

Cook's Tips

Purchase cooked turkey or chicken at the deli counter of the supermarket if you don't have leftover cooked turkey or chicken on hand.

Walnuts or pecans can be substituted for the water chestnuts to add crunch to this salad. Use ½ cup coarsely chopped nuts.

Cutting Up Turkey: Cut turkey into ½-inch pieces. Some pieces will be irregular in shape.

Italian Chopped Salad

PREP TIME: 20 Minutes • **START TO FINISH:** 20 Minutes • 4 servings

1 large bunch or 2 small bunches
romaine lettuce

2 large tomatoes

2 medium cucumbers

5 oz cooked chicken or turkey

3 oz Italian salami

1 can (15 oz) cannellini beans

1 cup fresh small basil leaves

⅔ cup red wine vinaigrette or
Italian dressing

1   Remove any limp outer leaves from the romaine and discard. Break remaining leaves off the core; rinse with cool water. Shake off excess water and blot to dry, or roll up the leaves in a clean kitchen towel or paper towel to dry. Chop the leaves to measure 6 cups.

2   Chop the tomatoes to measure about 2 cups. Peel the cucumbers, if you like, with a vegetable peeler. Chop the cucumbers to measure about 1½ cups.

3   Chop the chicken to measure about 1 cup. Chop the salami. Drain the beans in a strainer, then rinse with cool water.

4   In a large glass or plastic bowl, place the lettuce, tomatoes, cucumbers, chicken, salami, beans and basil leaves. Pour the vinaigrette over the salad, and toss until ingredients are coated.

1 Serving: Calories 500; Total Fat 29g; Cholesterol 55mg; Sodium 1050mg; Total Carbohydrate 33g (Dietary Fiber 9g); Protein 27g **Carbohydrate Choices:** 2

Cook's Tips

If your basil leaves are large, carefully tear them into about ¾-inch pieces before measuring.

If you like cheese, cut 4 ounces of mozzarella or cheddar cheese into ½-inch cubes and add to the other ingredients before tossing with the vinaigrette.

Chopping Romaine: Cut the leaves lengthwise into 1-inch pieces. Stack several pieces and cut crosswise into 1-inch pieces.

Chopping Cucumber: Cut cucumber lengthwise in half. Place half, cut side down, and cut lengthwise into ½-inch slices. Stack several slices and cut lengthwise into ½-inch strips. Cut strips crosswise to make about ½-inch pieces.

Turkey Caesar Salad Wraps

PREP TIME: 15 Minutes • **START TO FINISH:** 15 Minutes • 8 sandwiches

8 oz cooked turkey or chicken

1 small red onion

2 plum (Roma) tomatoes

1 bag (7.5 oz) Caesar salad kit with lettuce, dressing, Parmesan cheese and croutons

8 flour tortillas (10 inch)

1 Cut the turkey into ½-inch pieces. Chop enough of the onion to measure ¼ cup. Wrap any remaining onion with plastic wrap and refrigerate. Cut the tomatoes into slices.

2 Make the salad kit as directed on the bag, adding the turkey and onion.

3 Spoon salad mixture evenly down center of each tortilla to within 2 inches of bottom. Top with tomatoes. Fold up the bottom of the tortilla, then fold over the sides. Secure each with a toothpick if necessary.

1 Sandwich: Calories 320; Total Fat 11g; Cholesterol 30mg; Sodium 580mg; Total Carbohydrate 40g (Dietary Fiber 2g); Protein 15g **Carbohydrate Choices:** 2½

Cook's Tips

Caesar salad kit not available? In a large bowl, place 5 cups of bite-size pieces romaine, ½ cup bottled Caesar dressing, 2 tablespoons shredded Parmesan cheese and ½ cup seasoned croutons. Add the turkey and onions and toss until everything is evenly coated with the dressing.

Flour tortillas come in several varieties from regular, to fat-free, to whole wheat and a variety of flavors such as pumpkin, spinach, cilantro and tomato. The flavored tortillas, such as spinach and tomato, also add color.

Spooning Caesar Salad on Tortilla: Spoon salad mixture evenly down center of the tortilla.

Folding the Wrap: Fold up the bottom of the tortilla, then fold over the sides. Secure with a toothpick if necessary.

French Dip Sandwiches

PREP TIME: 5 Minutes • **START TO FINISH:** 4 Hours 5 Minutes • 10 sandwiches

1 boneless beef chuck roast (3 lb)

1 clove garlic or ⅛ teaspoon garlic powder

1 can (14 oz) beef broth

1½ cups water

⅓ cup soy sauce

1 teaspoon dried rosemary leaves

1 teaspoon dried thyme leaves

1 dried bay leaf

3 or 4 peppercorns

2 loaves (1 lb each) French bread

Slow Cooker French Dip Sandwiches:
Prepare as directed in steps 1 and 2—except omit beef broth and place beef roast in 3½- to 4-quart slow cooker. Cover; cook on Low heat setting 7 to 8 hours. Continue as directed in step 4.

1 Heat the oven to 325°F. Place the beef in an ovenproof 4-quart Dutch oven.

2 Peel and finely chop the garlic. In a medium bowl, mix garlic and remaining ingredients except bread. Pour the garlic mixture over beef.

3 Cover Dutch oven with lid; bake 2 to 3 hours or until beef is tender.

4 Carefully remove Dutch oven from the oven. Remove beef from Dutch oven and place on cutting board. Cover with foil to keep warm. Skim any fat from the surface of the cooking juices, using a spoon. Remove the bay leaf and peppercorns. Cut beef, across the grain, into thin slices. Heat cooking juices to boiling. Spoon juices from Dutch oven into individual bowls for dipping.

5 Cut each loaf of bread into 5 pieces, each about 4 inches long; cut bread pieces horizontally in half. Fill bread with beef. Serve sandwiches with broth for dipping.

1 Sandwich: Calories 500; Total Fat 19g; Cholesterol 80mg; Sodium 1080mg; Total Carbohydrate 46g (Dietary Fiber 2g); Protein 34g **Carbohydrate Choices:** 3

Cook's Tips

For carving roast beef, a sharp knife with a straight edge or an electric knife works best to cut thin, even slices. Keep beef from moving while cutting by holding it in place with a two-tined meat fork.

Ten sandwiches too many? Just carve enough beef roast to make the number of sandwiches you will need. Cover and refrigerate the remaining beef roast and broth to reheat and use another time.

Skimming Fat from Beef Juices: Using a spoon, skim any fat from the surface of the cooking juices.

Slicing Roast Beef: With a sharp straight-edge knife, cut beef into thin slices.

Beef-Pesto Panini

PREP TIME: 15 Minutes • **START TO FINISH:** 15 Minutes • 4 sandwiches

SPECIAL EQUIPMENT

grill pan

---

4 teaspoons butter or margarine, room temperature

8 slices (½ inch thick) Italian bread

4 slices (1 oz each) mozzarella cheese

4 tablespoons basil pesto (from 7-oz container)

½ lb thinly sliced cooked roast beef (from deli)

1 Thinly spread the butter over 1 side of each bread slice. Turn 4 bread slices so buttered sides are facing down; top each with 1 slice of the cheese, 1 tablespoon of the pesto and ¼ of the beef. Top with remaining bread slices, buttered sides up.

2 In a 12-inch grill pan or skillet, cook the sandwiches over medium heat 4 to 5 minutes, turning over once, until bread is golden brown and cheese is melted.

1 Sandwich: Calories 440; Total Fat 28g; Cholesterol 70mg; Sodium 570mg; Total Carbohydrate 22g (Dietary Fiber 1g); Protein 26g **Carbohydrate Choices:** 1½

Contact-Grill Beef-Pesto Panini: Heat closed medium-size contact grill for 5 minutes. Place sandwiches on grill. Close grill. Cook 3 to 5 minutes or until bread is toasted and cheese is melted.

Chicken-Pesto Panini: Use ½ pound thinly sliced cooked chicken or turkey instead of the roast beef.

Cook's Tips

A grill pan looks like a skillet but has ridges on the bottom. The ridges create brown lines on the food so it looks like it was cooked on an outdoor grill.

The pesto is placed between the cheese and the beef so it doesn't soak into the bread and make the sandwich soggy.

Checking Panini Doneness:
Lift corner of panini to check if bread is golden brown.

Tuna Salad Sandwiches

PREP TIME: 15 Minutes • **START TO FINISH:** 15 Minutes • 4 sandwiches

2 cans (6 oz each) tuna in water

1 medium stalk celery

1 small onion

½ cup mayonnaise or salad dressing

1 teaspoon lemon juice

¼ teaspoon salt

¼ teaspoon pepper

8 slices bread

1 Drain the tuna in a strainer in the sink. Chop the celery to measure ½ cup. Peel and chop the onion to measure ¼ cup.

2 In a medium bowl, mix the tuna, celery, onion, mayonnaise, lemon juice, salt and pepper.

3 Spread tuna mixture on 4 bread slices. Top with remaining bread slices.

1 Sandwich: Calories 410; Total Fat 24g; Cholesterol 30mg; Sodium 870mg; Total Carbohydrate 29g (Dietary Fiber 1g); Protein 21g **Carbohydrate Choices:** 2

Lighten Up Tuna Salad Sandwiches: Use fat-free mayonnaise for a tuna salad sandwich with 3 grams of fat and 240 calories.

Chicken Salad Sandwiches: Substitute 1½ cups chopped cooked chicken or turkey for the tuna. Omit the lemon juice.

Egg Salad Sandwiches: Substitute 6 Hard-Cooked Eggs (page 104), chopped, for the tuna. Omit the lemon juice.

Ham Salad Sandwiches: Substitute 1½ cups chopped cooked ham for the tuna. Omit the salt and pepper. Substitute 1 teaspoon yellow mustard for the lemon juice.

Cook's Tips

Make your sandwich heartier by topping with lettuce leaves, tomato slices, avocado slices and a slice of cheese.

Mayonnaise or salad dressing—what is the difference? They are both thick, creamy dressings that contain vegetable oil, lemon juice or vinegar and seasonings. Mayonnaise also contains egg yolk and is less sweet than salad dressing. They can be used interchangeably so you decide which you prefer.

Chopping Celery: Cut celery stalk lengthwise into about ½-inch pieces. Place several pieces together and cut crosswise into ¼- to ½-inch pieces.

Veggie Focaccia Sandwiches

PREP TIME: 20 Minutes • **START TO FINISH:** 20 Minutes • 4 sandwiches

½ medium yellow bell pepper

½ medium green bell pepper

1 small onion

2 plum (Roma) tomatoes

Cooking spray for greasing skillet

2 tablespoons balsamic vinaigrette or Italian dressing

1 round focaccia bread (8 inch)

2 tablespoons chopped fresh basil leaves

½ cup shredded mozzarella cheese (2 oz)

1   Cut out the seeds and membrane from the yellow and green bell peppers. Cut the bell peppers into ½-inch strips. Peel and cut the onion into ¼-inch slices. Cut the tomatoes into ¼-inch slices. Set tomatoes aside.

2   Spray an 8- or 10-inch skillet with the cooking spray; heat over medium-high heat. Add bell peppers, onion and vinaigrette to the skillet. Cook 4 to 5 minutes, stirring occasionally, until peppers are crisp-tender; remove from heat.

3   Cut the focaccia into 4 wedges; split each wedge horizontally. Spoon ¼ of the vegetable mixture onto each bottom half of focaccia wedge; sprinkle with basil and cheese. Top with tomatoes and tops of bread wedges.

1 Sandwich: Calories 280; Total Fat 12g; Cholesterol 10mg; Sodium 660mg; Total Carbohydrate 35g (Dietary Fiber 2g); Protein 9g **Carbohydrate Choices:** 2

Lighten Up Veggie Focaccia Sandwiches: Use fat-free balsamic vinaigrette to reduce the fat to 9 grams and the calories to 250 per serving.

Cook's Tip

Like a sandwich with warm bread? Heat the oven to 350°F. Place the uncut focaccia on the middle oven rack. Bake 5 to 7 minutes or until warm. Split the focaccia horizontally. Spoon the vegetable mixture on the bottom half and sprinkle with cheese and basil. Top with tomatoes and top of foccaccia and cut into 4 wedges.

Chopping Basil Leaves: Stack 3 or 4 basil leaves and roll up. Cut the basil into strips and chop the strips into small pieces using a chef's knife.

Chicken-Tortilla Soup

PREP TIME: 35 Minutes • **START TO FINISH:** 35 Minutes • 4 servings (1½ cups each)

1 medium avocado

10 oz cooked chicken or turkey

1 carton (32 oz) chicken broth
(4 cups)

1 cup chunky-style salsa

¾ cup broken tortilla chips

1½ cups shredded Monterey Jack
cheese (6 oz)

2 tablespoons chopped fresh
cilantro

Lime wedges, if desired

1 Cut the avocado in half lengthwise around the pit. Twist the halves in opposite directions to separate them. Place the avocado half with the pit on a countertop. Hit the pit with the sharp edge of a knife. Grasp the avocado half, then twist the knife to loosen and remove the pit. Using a paring knife, cut the avocado flesh (do not cut the peel) in a crosshatch pattern, then scoop the cut pieces with a spoon into a small bowl.

2 Chop the chicken to measure 2 cups.

3 In a 3-quart saucepan, heat the broth, salsa and chicken to boiling over medium-high heat, stirring occasionally.

4 Meanwhile, divide the broken chips among 4 serving bowls. Spoon hot soup over chips, then top with avocado, cheese and cilantro. Serve with lime wedges.

1 Serving: Calories 490; Total Fat 30g; Cholesterol 100mg; Sodium 1740mg; Total Carbohydrate 18g (Dietary Fiber 4g); Protein 38g **Carbohydrate Choices:** 1

Cook's Tips

If the avocados aren't ripe (or sometimes overripe) in the supermarket, use purchased guacamole instead. You'll find it in the dairy or frozen section and may be labeled "avocado dip" instead of "guacamole."

Use different flavored tortilla chips such as nacho cheese or lime white corn tortilla chips for the regular ones.

Scoring Avocado: Using the tip of the knife, cut the avocado flesh in a crisscross pattern, cutting just to the peel.

Removing Avocado Pieces: Run a small spoon next to the peel, rotating the avocado and squeezing slightly to release the pieces.

Chili

PREP TIME: 30 Minutes • **START TO FINISH:** 1 Hour 50 Minutes • 4 servings

1 large onion

2 cloves garlic or ¼ teaspoon garlic powder

1 lb lean (at least 80%) ground beef

1 tablespoon chili powder

2 teaspoons chopped fresh or 1 teaspoon dried oregano leaves

1 teaspoon ground cumin

½ teaspoon salt

½ teaspoon red pepper sauce

1 can (14.5 oz) diced tomatoes, undrained

1 can (15 to 16 oz) red kidney beans, undrained

1 Peel and chop the onion to measure 1 cup. Peel and finely chop the garlic.

2 In a 3-quart saucepan, cook the beef, onion and garlic over medium heat 8 to 10 minutes, stirring occasionally, until beef is thoroughly cooked. Place a strainer or colander in a large bowl; line strainer with a double thickness of paper towels. Pour the beef mixture into the strainer to drain. Return beef mixture to saucepan; discard paper towels and any juices in the bowl.

3 Into the beef, stir the chili powder, oregano, cumin, salt, pepper sauce and tomatoes with their liquid.

4 Heat the mixture to boiling over high heat. Once mixture is boiling, reduce heat just enough so mixture bubbles gently. Cover with lid; cook 1 hour, stirring occasionally.

5 Stir in the beans with their liquid. Heat to boiling over high heat. Once mixture is boiling, reduce heat just enough so mixture bubbles gently. Cook uncovered about 20 minutes, stirring occasionally, until desired thickness.

1 Serving: Calories 360; Total Fat 14g; Cholesterol 70mg; Sodium 720mg; Total Carbohydrate 31g (Dietary Fiber 8g); Protein 29g **Carbohydrate Choices:** 2

Lighten Up Chili: Use 1 pound lean ground turkey for the ground beef for chili with 7 grams of fat and 320 calories per serving.

Cincinnati-Style Chili: For each serving, spoon about ¾ cup beef mixture over 1 cup hot cooked spaghetti. Sprinkle each serving with ¼ cup shredded Cheddar cheese and 2 tablespoons chopped onion. Top with sour cream if desired.

Draining Cooked Ground Beef:
Pour the beef mixture into a strainer lined with a double thickness of paper towels.

Cook's Tip

If you only have chili powder in your cupboard just omit the cumin, oregano and pepper sauce and increase the chili powder to 2 tablespoons.

39

Vegetarian Chili

PREP TIME: 40 Minutes • **START TO FINISH:** 40 Minutes • 6 servings

2 medium white or red potatoes
(about 10 oz)

1 medium onion

1 small bell pepper (any color)

1 can (15 to 16 oz) garbanzo beans

1 can (15 to 16 oz) kidney beans

2 cans (14.5 oz each) diced
tomatoes, undrained

1 can (8 oz) tomato sauce

1 tablespoon chili powder

1 teaspoon ground cumin

1 medium zucchini

1 Scrub the potatoes thoroughly with a vegetable brush and water, but do not peel. Cut the potatoes into cubes that are ½ inch or slightly larger. Peel and chop the onion to measure ½ cup. In a 4-quart Dutch oven, place the potatoes and onion.

2 Cut the bell pepper in half lengthwise, and cut out seeds and membrane. Chop the bell pepper into small pieces. Add to the Dutch oven.

3 Drain the garbanzo and kidney beans in a strainer, then rinse with cool water. Add to the Dutch oven.

4 Add the tomatoes with their liquid, the tomato sauce, chili powder and cumin to the Dutch oven. Heat to boiling over high heat, stirring occasionally.

5 Once chili is boiling, reduce heat just enough so chili bubbles gently. Cover with lid; cook 10 minutes.

6 While chili is cooking, cut the zucchini into ½-inch slices; cut slices in half. Stir zucchini into chili. Cover; cook 5 to 7 minutes longer, stirring occasionally, until potatoes and zucchini are tender when pierced with a fork.

1 Serving: Calories 280; Total Fat 2.5g; Cholesterol 0mg; Sodium 650mg; Total Carbohydrate 51g (Dietary Fiber 12g); Protein 14g **Carbohydrate Choices:** 3½

Cook's Tips

You may notice that zucchini comes in many sizes. Choose a zucchini about 8 inches long because it will be younger and more tender than the bigger ones.

No garbanzo or kidney beans in your cupboard? You can use canned black, great northern, pinto or butter beans for one or both beans.

Cubing Potatoes: Cut potatoes into cubes that are ½ inch or slightly larger.

Black Bean Soup

PREP TIME: 40 Minutes • **START TO FINISH:** 40 Minutes • 2 servings

1 medium onion

2 cloves garlic or ¼ teaspoon garlic powder

1 medium carrot

1 medium stalk celery

Parsley sprigs

1 slice bacon

1 can (14 oz) chicken broth

½ teaspoon dried oregano leaves

½ teaspoon crushed red pepper flakes

1 can (15 oz) black beans

4 lemon wedges

1 Peel and chop the onion to measure ½ cup. Peel and finely chop the garlic. Peel and coarsely chop the carrot to measure ½ cup. Coarsely chop the celery to measure ½ cup.

2 Rinse sprigs of parsley with cool water, and pat dry with a paper towel. On a cutting board, chop enough parsley leaves into small pieces, using a chef's knife, to measure about 2 tablespoons; or place the parsley leaves in a small bowl or cup and snip into very small pieces with kitchen scissors. Discard the stems.

3 Cut the bacon slice crosswise into ½-inch strips. In a 2- or 3-quart saucepan, cook bacon strips over medium heat 1 minute, stirring constantly. Do not drain.

4 Add the onion and garlic to the bacon. Cook about 5 minutes, stirring frequently, until onion is tender when pierced with a fork. The bacon will still be soft. Remove the saucepan from the heat.

5 Stir in the chicken broth, carrot, celery, parsley, oregano and red pepper flakes. Heat to boiling over high heat. Once mixture is boiling, reduce heat just enough so mixture bubbles gently. Cover with lid; cook 10 minutes.

6 While broth mixture is cooking, drain the beans in a strainer, then rinse with cool water. Measure out ½ cup of the beans. Place the ½ cup beans in a small bowl, and mash them with a fork.

7 Stir the whole beans and the mashed beans into the broth mixture. Cook about 1 minute or until beans are heated. Serve soup with lemon wedges.

1 Serving: Calories 370; Total Fat 4g; Cholesterol 0mg; Sodium 1690mg; Total Carbohydrate 60g (Dietary Fiber 22g); Protein 22g **Carbohydrate Choices:** 4

Vegetarian Black Bean Soup: Omit the bacon. In step 4, heat 1 tablespoon vegetable oil in a 2- or 3-quart saucepan to cook the onion and garlic. Use vegetable broth instead of the chicken broth.

Cook's Tips

The bacon will be easier to cut into ½-inch strips if you place it in the freezer for 5 minutes first.

The mashed black beans will slightly thicken the soup without adding extra calories or fat.

Rinsing Black Beans: Empty beans into a strainer, and rinse with cool water.

Mashing Black Beans: Place ½ cup of the beans in a bowl, and mash with a fork.

French Onion Soup

PREP TIME: 20 Minutes • **START TO FINISH:** 1 Hour 30 Minutes • 4 servings

4 medium onions

2 tablespoons butter or margarine

2 cans (10.5 oz each) condensed beef broth

1½ cups water

⅛ teaspoon pepper

⅛ teaspoon dried thyme leaves

1 dried bay leaf

4 oz Gruyère, Swiss or mozzarella cheese

4 slices (¾ to 1 inch thick) French bread

¼ cup grated Parmesan cheese

Cook's Tip

The long, slow cooking of the onions gives this soup its rich caramelized-onion flavor and color.

1 Peel and cut the onions into slices to measure 4 cups. In a 4-quart nonstick Dutch oven, melt the butter over medium-high heat. Stir in onions to coat with butter. Cook uncovered 10 minutes, stirring every 3 to 4 minutes.

2 Reduce heat to medium-low. Cook uncovered 35 to 40 minutes longer, stirring well every 5 minutes, until onions are deep golden brown (onions will shrink during cooking).

3 Stir in broth, water, pepper, thyme and bay leaf. Heat to boiling over high heat. Once mixture is boiling, reduce heat just enough so mixture bubbles gently. Cover with lid; simmer 15 minutes. Meanwhile, shred the Gruyère cheese by rubbing it across the largest holes of a grater to measure 1 cup; set aside.

4 You may need to move the oven rack so it is near the broiler. Set the oven control to broil. On a cookie sheet, place the bread slices. Broil with tops about 5 inches from heat 1 to 2 minutes or until golden brown. Turn bread over; broil 1 to 2 minutes longer until golden brown. Place toasted bread in 4 ovenproof bowls or individual ceramic casseroles (do not use glass, which cannot withstand heat of broiler and may break).

5 Remove bay leaf from soup. Ladle soup into bowls. Top with Gruyère cheese. Sprinkle with Parmesan cheese. Place bowls in pan with shallow sides.

6 Broil soup bowls with tops about 5 inches from heat 1 to 2 minutes or just until cheese is melted and golden brown. Watch carefully so cheese does not burn. Serve with additional French bread if desired.

Caramelizing Onions Slowly cook the onions, stirring every 5 minutes to prevent burning, until deep golden brown.

Broiling French Onion Soup Place ovenproof bowls or individual ceramic casseroles in a pan with shallow sides. Broil until cheese is melted and golden brown.

1 Serving: Calories 450; Total Fat 19g; Cholesterol 50mg; Sodium 1390mg; Total Carbohydrate 46g (Dietary Fiber 4g); Protein 24g **Carbohydrate Choices:** 3

2 PASTA FAVORITES

Chicken- and Spinach-Stuffed Shells

PREP TIME: 30 Minutes • **START TO FINISH:** 1 Hour 10 Minutes • 6 servings (3 shells each)

½ teaspoon salt (for cooking pasta), if desired

18 jumbo pasta shells (from 12- or 16-oz package)

2 cups frozen cut leaf spinach, thawed

1 large egg

5 oz cooked chicken or turkey

1 container (15 oz) whole-milk ricotta cheese or 2 cups cottage cheese

¼ cup grated Parmesan cheese

1 jar (26 oz) tomato pasta sauce

2 cups shredded Italian cheese blend (8 oz)

1 Serving: Calories 580; Total Fat 27g; Cholesterol 130mg; Sodium 1060mg; Total Carbohydrate 49g (Dietary Fiber 4g); Protein 33g **Carbohydrate Choices:** 3

1   Heat the oven to 350°F. Fill a 4-quart Dutch oven about half full of water. Add ½ teaspoon salt if desired. Cover with lid; heat over high heat until the water is boiling rapidly. Add the pasta shells. Heat to boiling again. Boil uncovered 9 to 11 minutes, stirring frequently, until tender but not mushy.

2   While pasta water is heating and pasta is cooking, place thawed spinach in a strainer and squeeze with fingers to remove liquid. Place spinach on paper towels or clean kitchen towel and squeeze out any remaining liquid until spinach is dry. In a small bowl, beat the egg slightly with a fork. Chop the chicken to measure 1 cup.

3   In a medium bowl, mix the spinach, beaten egg, chicken, ricotta cheese and Parmesan cheese. Place a strainer in the sink. Pour the pasta shells in the strainer to drain. Rinse with cool water; drain.

4   In a 13 × 9-inch (3-quart) glass baking dish, spread 1 cup of the pasta sauce. Spoon about 2 tablespoons ricotta mixture into each pasta shell. Arrange shells, filled sides up, on sauce in baking dish. Spoon remaining sauce over stuffed shells.

5   Cover dish with foil. Bake 30 minutes. Carefully remove foil; sprinkle with Italian cheese blend. Bake uncovered 5 to 10 minutes longer or until cheese is melted.

Cook's Tips

Thaw the spinach overnight in the refrigerator or microwave about 2 minutes just until thawed.

This dish can be made up to 24 hours before baking. Cover with foil and refrigerate until ready to bake. Add 10 minutes to the first bake time in step 5 before topping with cheese.

Draining Thawed Spinach: Squeeze excess moisture from the spinach, using paper towels.

Filling Pasta Shells: Spoon about 2 tablespoons ricotta mixture into shell using a measuring spoon.

Cheesy Baked Rigatoni

PREP TIME: 25 Minutes • **START TO FINISH:** 1 Hour 5 Minutes • 8 servings

½ teaspoon salt (for cooking pasta), if desired

3 cups uncooked rigatoni pasta (8 oz)

1 lb bulk Italian pork sausage

1 jar (7 oz) roasted red bell peppers

3 cloves garlic or ⅜ teaspoon garlic powder

1 can (28 oz) crushed tomatoes, undrained

3 tablespoons chopped fresh or 3 teaspoons dried basil leaves

Cooking spray for greasing baking dish

1 package (8 oz) sliced fresh mushrooms (3 cups)

1 cup shredded Parmesan cheese (4 oz)

2½ cups shredded mozzarella cheese (10 oz)

1 Heat the oven to 375°F. Fill a 4-quart Dutch oven about half full of water. Add ½ teaspoon salt if desired. Cover with lid; heat over high heat until the water is boiling rapidly. Add the pasta. Heat to boiling again. Boil uncovered 14 to 16 minutes, stirring frequently, until tender but not mushy. While pasta is cooking, continue with the recipe.

2 In a 10-inch skillet, cook the sausage over medium heat 8 to 10 minutes, stirring occasionally, until no longer pink. Meanwhile, drain the roasted red peppers in a strainer; chop the peppers. Peel and finely chop the garlic. In a medium bowl, mix the tomatoes with their liquid, the basil and garlic.

3 Place a strainer or colander in the sink. Pour the pasta in the strainer to drain; return pasta to Dutch oven. Place the strainer in a bowl; line strainer with a double thickness of paper towels. Pour the sausage into the strainer to drain. (Discard paper towels and any juices in the bowl after using sausage in next step.)

4 Spray a 13 × 9-inch (3-quart) glass baking dish with the cooking spray. In the baking dish, layer half each of the pasta, sausage, mushrooms, roasted peppers, Parmesan cheese, tomato mixture and mozzarella cheese. Repeat layers.

5 Bake uncovered 35 to 40 minutes or until mixture is hot and cheese is golden brown.

1 Serving: Calories 410; Total Fat 20g; Cholesterol 55mg; Sodium 730mg; Total Carbohydrate 33g (Dietary Fiber 3g); Protein 26g **Carbohydrate Choices:** 2

Lighten Up Cheesy Baked Rigatoni: Use ¾ pound of Italian-seasoned ground turkey instead of the pork sausage to trim the fat to 17 grams per serving.

Peeling Garlic: With flat side of chef's knife, crush garlic clove to break the peel, which will slip off easily.

Chopping Garlic: Cut garlic clove lengthwise into thin slices. Using the chef's knife, chop the garlic into fine pieces.

Cook's Tip

If you don't have a jar of roasted red bell peppers on hand, go ahead and make this dish without them. It will still be tasty.

Vegetable Lasagna

PREP TIME: 30 Minutes • **START TO FINISH:** 1 Hour 25 Minutes • 6 servings

1 medium zucchini

2 cups tomato pasta sauce (from a 24- to 26-oz jar)

1 box (9 oz) frozen chopped spinach, thawed

1½ cups cottage cheese or ricotta cheese (12 oz)

⅓ cup grated Parmesan cheese

2 tablespoons chopped fresh or 1½ teaspoons dried oregano leaves

1 jar (4.5 oz) sliced mushrooms

8 purchased precooked or oven-ready lasagna noodles (each about 7 × 3 inches)

2 cups shredded mozzarella cheese (8 oz)

1 Heat the oven to 400°F. Shred the zucchini by rubbing it across the largest holes of a grater to measure about 1 cup. In a medium bowl, mix the pasta sauce and zucchini.

2 Drain the thawed spinach in a strainer, then squeeze out the excess moisture from the spinach, using paper towels or a clean kitchen towel, until the spinach is dry.

3 In another medium bowl, mix the spinach, cottage cheese, Parmesan cheese and oregano. Drain the mushrooms in a strainer. In an ungreased 8-inch square glass baking dish, spread ½ cup of the sauce mixture.

4 Top sauce mixture in dish with 2 noodles, placing them so they do not overlap or touch the sides of the dish because they will expand as they bake. Spread ¼ of the remaining sauce mixture (about ½ cup) over the noodles.

5 Drop ¼ of the spinach mixture by small spoonfuls over the sauce mixture; spread carefully, pulling with the tines of a fork if necessary. Sprinkle with ¼ of the mushrooms and ½ cup of the mozzarella cheese.

6 Repeat layering three more times, beginning with 2 more noodles and following directions in steps 4 and 5.

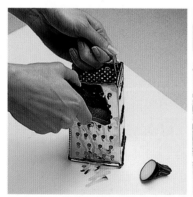

Shredding Zucchini: Rub zucchini across largest holes.

Layering the Lasagna: Assemble the lasagna, layer by layer.

7 Cover the dish with foil. Bake 35 minutes. Carefully remove the foil, and continue baking about 10 minutes longer or until lasagna is bubbly around the edges. Remove from the oven and let stand 10 minutes so the lasagna will become easier to cut and serve.

1 Serving: Calories 420; Total Fat 14g; Cholesterol 30mg; Sodium 1140mg; Total Carbohydrate 45g (Dietary Fiber 4g); Protein 27g **Carbohydrate Choices:** 3

Cook's Tips

The lasagna can be prepared and refrigerated up to 24 hours ahead of time. Assemble the lasagna through step 6. Cover with foil and refrigerate. Bake as directed in step 7 except bake 45 minutes before removing the foil.

Precooked or oven-ready lasagna noodles are available with the other dried pastas in the supermarket.

Spaghetti with Marinara Sauce

PREP TIME: 20 Minutes • **START TO FINISH:** 50 Minutes • 4 servings

1 medium onion

2 cloves garlic or ¼ teaspoon garlic powder

1 small green bell pepper

1 tablespoon olive or vegetable oil

1 can (14.5 oz) diced tomatoes, undrained

1 can (8 oz) tomato sauce

1 tablespoon chopped fresh or 1 teaspoon dried basil leaves

1½ teaspoons chopped fresh or ½ teaspoon dried oregano leaves

¼ teaspoon salt

¼ teaspoon fennel seed, if desired

⅛ teaspoon pepper

½ teaspoon salt (for cooking spaghetti), if desired

8 oz uncooked spaghetti

1 Peel and chop the onion to measure ½ cup. Peel and finely chop the garlic. Cut the bell pepper in half lengthwise, and cut out seeds and membrane. Chop enough bell pepper to measure ¼ cup. Wrap any remaining bell pepper with plastic wrap and refrigerate.

2 In a 2-quart saucepan, heat the oil over medium heat 1 to 2 minutes. Add the onion, garlic and bell pepper. Cook 2 minutes, stirring occasionally.

3 Stir in the tomatoes with their liquid, tomato sauce, basil, oregano, ¼ teaspoon salt, the fennel seed and pepper. Heat to boiling over high heat. Once mixture is boiling, reduce heat just enough so mixture bubbles gently and does not spatter.

4 Cover with lid; cook 35 minutes, stirring about every 10 minutes to make sure mixture is just bubbling gently and to prevent sticking. Lower the heat if the sauce is bubbling too fast.

5 After the sauce has been cooking about 20 minutes, fill a 4-quart Dutch oven about half full of water. Add ½ teaspoon salt if desired. Cover with lid; heat over high heat until the water is boiling rapidly. Add the spaghetti. Heat to boiling again. Boil uncovered 8 to 10 minutes, stirring frequently, until tender but not mushy.

6 Place a strainer or colander in the sink. Pour the spaghetti in the strainer to drain. Serve with the tomato sauce.

1 Serving: Calories 340; Total Fat 5g; Cholesterol 0mg; Sodium 580mg; Total Carbohydrate 62g (Dietary Fiber 5g); Protein 11g **Carbohydrate Choices:** 4

Spaghetti with Meat Sauce: In a 12-inch skillet, cook 1 pound lean (at least 80%) ground beef with the onion, garlic and bell pepper over medium heat 8 to 10 minutes, stirring occasionally, until beef is thoroughly cooked. Place a strainer or colander in a bowl; line strainer with a double thickness of paper towels. Pour the beef mixture into the strainer to drain. Return beef mixture to skillet; discard paper towels and any juices in the bowl. Continue with step 3.

Simmering Marinara Sauce: Heat to boiling. Reduce heat just enough so mixtures bubbles gently and doesn't spatter.

Cook's Tips

The sauce may look ready to eat after heating to a boil. However, the longer cook time over low heat is necessary to develop the flavors.

A tightly held bundle of spaghetti, about the diameter of a quarter, weighs about 4 ounces.

Rigatoni with Basil Pesto

PREP TIME: 30 Minutes • **START TO FINISH:** 30 Minutes • 4 servings

SPECIAL EQUIPMENT

blender or food processor

RIGATONI

½ teaspoon salt (for cooking pasta), if desired

3 cups uncooked rigatoni pasta (8 oz)

BASIL PESTO

1 cup fresh basil leaves

2 cloves garlic

⅓ cup grated Parmesan cheese

⅓ cup olive or vegetable oil

2 tablespoons pine nuts or walnut pieces

Cook's Tip

Use pesto immediately because it will darken as it is exposed to the air. Or store the pesto immediately by placing in an airtight container and refrigerate up to 5 days or freeze up to 1 month.

1   Fill a 4-quart Dutch oven about half full of water. Add ½ teaspoon salt if desired. Cover with lid; heat over high heat until the water is boiling rapidly. Add the pasta. Heat to boiling again. Boil uncovered 14 to 16 minutes, stirring frequently, until tender but not mushy. While the water is heating and the pasta is cooking, continue with the recipe to make the pesto.

2   To measure basil, firmly pack basil leaves into a measuring cup. Use a measuring cup for measuring dry ingredients. Rinse the basil leaves with cool water, and pat dry thoroughly with a paper towel or clean, dry kitchen towel. Peel the garlic cloves.

3   In a food processor or blender, place the basil leaves, garlic, cheese, oil and pine nuts. Cover and process, stopping occasionally to scrape sides with rubber spatula, until smooth.

4   Place a strainer or colander in the sink. Pour the pasta in the strainer to drain, and place in a large serving bowl or back in the Dutch oven. Immediately pour the pesto over the hot pasta, and toss until pasta is well coated. Serve with additional grated Parmesan cheese if desired.

1 Serving: Calories 470; Total Fat 25g; Cholesterol 5mg; Sodium 135mg; Total Carbohydrate 50g (Dietary Fiber 3g); Protein 13g **Carbohydrate Choices:** 3

Rigatoni with Cilantro Pesto: Substitute ¾ cup firmly packed fresh cilantro leaves and ¼ cup firmly packed fresh parsley leaves for the fresh basil.

Rigatoni with Spinach Pesto: Substitute 1 cup firmly packed fresh spinach leaves and ¼ cup firmly packed fresh basil leaves (or 2 tablespoons dried basil leaves) for the 1 cup fresh basil.

Measuring Basil Leaves: Firmly pack basil leaves into dry measuring cup.

Making Pesto: Place pesto ingredients into food processor. Cover and process until smooth.

Fettuccine Alfredo

PREP TIME: 30 Minutes • **START TO FINISH:** 30 Minutes • 4 servings

½ teaspoon salt (for cooking fettuccine), if desired

8 oz uncooked fettuccine

½ cup butter or margarine (1 stick)

½ cup whipping cream

¾ cup grated Parmesan cheese

½ teaspoon salt

Dash of pepper

Chopped fresh parsley, if desired

1 Fill a 4-quart Dutch oven about half full of water. Add ½ teaspoon salt if desired. Cover with lid; heat over high heat until the water is boiling rapidly. Add the fettuccine. Heat to boiling again. Boil uncovered 11 to 13 minutes, stirring frequently. While the fettuccine is cooking, continue with the recipe to make the Alfredo sauce.

2 In a 2-quart saucepan, heat the butter and whipping cream over low heat, stirring constantly, until butter is melted. Stir in the cheese, ½ teaspoon salt and dash of pepper until mixture is smooth.

3 To test if fettuccine is done, use a fork to lift one strand of fettuccine and press gently against inside of Dutch oven. Fettuccine should be tender but not mushy. Place a strainer or colander in the sink. Pour the fettuccine in the strainer to drain, and place in a large serving bowl or back in the Dutch oven.

4 Pour the sauce over the hot fettuccine, and stir until fettuccine is well coated. Sprinkle with parsley.

1 Serving: Calories 580; Total Fat 41g; Cholesterol 155mg; Sodium 760mg; Total Carbohydrate 39g (Dietary Fiber 2g); Protein 15g **Carbohydrate Choices:** 2½

Cooking Fettuccine: To test, use a fork to lift one strand of fettuccine and press gently against inside of the Dutch oven. It should be tender but not mushy.

Lighten Up Fettuccine Alfredo: For 24 grams of fat and 440 calories per serving, decrease butter to ⅓ cup and substitute fat-free half-and-half for the whipping cream.

Chicken Fettuccine Alfredo: In step 2, stir in 2 cups chopped cooked chicken or turkey with the cheese.

Cook's Tips

Freshly grated Parmesan cheese will make a thinner sauce than will canned grated cheese. The canned cheese is grated finer so there is slightly more in ¾ cup.

Other pastas may be substituted for the fettuccine. The sauce will cling best to a flat, narrow shape, such as linguine or spaghetti.

Pasta Primavera

PREP TIME: 30 Minutes · **START TO FINISH:** 30 Minutes · 4 servings

½ teaspoon salt (for cooking fettuccine), if desired

8 oz uncooked fettuccine

2 medium carrots

1 small onion

1 tablespoon olive or vegetable oil

1 cup broccoli florets

1 cup cauliflower florets

1 cup frozen green peas

1 container (10 oz) refrigerated Alfredo pasta sauce

Grated Parmesan cheese, if desired

1   Fill a 4-quart Dutch oven about half full of water. Add ½ teaspoon salt if desired. Cover with lid; heat over high heat until the water is boiling rapidly. Add the fettuccine. Heat to boiling again. Boil uncovered 11 to 13 minutes, stirring frequently. While the water is heating and the fettuccine is cooking, continue with the recipe.

2   Peel the carrots, and cut crosswise into thin slices to measure about 1 cup. Peel and chop the onion to measure about ¼ cup.

3   In a 12-inch skillet, heat the oil over medium-high heat 1 to 2 minutes. Add the carrots, onion, broccoli, cauliflower and frozen peas. Stir-fry with a turner or large spoon 6 to 8 minutes, lifting and stirring constantly, until vegetables are crisp-tender when pierced with a fork.

4   Stir the Alfredo sauce into the vegetable mixture. Cook over medium heat, stirring constantly, until hot.

5   To test if fettuccine is done, use a fork to lift one strand of fettuccine and press gently against inside of Dutch oven. Fettuccine should be tender but not mushy. Place strainer or colander in the sink. Pour the fettuccine in the strainer to drain.

6   Stir drained fettuccine into the vegetable mixture. Serve with cheese.

1 Serving: Calories 540; Total Fat 29g; Cholesterol 115mg; Sodium 330mg; Total Carbohydrate 54g (Dietary Fiber 5g); Protein 15g **Carbohydrate Choices:** 3½

Stir-Frying Vegetables: Using a turner or large spoon, lift and stir vegetables constantly, until they are crisp-tender.

Cook's Tips

Other flat, long pasta, such as linguine or spaghetti, can be used for the fettuccine.

Look for the refrigerated Alfredo sauce next to the fresh pasta. Alfredo sauce is also available in 16-ounce jars near the dried pasta. Use 1¼ cups of the sauce. Refrigerate leftover sauce and toss with hot cooked pasta or vegetables.

Pad Thai

PREP TIME: 40 Minutes • **START TO FINISH:** 40 Minutes • 4 servings

SPECIAL EQUIPMENT

nonstick wok or 12-inch nonstick skillet

⅓ cup lime juice (2 or 4 medium limes)

3 cloves garlic or ⅜ teaspoon garlic powder

1 medium shallot or 1 small onion

4 medium green onions with tops

3 cups fresh bean sprouts or 2 cans (14.5 oz each) bean sprouts

¼ cup dry-roasted peanuts

2 large eggs

4 cups water

1 package (7 oz) linguine-style stir-fry rice noodles (rice stick noodles)

⅓ cup water

3 tablespoons packed brown sugar

3 tablespoons fish sauce or soy sauce

3 tablespoons soy sauce

1 tablespoon rice vinegar or white vinegar

¾ teaspoon ground red pepper (cayenne)

3 tablespoons vegetable oil

¼ cup firmly packed fresh cilantro leaves, coarsely chopped

Cook's Tip

If rice noodles aren't available you can substitute 7 ounces uncooked linguine. Omit step 3; cook and drain linguine as directed on package.

1 Peel and finely chop the garlic. Peel and finely chop the shallot (or peel and finely chop the onion to measure ¼ cup). Peel and thinly slice the green onions to measure ¼ cup. Rinse the fresh bean sprouts with cool water, then drain in a strainer (or drain and rinse the canned bean sprouts in a strainer). Finely chop the peanuts. In a small bowl, beat the eggs slightly with a fork.

2 In a 3-quart saucepan, heat 4 cups water to boiling. Remove saucepan from heat and add the noodles, push noodles into water with back of spoon to cover completely with water if necessary. Soak noodles 3 to 5 minutes or until noodles are soft yet firm.

3 While noodles are soaking, in a small bowl, mix lime juice, ⅓ cup water, brown sugar, fish sauce, soy sauce, vinegar, red pepper and 1 tablespoon of the oil; set aside. Place strainer in the sink. Pour noodles in the strainer to drain. Rinse with cold water; drain.

4 In a nonstick wok or 12-inch nonstick skillet, heat remaining 2 tablespoons oil over medium heat. Add garlic and shallot; cook about 30 seconds, stirring constantly, until they begin to brown. Stir in beaten eggs, cooking and stirring gently about 2 minutes until scrambled but still moist.

5 Stir in noodles and lime juice mixture. Increase heat to high; cook about 1 minute, tossing constantly with 2 wooden spoons, until sauce begins to thicken. Add green onions, bean sprouts and peanuts; cook 1 to 2 minutes, tossing with wooden spoons. Place on serving platter. Sprinkle with cilantro. If desired, garnish with additional chopped dry-roasted peanuts and green onions.

1 Serving: Calories 520; Total Fat 21g; Cholesterol 105mg; Sodium 1300mg; Total Carbohydrate 65g (Dietary Fiber 4g); Protein 15g **Carbohydrate Choices:** 4

Pad Thai with Chicken: Add 2 cups chopped cooked chicken with the green onions, bean sprouts and peanuts in step 6.

Pad Thai with Shrimp: Add 12 ounces cooked deveined peeled medium shrimp, thawed if frozen, with the green onions, bean sprouts and peanuts in step 6.

Chopping Shallots: Cut the shallot in half. Place cut side down on cutting board. Starting ¼-inch from the root end, make length-wise cuts. Cut crosswise into pieces; chop into small pieces.

Pushing Noodles into Water: Using a spoon, push noodles into the hot water to cover them completely with water.

Asian Noodle Bowl

PREP TIME: 25 Minutes • **START TO FINISH:** 25 Minutes • 4 servings

1 small onion

¼ of a medium red bell pepper

2 cups fresh broccoli florets or 2 cups frozen (thawed) broccoli florets

1 can (14 to 15 oz) baby corn nuggets

¼ cup salted peanuts

¼ cup barbecue sauce

2 tablespoons hoisin sauce or barbecue sauce

1 tablespoon peanut butter

Dash of ground red pepper (cayenne), if desired

1 tablespoon vegetable oil

½ cup water

½ teaspoon salt (for cooking noodles), if desired

1 package (10 oz) Chinese noodles (curly)

1 Peel the onion and cut into thin wedges. Cut out the seeds and membrane from the bell pepper, and chop enough of the bell pepper to measure ¼ cup. Wrap and refrigerate any remaining bell pepper. Place fresh broccoli in a strainer; rinse with cold water (or drain thawed frozen broccoli in strainer). Drain the corn nuggets in a strainer. Coarsely chop the peanuts.

2 In a small bowl, mix the barbecue sauce, hoisin sauce, peanut butter and ground red pepper; set aside.

3 In a 12-inch skillet, heat the oil over medium heat 1 to 2 minutes. Add the onion and bell pepper. Cook 2 minutes, stirring frequently. Stir in the broccoli and ½ cup water. Cover with lid; cook 2 to 4 minutes, stirring occasionally, until broccoli is crisp-tender.

4 While vegetables are cooking, fill a 4-quart Dutch oven about half full with water. Add ½ teaspoon salt if desired. Cover with lid; heat over high heat until the water is boiling rapidly. Add the noodles. Heat to boiling again. Boil uncovered 4 to 5 minutes, stirring frequently, until tender but not mushy.

5 While noodles are cooking, stir corn and sauce mixture into vegetable mixture. Cook uncovered 3 to 4 minutes, stirring occasionally, until mixture is hot and bubbly.

6 Place a strainer or colander in the sink. Pour the noodles in the strainer to drain. Divide noodles among 4 individual serving bowls. Spoon vegetable mixture over noodles. Sprinkle with the chopped peanuts.

1 Serving: Calories 520; Total Fat 13g; Cholesterol 0mg; Sodium 590mg; Total Carbohydrate 83g (Dietary Fiber 8g); Protein 19g **Carbohydrate Choices:** 5½

Cutting Onion into Wedges:
Peel the onion and cut lengthwise in half. Cut each half lengthwise into thin wedges.

Mom's Macaroni and Cheese

PREP TIME: 10 Minutes • **START TO FINISH:** 40 Minutes • 5 servings

1 small onion

6 oz American cheese loaf
(from 8-oz package)

½ teaspoon salt (for cooking
macaroni), if desired

1½ cups uncooked elbow macaroni
(5 oz)

2 tablespoons butter or margarine

¼ cup all-purpose flour

½ teaspoon salt

¼ teaspoon pepper

1¾ cups milk

1 Heat the oven to 375°F. Peel and chop the onion to measure ¼ cup. Cut the cheese loaf into ½-inch cubes.

2 Fill a 2-quart saucepan about half full of water. Add ½ teaspoon salt if desired. Cover with lid; heat over high heat until the water is boiling rapidly. Add the macaroni. Heat to boiling again. Boil uncovered 6 to 8 minutes, stirring frequently, until tender but not mushy. While macaroni is cooking, continue with the recipe.

3 In a 3-quart saucepan, melt the butter over medium heat. Add the onion. Cook about 2 minutes, stirring occasionally, until onion is softened. Stir in the flour, salt and pepper. Cook 1 to 2 minutes, stirring constantly, until smooth and bubbly. Remove the saucepan from the heat. Stir in the milk with a wire whisk. Return saucepan to medium heat and heat to boiling, stirring constantly. Continue boiling and stirring 1 minute.

4 Remove the saucepan from the heat again. Stir in the cheese until it is melted and smooth.

5 Place a strainer or colander in the sink. Pour the macaroni in the strainer to drain. Stir macaroni into the cheese sauce.

6 Into an ungreased 1½-quart casserole, spoon the macaroni mixture. Bake uncovered about 30 minutes or until bubbly and light brown.

1 Serving: Calories 360; Total Fat 18g; Cholesterol 50mg; Sodium 810mg; Total Carbohydrate 35g (Dietary Fiber 2g); Protein 16g **Carbohydrate Choices:** 2

Cutting Cheese into Cubes:
Cut the cheese into ½-inch slices and stack; cut into ½-inch strips. Cut across the strips into ½-inch cubes.

Making Cheese Sauce: Stir the flour, salt and pepper into the cooked onion. Cook, stirring constantly, until smooth and bubbly.

Cook's Tips

American cheese loaf (the loaf of cheese in a box) is used in this recipe because it melts easily and won't curdle during baking. The cheese will be easier to cut into cubes if it is cold rather than room temperature.

There are many shapes of pasta available, so use any short-cut pasta in place of the elbow macaroni such as rotini, gemelli or fusilli.

PASTA BASICS

LONG PASTA

Capellini (Angel Hair): Thin strands that are the thinnest spaghetti.

Egg Noodles: Long or short strips, which can be flat or curly.

Fettuccine: Flat noodles usually ⅜ to ¼ inch wide.

Linguine: Flat noodles, usually ⅛ inch wide.

Spaghetti: Long, thin strands that are round and solid.

Vermicelli: Long strands, thinner than spaghetti.

Lasagna: About 2 inches wide, with ruffled or straight edges.

SHAPED PASTA

Conchigle (Shells): Shell-shaped in small, medium and large sizes and usually has ridges.

Farfalle (Bow-Tie): Butterfly-shaped pasta in small and large sizes.

Gemelli: Looks like two strands of spaghetti twisted together.

Orecchiette: Small disk-shape and means "little ear."

Radiatore: Looks like old-fashioned radiator with ruffled edges.

Rotelle: Wide corkscrew-shaped pasta.

Rotini: Short-cut corkscrew-shaped and not as wide as rotelle.

Wagon Wheel: Round resembling a wheel with spokes.

Acini De Pepe: Peppercorn-size pieces of cut spaghetti.

Couscous: Tiniest pasta made from granular semolina wheat.

Rosamarina: Pumpkin seed-shaped pasta.

Orzo: Rice-shaped pasta. Orzo and rosamarina are similar in shape but orzo is smaller.

Ditalini (Ditali): Very tiny short tubes either grooved or smooth.

TUBULAR PASTA

Bucatini: Long with a smooth surface.

Cannelloni: Large with smooth surface.

Cavatappi: Short-cut that is corkscrew-shaped.

Elbow Macaroni: Short-cut that is curved in the middle.

Fusilli: Short-cut that is spring-shaped.

Manicotti: Large 4-inch-long tube with lengthwise grooves.

Mostaccioli: About 2-inch-long tube and can be smooth surface or with grooves.

Penne: Short-cut, about 1¼ inches long, with smooth surface or with grooves.

Rigatoni: Short-cut, about 1 inch long, with grooves.

Ziti: Short-cut, about 2 inches long, with smooth surface.

FILLED PASTA

Ravioli: Pillow-shaped filled with cheese, meat or vegetable filling.

Tortellini: Little rings filled with cheese, meat or vegetable filling.

ASIAN NOODLES

Cellophane (Bean Thread): Thin transparent noodle made from starch of mung beans. Substitute rice noodles.

Chinese Noodles (Stir-Fry): Range from very thin to thick and round. Substitute spaghetti or linguine.

Chinese or Japanese Noodles (Curly): Wavy, thin, long noodles sold in rectangular "bricks."

Ramen Noodles: Instant, deep-fried noodles sold with a seasoning packet.

Rice Noodles (Rice Sticks): Thin translucent strands made from rice flour. Substitute capellini or linguine.

Soba: Round or flat noodle made from buckwheat flour. Substitute whole wheat spaghetti.

Somen: Very thin strands made from wheat flour. substitute vermicelli or capellini.

Udon: Fat noodle made from wheat flour that can be flat, square or round. Substitute fettuccine or linguine.

3 MAIN DISHES, MEAT to MEATLESS

Thyme-Roasted Chicken with Vegetables

PREP TIME: 25 Minutes • **START TO FINISH:** 2 Hours 10 Minutes • 6 servings

SPECIAL EQUIPMENT

shallow roasting pan
(about 13 × 9-inch rectangle)

---

1 whole chicken (3 to 3½ lb)

6 medium carrots

4 medium stalks celery

3 large baking potatoes (russet or
    Idaho), about 8 oz each

3 medium onions

2 tablespoons butter or margarine

1 tablespoon chopped fresh or
    1 teaspoon dried thyme leaves

1 Serving: Calories 400; Total Fat 17g;
Cholesterol 95mg; Sodium 180mg; Total
Carbohydrate 32g (Dietary Fiber 5g);
Protein 30g **Carbohydrate Choices:** 2

1 Heat the oven to 375°F. Fold the wings of the chicken across the back so tips are touching. There may be a little resistance, but once they are in this position, they will stay. Tie the legs to the tail with string or use skewers; if the tail is missing, tie the legs together.

2 In a shallow roasting pan, place the chicken with the breast side up. Insert an ovenproof meat thermometer so the tip is in the thickest part of inside thigh and does not touch bone. Roast chicken uncovered 45 minutes.

3 While the chicken is roasting, peel the carrots, and cut into 1-inch pieces. Cut the celery into 1-inch pieces. Scrub the potatoes thoroughly with a vegetable brush or peel the potatoes, and cut into 1½-inch pieces. Peel the onions, and cut into wedges.

4 Remove the chicken from the oven. Arrange the carrots, celery, potatoes and onions around the chicken. In a 1-quart saucepan, heat the butter over low heat just until melted. (Or place the butter in a small microwavable bowl; cover with a microwavable paper towel and microwave on High 10 to 20 seconds or until melted.) Stir the thyme into the butter, then drizzle over the chicken and vegetables.

5 Cover the chicken and vegetables with foil; roast 45 to 60 minutes longer or until the thermometer reads 180°F and vegetables are tender when pierced with a fork. Or check by wiggling the legs; if they move easily, the chicken is done.

6 Remove the vegetables from the pan, and cover with foil to keep warm while carving the chicken.

7 Place the chicken, breast up and with its legs to your right if you're right-handed or to the left if left-handed, on cutting board. Remove ties from legs. To carve chicken, see Carving Roast Chicken and Turkey (page 257).

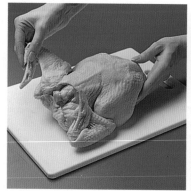

Folding Chicken Wings: Fold wings of the chicken across its back so that tips are touching.

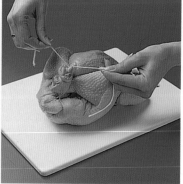

Tying Chicken Legs: Tie the legs to the tail with string or use skewers; if the tail is missing, tie the legs together.

Cook's Tips

For easy cleanup, use a disposable foil roasting pan. For easier handling of the heavy chicken and vegetables, buy a heavy-duty roasting pan or use two lighter-weight pans.

If you have an ovenproof platter, place the vegetables on the platter, cover with foil and place in the oven, which has been turned off, while you carve the chicken.

Oven-Fried Chicken

PREP TIME: 20 Minutes • **START TO FINISH:** 1 Hour 20 Minutes • 6 servings

1 cut-up whole chicken
   (3 to 3½ lb)

¼ cup butter or margarine
   (½ stick)

½ cup all-purpose flour

1 teaspoon paprika

½ teaspoon salt

¼ teaspoon pepper

1   Cut fat from chicken with kitchen scissors or a knife and discard.

2   Heat the oven to 425°F. Place the butter in a 13 × 9-inch pan, and melt it in the oven, which will take about 3 minutes.

3   In a large food-storage plastic bag, mix the flour, paprika, salt and pepper. Place a few pieces of chicken at a time in the bag, seal the bag and shake to coat with flour mixture. Place the chicken, skin sides down, in a single layer in the butter in the pan.

4   Bake uncovered 30 minutes. Remove the pan from the oven; turn chicken pieces over, using tongs. Continue baking uncovered about 30 minutes longer or until juice of chicken is clear when you cut to the bone of the thickest pieces (170°F for breasts; 180°F for thighs and legs on instant-read thermometer). If the chicken sticks to the pan, loosen it gently with a turner or fork.

1 Serving: Calories 330; Total Fat 21g; Cholesterol 105mg; Sodium 330mg; Total Carbohydrate 8g (Dietary Fiber 0g); Protein 28g **Carbohydrate Choices:** ½

Cook's Tips

You can use your favorite chicken pieces instead of the cut-up whole chicken. Use 3 to 3½ pounds breasts, thighs or legs for the cut-up chicken.

For a crunchy coating, substitute 1 cup cornflake crumbs for the ½ cup flour. Dip chicken into ¼ cup butter or margarine, melted, before coating with crumb mixture.

Turning Chicken Pieces: Turn chicken pieces over, using tongs or turner. If chicken pieces stick to the pan, loosen them gently to prevent pulling off the skin.

Lighten Up Oven-Fried Chicken: Remove the skin from chicken before cooking. Do not melt butter in pan; instead, spray pan with cooking spray. Decrease butter to 2 tablespoons; melt the butter and drizzle over chicken after turning in step 4 for 11 grams of fat and 240 calories per serving.

Zesty Roasted Chicken and Potatoes

PREP TIME: 10 Minutes • **START TO FINISH:** 45 Minutes • 6 servings

SPECIAL EQUIPMENT

15 × 10 × 1-inch pan

6 boneless skinless chicken breasts (about 1¾ lb)

Cooking spray for greasing pan

8 small (new) red potatoes (about 1 lb)

2 cloves garlic or ¼ teaspoon garlic powder

⅓ cup mayonnaise or salad dressing

3 tablespoons Dijon mustard

½ teaspoon pepper

Chopped fresh chives, if desired

1 Cut fat from chicken with kitchen scissors or a knife and discard.

2 Heat the oven to 350°F. Spray a 15 × 10 × 1-inch pan with the cooking spray. Scrub the potatoes thoroughly with a vegetable brush and water to remove any dirt, but do not peel. Cut the potatoes into quarters. Peel and finely chop the garlic.

3 Place the chicken and potatoes in the pan. In a small bowl, mix the mayonnaise, mustard, pepper and garlic; brush mixture over chicken and potatoes.

4 Roast uncovered 30 to 35 minutes or until potatoes are tender when pierced with a fork and juice of chicken is clear when you cut into the center of thickest part (170°F on instant-read thermometer). Sprinkle with chives.

1 Serving: Calories 310; Total Fat 14g; Cholesterol 85mg; Sodium 330mg; Total Carbohydrate 15g (Dietary Fiber 2g); Protein 31g **Carbohydrate Choices:** 1

Lighten Up Zesty Roasted Chicken and Potatoes: Use low-fat mayonnaise for 9 grams of fat and 270 calories per serving.

Cook's Tips

Choose potatoes similar in size, about 1½ inches in diameter, so they get tender at the same time.

A coarse-grained, spicy brown or honey mustard can be substituted for the Dijon mustard.

Scrubbing Small Potatoes: Scrub potatoes thoroughly with a vegetable brush and water to remove any dirt.

Chopping Garlic: Hit garlic clove with flat side of a chef's knife to crack the skin, which will slip off easily. Finely chop garlic with the knife.

Parmesan-Dijon Chicken

PREP TIME: 15 Minutes • **START TO FINISH:** 45 Minutes • 6 servings

SPECIAL EQUIPMENT

shallow microwavable dish
or pie plate

---

6 boneless skinless chicken
breasts (about 1¾ lb)

¼ cup butter or margarine
(½ stick)

¾ cup dry bread crumbs

¼ cup grated Parmesan cheese

2 tablespoons Dijon mustard

1 Cut fat from chicken with kitchen scissors or a knife and discard.

2 Heat the oven to 375°F. Either place the butter in a shallow microwavable dish and microwave uncovered on High about 15 seconds until melted, or place the butter in a pie plate and place in the oven about 4 minutes until melted.

3 In a large food-storage plastic bag, mix the bread crumbs and cheese. Stir the mustard into the melted butter until well mixed.

4 Pat the chicken dry with paper towels. Dip 1 piece of chicken at a time into the butter mixture, coating all sides. Then place in the bag of crumbs, seal the bag and shake to coat with crumb mixture. In an ungreased 13 × 9-inch pan, place the chicken in a single layer.

5 Bake uncovered 20 to 30 minutes, turning chicken over once with tongs, until juice of the chicken is clear when you cut into the center of the thickest part (170°F on instant-read thermometer). If chicken sticks to the pan during baking, loosen it gently with a turner or fork.

1 Serving: Calories 330; Total Fat 17g; Cholesterol 110mg; Sodium 540mg; Total Carbohydrate 11g (Dietary Fiber 0g); Protein 36g **Carbohydrate Choices:** 1

Cook's Tip

If you're a mustard fan, you might try varying the mustard for coating the chicken by using tarragon, coarse-grained or country-style Dijon mustard.

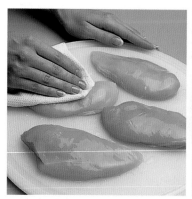

Patting Chicken: Pat chicken with paper towel to remove excess moisture so crumb coating will stick.

Coating Chicken: Dip chicken into butter mixture, then shake in bag of crumb coating.

Lemon Chicken Stir-Fry

PREP TIME: 30 Minutes • **START TO FINISH:** 30 Minutes • 4 servings

1 lb uncooked chicken breast tenders (not breaded)

1 medium onion

2 cups small broccoli florets

½ cup sugar snap pea pods

1 cup cherry or grape tomatoes

½ teaspoon salt (for cooking pasta), if desired

8 oz uncooked angel hair (capellini) pasta

1 tablespoon vegetable oil

1 cup chicken broth

1 tablespoon chopped fresh or 1 teaspoon dried thyme leaves

1 teaspoon grated lemon peel

4 teaspoons cornstarch

1½ teaspoons lemon-pepper seasoning

1 Cut the chicken into 1-inch pieces.

2 Peel the onion and cut into 8 wedges. Prepare the broccoli (page 169). Snap off the stem end of each pea pod, then pull the string across the pea pod to remove it. Cut the tomatoes in half.

3 Fill a 4-quart Dutch oven about half full of water. Add ½ teaspoon salt if desired. Cover with lid; heat over high heat until the water is boiling rapidly. Add the pasta. Heat to boiling again. Boil uncovered 5 to 6 minutes, stirring frequently, until pasta is tender but still firm to the bite.

4 While pasta is cooking, in a 12-inch skillet, heat the oil over medium-high heat. Add the chicken and onion; stir-fry 5 to 6 minutes or until chicken is brown.

5 Add the broccoli and pea pods to chicken mixture. Cook over medium-high heat 4 to 5 minutes, stirring frequently, until vegetables are crisp-tender.

6 Meanwhile, in a small bowl, stir together the broth, thyme, lemon peel, cornstarch and lemon-pepper seasoning; stir into the chicken mixture. Cook over medium-high heat 1 to 2 minutes or until sauce is thickened and vegetables are coated.

7 Stir in the tomatoes; cook until thoroughly heated. Place a strainer or colander in the sink. Pour the pasta in the strainer to drain. Serve chicken mixture over pasta.

1 Serving: Calories 440; Total Fat 6g; Cholesterol 50mg; Sodium 530mg; Total Carbohydrate 61g (Dietary Fiber 5g); Protein 37g **Carbohydrate Choices:** 4

Stringing Pea Pods: Snap off the stem end and pull the string along the straight edge of the pea pod to remove it.

Stir-Frying Chicken and Onions: Cook chicken and onion, turning constantly with a large spoon, until chicken is brown.

Cook's Tips

If you don't have lemon-pepper seasoning, use 1 teaspoon black pepper and increase the grated lemon peel to 1½ teaspoons.

A pound of boneless skinless chicken breasts can be substituted for the chicken tenders. Cut each breast lengthwise into about 1-inch strips and then crosswise into 1-inch pieces.

Meat Loaf

PREP TIME: 20 Minutes • **START TO FINISH:** 1 Hour 25 Minutes • 4 servings

SPECIAL EQUIPMENT

baking pan, such as square or rectangle pan

---

1 lb lean (at least 80%) ground beef

1 clove garlic or ⅛ teaspoon
 garlic powder

1 small onion

2 slices bread with crust

¼ cup milk

2 teaspoons Worcestershire sauce

1 teaspoon chopped fresh or
 ¼ teaspoon dried sage leaves

¼ teaspoon salt

¼ teaspoon ground mustard

⅛ teaspoon pepper

1 large egg

⅓ cup ketchup, chili sauce
 or barbecue sauce

Checking Meat Loaf Doneness:
Cut a small slit near center of loaf; meat and juices should no longer be pink.

1 Heat the oven to 350°F. In a large bowl, break up the beef into small pieces, using a fork or spoon.

2 Peel and finely chop the garlic. Peel the onion, and chop enough of the onion into small pieces to measure 3 tablespoons. Wrap remaining piece of onion, and refrigerate for another use. Add the garlic and onion to the beef.

3 Tear the bread into small pieces and add to beef mixture.

4 Add the milk, Worcestershire sauce, sage, salt, mustard, pepper and egg to the beef mixture. Mix with a fork, large spoon or your hands until the ingredients are well mixed.

5 Place the beef mixture in an ungreased baking pan. Shape the mixture into an 8 × 4-inch loaf in the pan, then spread the ketchup over the top.

6 Bake uncovered 50 to 60 minutes until meat and juices are no longer pink or until a meat thermometer inserted in the center of the loaf reads 160°F and center of loaf is no longer pink*. Let the loaf stand 5 minutes so it will be easier to remove from the pan. Remove loaf from pan and cut into slices.

1 Serving: Calories 290; Total Fat 15g; Cholesterol 125mg; Sodium 560mg; Total Carbohydrate 15g (Dietary Fiber 0g); Protein 23g **Carbohydrate Choices:** 1

* If you like bell pepper, onions and celery in your meat loaf, you may find that it may remain pink even though the beef is cooked to 160°F in the center. It's due to the natural nitrate content of these ingredients. So it is best to always check meat loaf with a thermometer to make sure it is thoroughly cooked.

Turkey Loaf: Substitute ground turkey for the ground beef. Bake about 60 minutes or until a meat thermometer inserted in the center of the loaf reads 165°F.

Cook's Tips

You can use ⅓ cup dry bread crumbs or ½ cup quick-cooking oats for the 2 slices bread. Just add it to the beef mixture.

Almost any size pan will work; just be sure the pan has sides to catch the juices that will accumulate while the meat loaf bakes.

Fiesta Taco Casserole

PREP TIME: 15 Minutes • **START TO FINISH:** 45 Minutes • 4 servings

4 medium green onions with tops

1 medium tomato

1 lb lean (at least 80%) ground beef

1 can (15 to 16 oz) spicy chili beans in sauce, undrained

1 cup salsa

2 cups coarsely broken tortilla chips

¾ cup sour cream

1 cup shredded Cheddar cheese (4 oz)

Shredded lettuce, if desired

Additional salsa, if desired

1   Heat the oven to 350°F. Peel and slice the green onions to measure ¼ cup. Chop the tomato to measure ¾ cup.

2   In a 10-inch skillet, cook the beef over medium heat 8 to 10 minutes, stirring occasionally, until thoroughly cooked. Place a strainer or colander in a large bowl; line strainer with a double thickness of paper towels. Pour the beef into the strainer to drain. Return beef to skillet. Discard paper towel and any juices in the bowl. Stir in the beans and 1 cup salsa. Heat to boiling, stirring occasionally.

3   In an ungreased 2-quart casserole, place the broken tortilla chips. Top with the beef mixture. Spread with the sour cream. Sprinkle with the onions, tomato and cheese.

4   Bake uncovered 20 to 30 minutes or until hot and bubbly. Serve with the lettuce and additional salsa.

1 Serving: Calories 650; Total Fat 38g; Cholesterol 130mg; Sodium 1550mg; Total Carbohydrate 42g (Dietary Fiber 7g); Protein 37g **Carbohydrate Choices:** 3

Lighten Up Fiesta Taco Casserole: Substitute ground turkey breast for the ground beef, and use reduced-fat sour cream and reduced-fat Cheddar cheese for 21 grams of fat and 520 calories per serving.

Cook's Tips

Tortilla chips at the bottom of the bag are perfect for this casserole. They're already "coarsely broken." But if you need more, place the tortilla chips in a heavy-duty plastic bag and crush them with your hand or rolling pin.

Looking for a different cheese to try? Shredded Mexican cheese blend or Monterey Jack are good choices.

Cutting Green Onions: Peel onions and cut off root end. Cut the onions into thin slices, including some of the green part.

Shredding Lettuce: Cut head of iceberg lettuce in half. Place one half, cut side down, on cutting board and cut into long pieces.

Beef Pot Roast

PREP TIME: 15 Minutes • **START TO FINISH:** 3 Hours 15 Minutes • 6 servings

ROAST

1 tablespoon vegetable oil

1 boneless beef bottom round (rump) roast, beef tip or chuck eye roast (2 to 2½ lb)

¾ teaspoon salt

½ teaspoon pepper

¼ cup prepared horseradish

¾ cup water

8 small (new) red or white potatoes (about 1 lb)

6 medium carrots

4 small onions

POT ROAST GRAVY

Water

¼ cup cold water

2 tablespoons all-purpose flour

Salt and pepper to taste, if desired

1 In a 4-quart Dutch oven, add the oil. Place the beef roast in the Dutch oven. Cook over medium heat, turning occasionally, until all sides are brown. Browning is important because it helps develop the rich flavor of the roast. If the roast sticks to the Dutch oven, loosen it carefully with a fork or turner. Remove Dutch oven from the heat.

2 Sprinkle ¾ teaspoon salt and ½ teaspoon pepper over the roast. Measure ¾ cup water in a 1-cup glass measuring cup. Add horseradish and stir until mixed. Pour over roast in Dutch oven. Heat to boiling over high heat. Once water is boiling, reduce heat just enough so water bubbles gently. Cover with lid; cook 1 hour 30 minutes. If more water is needed to keep the Dutch oven from becoming dry, add ¼ cup at a time.

3 After the roast has been cooking for 1 hour 30 minutes, scrub the potatoes thoroughly with a vegetable brush and water, but do not peel. Cut each potato into quarters. Peel the carrots, and cut each into 4 equal lengths. Peel the onions and cut each in half. Add the potatoes, carrots and onions to the Dutch oven around the roast. Cover; cook about 1 hour or until the roast and vegetables are tender when pierced with a fork. Vegetables that are in the cooking liquid will cook more quickly, so you may want to move some of the vegetables from the top of the roast into the liquid so all cook uniformly.

Cook's Tip

The horseradish blends in and mellows, leaving a flavor you can't quite put your finger on. Be sure to use prepared horseradish, and not horseradish sauce which is creamy, which you'll find in the refrigerator section of your supermarket.

Browning Pot Roast: Brown the pot roast, turning occasionally with a fork or tongs, until all sides are brown. If necessary, hold the roast with the fork to brown the sides.

Making Pot Roast Gravy: Shake water and flour in a tightly covered jar. Gradually pour flour mixture into liquid, stirring constantly.

4 Remove the roast and vegetables to a warm platter or pan and cover with foil to keep warm while making the gravy.

5 Pour liquid from Dutch oven into a 2-cup glass measuring cup. Remove the fat from the liquid by skimming off the fat with a large spoon; return 1 tablespoon fat to Dutch oven and discard remaining fat. You will need 1 cup liquid to make gravy. If needed, add enough water to the liquid to measure 1 cup. Return 1 cup liquid to the Dutch oven.

6 In a tightly covered jar, shake ¼ cup cold water and the flour. Gradually stir this mixture into the liquid in the Dutch oven. Heat to boiling over high heat, stirring constantly. Continue boiling 1 minute, stirring constantly, until thickened. Season with salt and pepper to taste if desired. While keeping the gravy warm over low heat, cut the roast into ¼-inch slices. Serve with the gravy and vegetables.

1 Serving: Calories 310; Total Fat 5g; Cholesterol 85mg; Sodium 420mg; Total Carbohydrate 28g (Dietary Fiber 5g); Protein 37g **Carbohydrate Choices:** 2

Oven Beef Pot Roast: Heat the oven to 325°F. Using an ovenproof 5-quart Dutch oven, brown the roast as directed in step 1. Continue as directed in step 2—except after adding the water, place Dutch oven in 325°F oven. Cover; bake 2 hours. Prepare the vegetables as directed in step 3. Add the vegetables around the roast. Cover; bake 45 minutes to 1 hour longer or until roast and vegetables are tender. Continue as directed in steps 4, 5 and 6.

Beef Stew

PREP TIME: 30 Minutes • **START TO FINISH:** 3 Hours 30 Minutes • 4 servings

1 boneless beef chuck, tip or round roast (1 lb)

1 tablespoon vegetable oil

3 cups water

½ teaspoon salt

⅛ teaspoon pepper

2 medium carrots

1 large baking potato (russet or Idaho), about 8 oz

1 medium green bell pepper

1 medium stalk celery

1 small onion

1 teaspoon salt

1 dried bay leaf

½ cup cold water

2 tablespoons all-purpose flour

1 Cut most of the fat from the beef, if necessary, and discard. Cut the beef into 1-inch cubes.

2 In a 12-inch skillet or 4-quart Dutch oven, heat the oil over medium heat 1 to 2 minutes. Add the beef; cook 10 to 15 minutes, stirring occasionally, until brown on all sides.

3 Remove the skillet from the heat, then add the water, ½ teaspoon salt and the pepper. Heat to boiling over high heat. Once mixture is boiling, reduce heat just enough so mixture bubbles gently. Cover with lid; cook 2 hours to 2 hours 30 minutes or until beef is almost tender.

4 Peel the carrots, and cut into 1-inch pieces. Scrub the potato thoroughly with a vegetable brush and water, but do not peel. Cut the potato into 1½-inch pieces. Cut the bell pepper in half lengthwise, and cut out seeds and membrane. Cut the bell pepper into 1-inch pieces. Cut the celery into 1-inch pieces. Peel and chop the onion.

5 Stir the vegetables, 1 teaspoon salt and the bay leaf into the beef mixture. Cover; cook about 30 minutes longer or until vegetables are tender when pierced with a fork. Remove and discard bay leaf.

6 In a tightly covered jar or container, shake the cold water and flour. Gradually stir flour mixture into beef mixture. Heat to boiling over high heat, stirring constantly. Continue boiling 1 minute, stirring constantly, until stew is thickened.

1 Serving: Calories 350; Total Fat 17g; Cholesterol 65mg; Sodium 980mg; Total Carbohydrate 25g (Dietary Fiber 4g); Protein 24g **Carbohydrate Choices:** 1½

Browning Beef Stew Meat:
Cook the beef in the oil about 15 minutes, stirring occasionally, until brown on all sides. Browning helps develop the flavor of the stew.

Cook's Tips

Save time and use 1 pound of beef stew meat for the roast. If some pieces are large, cut into about 1-inch pieces.

You can use a 1-pound bag of frozen mixed vegetables instead of the carrots, potato, bell pepper, celery and onion. There's no need to thaw the vegetables; just stir them into the beef mixture in step 5.

Italian Beef Kabobs

PREP TIME: 25 Minutes • **START TO FINISH:** 1 Hour 25 Minutes • 2 servings

SPECIAL EQUIPMENT

four 10-inch metal or bamboo skewers; broiler pan with rack

¾ lb boneless beef sirloin or round steak (1 inch thick)

2 cloves garlic or ¼ teaspoon garlic powder

¼ cup balsamic vinegar

¼ cup water

1 tablespoon chopped fresh or 1 teaspoon dried oregano leaves

2 tablespoons olive or vegetable oil

1½ teaspoons chopped fresh or ½ teaspoon dried marjoram leaves

1 teaspoon granulated sugar

1 Cut most of the fat from the beef, if necessary, and discard. Cut beef into 1-inch pieces.

2 Peel and finely chop the garlic. In a medium glass or plastic bowl, make a marinade by mixing the vinegar, water, oregano, oil, marjoram, sugar and garlic. Stir in the beef until coated. Cover; refrigerate, stirring occasionally, at least 1 hour but no longer than 12 hours. If you are using bamboo skewers, soak them in water for 30 minutes before using to prevent burning.

3 Move the rack so the kabobs are about 4 inches from the broiler heating unit. Set the oven control to broil.

4 Remove the beef from the marinade, reserving the marinade. On 4 (10-inch) metal or bamboo skewers, thread the beef, leaving a ½-inch space between each piece. Brush the kabobs with the marinade.

5 Place the kabobs on the rack in the broiler pan. Broil kabobs with tops about 3 inches from the heat 6 to 8 minutes for medium-rare to medium doneness, turning and brushing with marinade after 3 minutes. Discard any remaining marinade.

1 Serving: Calories 270; Total Fat 12g; Cholesterol 95mg; Sodium 50mg; Total Carbohydrate 2g (Dietary Fiber 0g); Protein 39g **Carbohydrate Choices:** 0

Cook's Tips

To save time, omit the garlic, vinegar, water, oregano, oil, marjoram and sugar, and instead, marinate the beef in ⅔ cup purchased Italian dressing in step 2.

Be sure to discard any left-over marinade that has been in contact with raw meat. Bacteria from the raw meat could transfer to the marinade.

Broiling Kabobs: Measure the distance from the kabobs to the heating unit. If too close, the meat will become too dark and dry before the inside is done.

Grilled Italian Beef Kabobs: Prepare the coals or a gas grill for direct heat (page 267). Heat to medium heat, which will take about 40 minutes for charcoal or about 10 minutes for a gas grill. Make the kabobs as directed in steps 1, 2 and 4. Place the kabobs on the grill over medium heat. Cover the grill; cook 6 to 8 minutes, turning and brushing kabobs 3 or 4 times with marinade, until beef is desired doneness. Discard any remaining marinade.

Thai Beef Stir-Fry

PREP TIME: 30 Minutes • **START TO FINISH:** 30 Minutes • 4 servings

SPECIAL EQUIPMENT

wok or 12-inch skillet

1 cup uncooked jasmine rice

1¾ cups water

1 lb boneless beef sirloin steak, 1 inch thick

2 teaspoons finely chopped gingerroot or ½ teaspoon ground ginger

2 cloves garlic

7 medium carrots

6 green onions with tops

1 can (8 oz) sliced water chestnuts

½ cup beef broth

2 tablespoons fish sauce or soy sauce

1 tablespoon cornstarch

1 tablespoon white vinegar

2 teaspoons packed brown sugar

2 tablespoons vegetable oil

1 tablespoon grated lemon peel

1 In a 2-quart saucepan, heat the rice and water to boiling over medium-high heat, stirring occasionally to prevent sticking. Once mixture is boiling, reduce heat just enough so mixture bubbles gently. Cover with lid; cook 15 to 20 minutes or until rice is fluffy and tender.

2 While the rice is cooking, cut most of the fat from the beef, if necessary, and discard. Cut beef with the grain into 2-inch strips, then cut strips across the grain into ⅛-inch slices.

3 Prepare the gingerroot. Peel and finely chop the garlic. Peel and thinly slice the carrots to measure 3½ cups. Peel the onions and cut into ½-inch pieces. Drain the water chestnuts in a strainer.

4 In a small bowl, mix the broth, fish sauce, cornstarch, vinegar and brown sugar; set aside.

5 Heat a wok or 12-inch skillet over high heat. Add 1 tablespoon of the oil; rotate the wok to coat the side with oil. Add the beef, gingerroot and garlic; stir-fry about 3 minutes or until beef is brown. Remove beef from wok with a slotted spoon and place on a plate.

6 Add remaining 1 tablespoon oil to the wok; rotate the wok to coat the side with oil. Add the carrots; stir-fry about 5 minutes or until crisp-tender.

7 Stir in the beef, onions, water chestnuts and lemon peel; heat to boiling. Stir in the broth mixture. Cook and stir about 1 minute or until thoroughly heated. Serve beef mixture over rice.

1 Serving: Calories 480; Total Fat 11g; Cholesterol 65mg; Sodium 940mg; Total Carbohydrate 63g (Dietary Fiber 5g); Protein 32g **Carbohydrate Choices:** 4

Cutting Beef Steak Slices: Cut beef with the grain into 2-inch strips, then cut strips across the grain into ⅛-inch slices.

Chopping Gingerroot: Peel gingerroot using a paring knife or vegetable peeler. Cut into thin slices; cut slices into thin pieces. Finely chop using a chef's knife.

Cook's Tips

Place beef in the freezer for 1 hour before slicing. It will be easier to cut into ⅛-inch slices when partially frozen.

If you don't have jasmine rice, you can use regular long-grain white rice. Use 1 cup uncooked rice and 2 cups water; prepare as directed in step 1, cooking 15 minutes.

Pork Tenderloin with Rosemary

PREP TIME: 5 Minutes • **START TO FINISH:** 35 Minutes • 3 servings

SPECIAL EQUIPMENT

garlic press

Cooking spray for greasing pan

1 clove garlic

¼ teaspoon salt

⅛ teaspoon pepper

1 pork tenderloin (about ¾ lb)

1½ teaspoons finely chopped or
    ½ teaspoon dried rosemary
    leaves, crushed

1 Heat the oven to 425°F. Spray an 8-inch square or 11 × 7-inch pan with the cooking spray.

2 Peel and crush the garlic in a garlic press. Sprinkle salt and pepper over all sides of the pork tenderloin. Rub the rosemary and garlic on all sides of pork. Place pork in the pan.

3 Bake uncovered 20 to 30 minutes or until pork has a slight blush of pink in the center and a meat thermometer inserted in the center reads 160°F. Cut pork crosswise into thin slices.

1 Serving: Calories 150; Total Fat 5g; Cholesterol 70mg; Sodium 250mg; Total Carbohydrate 0g (Dietary Fiber 0g); Protein 26g **Carbohydrate Choices:** 0

Cook's Tips

If you're having trouble getting the garlic and rosemary to stick to the tenderloin, rub a little olive oil on the tenderloin.

Some meat thermometers are too top-heavy to stand up in a pork tenderloin so try inserting it almost horizontally, or sideways, into the pork. Using an instant-read thermometer is another option but it isn't ovenproof and can't be left in the pork.

Crushing Garlic: Crush garlic by placing the clove in a garlic press and pushing down on the handle. If you don't have a garlic press, finely chop the garlic with a chef knife.

Crumbling Rosemary Leaves: When using dried rosemary, crumble the leaves in the palm of your hand to release more flavor before rubbing them over the pork.

Pork Chops and Apples

PREP TIME: 15 Minutes • **START TO FINISH:** 1 Hour • 2 servings

1 medium apple, such as Braeburn, Rome Beauty or Granny Smith

2 tablespoons packed brown sugar

¼ teaspoon ground cinnamon

2 pork rib chops, ½ to ¾ inch thick (about ¼ lb each)

Cooking spray for greasing skillet

1 Heat the oven to 350°F. Cut the apple into quarters, and remove the core and seeds. Cut each quarter into 3 or 4 wedges. Place apple wedges in a 1½-quart casserole. Sprinkle the brown sugar and cinnamon over the apples.

2 Cut most of the fat from the pork chops, if necessary, and discard. Spray an 8-inch or 10-inch skillet with the cooking spray, and heat over medium heat 1 to 2 minutes. Cook the pork chops in the hot skillet about 5 minutes, turning once, until light brown.

3 Place the pork chops in a single layer on the apple wedges. Cover with lid or foil; bake about 45 minutes or until the pork is no longer pink when you cut into the center and apples are tender when pierced with a fork. (For pork chops that are ¾ inch thick, a meat thermometer inserted in center should read 160°F.)

1 Serving: Calories 260; Total Fat 9g; Cholesterol 65mg; Sodium 45mg; Total Carbohydrate 23g (Dietary Fiber 2g); Protein 22g **Carbohydrate Choices:** 1½

Cook's Tips

Serve with Garlic Mashed Potatoes (page 226), cooked broccoli (page 169) and whole-grain rolls.

Carefully follow cooking times for pork and use a meat thermometer to test for doneness. Overcooking pork will make it tough and dry.

Cutting Fat from Pork Chop: Use a sharp knife to cut most of the fat from pork chop, being careful not to cut into the meat.

Cutting Apple into Wedges: Cut apple into quarters, and remove core and seeds. Cut each quarter into wedges.

Barbecued Ribs

PREP TIME: 15 Minutes   •   **START TO FINISH:** 2 Hours   •   6 servings

SPECIAL EQUIPMENT
shallow roasting pan (about 13 × 9-inch rectangle); pastry brush

RIBS
4½ lb pork spareribs

SPICY BARBECUE SAUCE
⅓ cup butter or margarine

2 tablespoons white vinegar

2 tablespoons water

1 teaspoon granulated sugar

½ teaspoon garlic powder

½ teaspoon onion powder

½ teaspoon pepper

Dash of ground red pepper (cayenne)

1   Heat the oven to 325°F. Cut the ribs into 6 serving pieces. Place the ribs, meaty sides down, in a shallow roasting pan, about 13 × 9 inches.

2   Bake uncovered 1 hour.

3   While the ribs are baking, in a 1-quart saucepan, heat the sauce ingredients over medium heat, stirring frequently, until butter is melted. (Or microwave the sauce ingredients in a 1-cup microwavable measuring cup on High about 30 seconds or until butter is melted.)

4   Brush the sauce over the ribs, using a pastry brush. Turn ribs over, using tongs. Brush meaty sides of ribs with sauce.

5   Bake uncovered about 45 minutes longer, brushing frequently with sauce, until ribs are tender and no longer pink next to bones. To serve any remaining sauce with the ribs, heat the sauce to boiling, stirring constantly, then continue to boil and stir 1 minute.

1 Serving: Calories 610; Total Fat 51g; Cholesterol 190mg; Sodium 200mg; Total Carbohydrate 1g (Dietary Fiber 0g); Protein 39g **Carbohydrate Choices:** 0

Country-Style Saucy Ribs: Use 3 pounds pork country-style ribs; cut into 6 serving pieces if it is a rack of ribs. Place in 13 × 9-inch pan. Cover with foil; bake at 325°F for 2 hours; drain. Pour sauce over the ribs. Bake uncovered about 30 minutes longer or until ribs are tender and no longer pink next to bones.

Slow Cooker Barbecued Ribs: Use 3½ pounds spareribs and cut into 2- or 3-rib portions. Place ribs in 5- to 6-quart slow cooker. Sprinkle with ½ teaspoon salt and ¼ teaspoon pepper; add ½ cup water. Cover; cook on Low heat setting 8 to 9 hours or until tender. Remove ribs. Drain and discard liquid from slow cooker. Dip ribs into sauce to coat. Place ribs in slow cooker. Pour any remaining sauce over ribs. Cover; cook on Low heat setting 1 hour.

Cutting Ribs: Using kitchen scissors or a sharp knife, cut pork ribs into 6 serving pieces.

Brushing Barbecue Sauce on Ribs: Coat the ribs liberally with sauce, using a pastry brush. Turn ribs with tongs, and brush the other side.

Cook's Tip

This is a vinegar-base barbecue sauce rather than the
more common tomato-base
sauce. If you prefer a tomato
sauce, use ¾ cup of your
favorite barbecue sauce.

Shrimp Scampi

PREP TIME: 15 Minutes • **START TO FINISH:** 15 Minutes • 2 servings

¾ lb uncooked deveined peeled medium shrimp, thawed if frozen

1 medium green onion with top

1 clove garlic or ⅛ teaspoon garlic powder

1 tablespoon olive or vegetable oil

2 teaspoons chopped fresh or ½ teaspoon dried basil leaves

2 teaspoons chopped fresh parsley or ¾ teaspoon parsley flakes

1 tablespoon lemon juice

⅛ teaspoon salt

Grated or shredded Parmesan cheese, if desired

1 Rinse the shrimp with cool water, and pat dry with paper towels. If the shrimp have tails, remove tails with knife. Peel the green onion, and cut into ¼-inch slices. Peel and finely chop the garlic.

2 In a 10-inch skillet, heat the oil over medium heat 1 to 2 minutes. Add the shrimp, onion, garlic, basil, parsley, lemon juice and salt; cook 2 to 3 minutes, stirring frequently, until shrimp are pink. Do not overcook the shrimp or they will become tough.

3 Sprinkle the cheese over the shrimp.

1 **Serving:** Calories 190; Total Fat 8g; Cholesterol 240mg; Sodium 430mg; Total Carbohydrate 2g (Dietary Fiber 0g); Protein 26g **Carbohydrate Choices:** 0

Cook's Tips

Serve these succulent shrimp over hot cooked fettuccine, angel hair pasta or rice and garnish with freshly chopped parsley and fresh lemon.

Uncooked shrimp is very perishable so store it in the refrigerator no longer than 1 to 2 days. Store it in a leakproof plastic bag or plastic container with a tight lid.

Cooking Shrimp: Cook the shrimp only 2 to 3 minutes, stirring frequently. Shrimp will turn pink when done.

Stir-Fried Scallops with Broccoli

PREP TIME: 35 Minutes • **START TO FINISH:** 35 Minutes • 4 servings

½ lb fresh broccoli

¼ lb fresh mushrooms

1 lb uncooked sea scallops

¼ cup roasted red bell peppers (from 7-oz jar)

1 cup uncooked regular long-grain white rice

2 cups water

2 tablespoons butter or margarine

3 tablespoons cornstarch

1 can (10½ oz) condensed chicken broth

2 teaspoons soy sauce

Stir-Fried Shrimp with Broccoli:
Substitute 1 pound uncooked peeled and deveined medium shrimp (thawed if frozen) for the scallops. In step 5, cook the shrimp, broccoli and roasted red peppers 4 to 5 minutes, stirring frequently, until shrimp are pink.

---

1 Trim the large leaves from the broccoli, and cut off any tough ends of lower stems. Rinse broccoli with cool water. Cut stems and florets into bite-size pieces. Cut stem ends from the mushrooms, and cut the mushrooms into ¼-inch slices.

2 If the scallops are larger than 1 inch in diameter, cut each in half. Rinse with cool water, and pat dry with paper towels. Drain the roasted red peppers in a strainer; cut the red peppers into slices.

3 In a 2-quart saucepan, heat the rice and water to boiling over medium-high heat, stirring occasionally to prevent sticking. Once mixture is boiling, reduce heat just enough so mixture bubbles gently. Cover with lid; cook about 15 minutes or until rice is fluffy and tender. While the rice is cooking, continue with the recipe.

4 In a 3-quart saucepan or 12-inch skillet, melt the butter over medium heat. Add the mushrooms; cook about 5 minutes, stirring frequently, until tender when pierced with a fork.

5 Stir in the scallops, broccoli and roasted red peppers. Cook 3 to 4 minutes, stirring frequently, until scallops are white and opaque. Remove the saucepan from the heat.

6 Place the cornstarch in a medium bowl. Gradually stir the chicken broth into the cornstarch until the mixture is smooth. Stir the broth mixture and soy sauce into the scallop mixture. Heat to boiling over high heat, stirring constantly. Continue boiling 1 minute, stirring constantly. Serve over rice.

1 Serving: Calories 360; Total Fat 8g; Cholesterol 45mg; Sodium 820mg; Total Carbohydrate 50g (Dietary Fiber 2g); Protein 22g **Carbohydrate Choices:** 3

Cutting Broccoli into Pieces:
Cut the broccoli into ½-inch stalks and cut the stalks crosswise into 1-inch pieces.

Checking Scallop Doneness:
Scallops are done when they turn white and opaque. Longer cooking results in tough scallops.

Cook's Tips

Scallops are classified as either bay or sea scallops. Bay scallops are much smaller and sweeter than their counterparts. Sea scallops are more readily available and less expensive than bay scallops.

If sea scallops aren't available you can use 1 pound bay scallops. In step 5, cook the broccoli and peppers 2 minutes and then add the scallops. Cook 2 to 3 minutes or until scallops are white and opaque.

Hard-Cooked (Hard-Boiled) Eggs

PREP TIME: 5 Minutes • **START TO FINISH:** 35 Minutes • 4 servings

4 eggs

1 In a 2-quart saucepan, place the eggs in a single layer. Add enough cold water until it is at least 1 inch above the eggs. Heat uncovered to boiling over high heat. Remove the saucepan from the heat. Cover with lid; let stand 18 minutes.

2 Immediately pour off the hot water from the eggs, then run cool water over them in the saucepan until completely cool.

3 Tap each egg lightly on the kitchen counter to crackle the shell. Roll the egg between your hands to loosen the shell, then peel starting at the large end. If the shell is hard to peel, hold egg under cold water while peeling.

1 Serving: Calories 80; Total Fat 5g; Cholesterol 210mg; Sodium 60mg; Total Carbohydrate 0g (Dietary Fiber 0g); Protein 6g **Carbohydrate Choices:** 0

Cook's Tip

Avoid keeping hard-cooked eggs at room temperature for more than 2 hours. If you do, don't eat the eggs.

Peeling Hard-Cooked Eggs:
Roll the egg between your hands to loosen shell, then peel. If shell is hard to peel, hold egg under cold water while peeling.

Fried Eggs, Sunny Side Up

PREP TIME: 10 Minutes • **START TO FINISH:** 10 Minutes • 4 servings

2 tablespoons butter or margarine
4 eggs

1 In a heavy 10-inch skillet, heat the butter over medium heat until it begins to sizzle and look hot.

2 Break an egg into a custard cup, small bowl or saucer. Slip the egg carefully into the skillet. Repeat with the remaining eggs. Reduce heat to low. You should still be able to see and hear the eggs sizzle as they cook. If they stop sizzling, turn up the heat a little.

3 Cook uncovered 5 to 7 minutes, frequently spooning butter from the skillet over the eggs, until the whites are set, a film forms over the yolks and the yolks are thickened.

1 Serving: Calories 130; Total Fat 11g; Cholesterol 225mg; Sodium 105mg; Total Carbohydrate 0g (Dietary Fiber 0g); Protein 6g **Carbohydrate Choices:** 0

Lighten Up Fried Eggs: Omit butter and use a nonstick pan. Cook eggs over low heat about 1 minute or until edges turn white. Add 2 teaspoons water for each egg. Cover and cook about 5 minutes longer or until a film forms over the top and whites and yolks are firm, not runny.

Fried Eggs, Over Easy: Follow directions for Fried Eggs, Sunny Side Up, but after cooking 3 minutes, gently turn eggs over with a turner and cook 1 to 2 minutes longer or until yolks are thickened.

Cook's Tip

Store eggs in their carton in the refrigerator. Keeping them in the carton protects them from absorbing refrigerator odors. Store the carton on a refrigerator shelf, where it is colder, rather than in the door.

Frying Eggs: Break each egg into a custard cup, small bowl or saucer. Slip the egg carefully into the skillet.

Poached Eggs

PREP TIME: 10 Minutes • **START TO FINISH:** 15 Minutes • 4 servings

4 eggs

1 In a 10-inch skillet or 2-quart saucepan, heat 2 to 3 inches of water to boiling. When the water comes to a rolling boil, reduce the heat until water is just simmering (bubbles rise slowly and break just below the surface).

2 Break an egg into a custard cup, small bowl or saucer. Hold the custard cup close to the water's surface and carefully slip the egg into the water. Repeat with the remaining eggs.

3 Cook eggs 3 to 5 minutes or until whites and yolks are firm and not runny. Carefully remove eggs with a slotted spoon.

1 Serving: Calories 80; Total Fat 5g; Cholesterol 210mg; Sodium 60mg; Total Carbohydrate 0g (Dietary Fiber 0g); Protein 6g **Carbohydrate Choices:** 0

Cook's Tip

Whether the eggshell is white or brown depends on the breed and diet of the hen. Flavor, nutritive value and the way the egg cooks are the same for both kinds.

Poaching Eggs: Break each egg into a custard cup, small bowl or saucer. Hold the custard cup close to the water's surface and carefully slip the egg into the water.

Scrambled Eggs

PREP TIME: 15 Minutes • **START TO FINISH:** 15 Minutes • 4 servings

6 eggs
⅓ cup water, milk or half-and-half
¼ teaspoon salt
⅛ teaspoon pepper
1 tablespoon butter or margarine

1 In a medium bowl, beat the eggs, water, salt and pepper with a fork or wire whisk until well mixed.

2 In a 10-inch skillet, heat the butter over medium heat just until it begins to sizzle and look hot.

3 Pour egg mixture into skillet. The egg mixture will become firm at the bottom and side very quickly. When this happens, gently lift the cooked portions around the edge with a turner so that the thin, uncooked portion can flow to the bottom. Avoid constant stirring because the eggs will become dry and rubbery rather than light and fluffy.

4 Cook 3 to 4 minutes or until eggs are thickened throughout but still moist and creamy. Serve immediately.

1 Serving: Calories 140; Total Fat 11g; Cholesterol 325mg; Sodium 260mg; Total Carbohydrate 0g (Dietary Fiber 0g); Protein 9g **Carbohydrate Choices:** 0

Cook's Tip

Before buying eggs, open the carton and check that the eggs are clean and uncracked. Gently move each egg to be sure it hasn't cracked and stuck to the carton. If an egg cracks on the way home, throw it away.

Scrambling Eggs: Gently lift the cooked portions with a turner so the thin, uncooked portion can flow to the bottom and cook.

French Omelet

PREP TIME: 10 Minutes • **START TO FINISH:** 10 Minutes • 1 serving

SPECIAL EQUIPMENT

8-inch skillet

---

2 large eggs

2 teaspoons butter or margarine

⅛ teaspoon salt

Dash of pepper

1 In a small bowl, beat the eggs with a fork or wire whisk until yolks and whites are well mixed.

2 In an 8-inch skillet, heat the butter over medium-high heat until hot and sizzling. As butter melts, tilt skillet to coat bottom with butter.

3 Quickly pour the eggs into the skillet. While sliding the skillet back and forth rapidly over the heat, quickly stir the eggs with a fork to spread them continuously over the bottom of the skillet as they thicken. When they are thickened, let stand over the heat a few seconds to lightly brown the bottom. Do not overcook— the omelet will continue to cook after being folded.

4 Tilt the skillet and run a spatula or fork under the edge of the omelet, then jerk the skillet sharply to loosen omelet from bottom of skillet. Add favorite filling if desired. Fold the portion of the omelet nearest you just to the center. Allow for a portion of the omelet to slide up the side of the skillet. Turn the omelet onto a warm plate, flipping folded portion of omelet over so the far side is on the bottom. Sprinkle with salt and pepper.

1 Serving: Calories 220; Total Fat 18g; Cholesterol 445mg; Sodium 470mg; Total Carbohydrate 1g (Dietary Fiber 0g); Protein 13g **Carbohydrate Choices:** 0

Cheese Omelet: Before folding omelet, sprinkle with ¼ cup shredded Cheddar, Monterey Jack or Swiss cheese or ¼ cup crumbled blue cheese.

Denver Omelet: Cook 2 tablespoons chopped cooked ham, 1 tablespoon finely chopped bell pepper and 1 tablespoon finely chopped onion in the butter about 2 minutes, stirring frequently, before adding eggs.

Folding an Omelet: After loosening the omelet from the skillet, fold portion of omelet nearest you just to center.

Turning Omelet onto Plate: Tilt skillet, letting flat unfolded side of omelet slide out onto plate. Flip folded edge of omelet over the flat portion on the plate.

Cook's Tips

To warm a plate for serving the omelet, run hot water over the serving plate and dry it thoroughly, just before cooking the omelet.

Omelets cook quickly, so always have your filling ingredients ready before you begin cooking the eggs. The butter should be sizzling before the egg mixture is added.

Cheese Enchiladas

PREP TIME: 20 Minutes • **START TO FINISH:** 45 Minutes • 4 servings

SPECIAL EQUIPMENT

rectangular baking dish or casserole (about 11 × 7 inches)

---

1 small green bell pepper

1 clove garlic or ⅛ teaspoon garlic powder

1 medium onion

1 tablespoon chili powder

1½ teaspoons chopped fresh or ½ teaspoon dried oregano leaves

¼ teaspoon ground cumin

1 can (15 oz) tomato sauce

2 cups shredded Monterey Jack cheese (8 oz)

1 cup shredded Cheddar cheese (4 oz)

½ cup sour cream

2 tablespoons chopped fresh parsley, if desired

¼ teaspoon pepper

8 corn tortillas (5 or 6 inch)

Additional sour cream and chopped green onions, if desired

1 Heat the oven to 350°F. Cut the bell pepper in half lengthwise, and cut out seeds and membrane. Chop enough of the bell pepper to measure ⅓ cup. Wrap and refrigerate any remaining bell pepper. Peel and finely chop the garlic. Peel and chop the onion; set aside.

2 In a medium bowl, mix the bell pepper, garlic, chili powder, oregano, cumin and tomato sauce; set aside. In a large bowl, mix the onion, Monterey Jack cheese, Cheddar cheese, ½ cup sour cream, the parsley and pepper.

3 Place 2 tortillas between dampened microwavable paper towels or microwavable plastic wrap; microwave on High 15 to 20 seconds to soften them. Immediately spoon about ⅓ cup of the cheese mixture down one side of each softened tortilla to within 1 inch of edge. Roll tortilla around filling; place seam side down in an ungreased 11 × 7-inch glass baking dish. Repeat with the remaining tortillas and cheese mixture.

4 Pour the tomato sauce mixture over the tortillas. Bake uncovered about 25 minutes or until hot and bubbly. Garnish with additional sour cream and chopped green onions.

1 Serving: Calories 560; Total Fat 34g; Cholesterol 100mg; Sodium 1090mg; Total Carbohydrate 36g (Dietary Fiber 6g); Protein 27g **Carbohydrate Choices:** 2½

Filling Tortillas: Spoon about ⅓ cup of the cheese mixture down one side of each softened tortilla to within 1 inch of edge. Roll tortilla around filling; place seam side down in baking dish.

Beef Enchiladas: Add 1½ cups shredded or chopped cooked beef. In step 3, spoon about 2 tablespoons beef over the cheese mixture on each tortilla.

Chicken Enchiladas: Add 1½ cups shredded or chopped cooked chicken or turkey. In step 3, spoon about 2 tablespoons chicken over the cheese mixture on each tortilla.

Cook's Tips

Save a few minutes and use a 16-ounce jar of salsa, which is about 2 cups. Just omit the bell pepper, garlic, chili powder, oregano, cumin and tomato sauce and pour the salsa over the rolled tortillas.

If you like enchiladas with a hotter flavor, seed and finely chop 2 green jalapeño chiles, and add to the tomato sauce.

Chipotle and Black Bean Burritos

PREP TIME: 20 Minutes • **START TO FINISH:** 20 Minutes • 4 servings

1 large onion

6 cloves garlic or ¾ teaspoon garlic powder

1 can (15 oz) black beans

2 to 3 chipotle chiles in adobo sauce (from a 7-oz can), drained

1 large tomato

2 tablespoons vegetable oil

4 flour tortillas (8 or 10 inch)

1 cup shredded mozzarella cheese (4 oz)

Salsa, if desired

Sour cream, if desired

1   Peel and chop the onion to measure 1 cup. Peel and finely chop the garlic. Drain and rinse the beans in a strainer; in a medium bowl, mash the beans with a fork. Finely chop chipotle chiles to measure 2 teaspoons. Chop the tomato to measure 1 cup.

2   In a 10-inch nonstick skillet, heat the oil over medium-high heat. Add the onion and garlic; cook 6 to 8 minutes, stirring occasionally, until onion is tender. Stir in the mashed beans and chiles. Cook, stirring frequently, until hot.

3   Place ¼ of the bean mixture on center of each tortilla. Top with cheese and tomato.

4   Fold one end of each tortilla up about 1 inch over filling; fold right and left sides over folded end, overlapping. Fold remaining end down. Place seam side down on serving platter or plate. Spoon on salsa and a dollop of sour cream.

1 Serving: Calories 450; Total Fat 17g; Cholesterol 15mg; Sodium 820mg; Total Carbohydrate 56g (Dietary Fiber 12g); Protein 20g **Carbohydrate Choices:** 4

Cook's Tips

Use shredded Monterey Jack or Cheddar cheese for a flavor change. Top with a generous sprinkle of chopped cilantro before folding the burrito.

Chipotle chiles are dried, smoked jalapeño chiles and have a smoky, sweet flavor. In addition to dried, chipotle chiles are available canned in adobo sauce which is a spicy tomato-based sauce. For an extra burst of flavor, add 1 or 2 teaspoons of adobo sauce with the chiles.

Folding Burrito: Fold one end of the tortilla up about 1 inch over the filling. Fold right and left sides over folded end, overlapping. Fold remaining end down.

Chopping Chipotle Chiles: Remove chipotle chiles from adobo sauce with fork, shaking off excess sauce. Cut chiles into thin strips and chop strips into small pieces.

Curried Peppers and Edamame

PREP TIME: 20 Minutes • **START TO FINISH:** 20 Minutes • 4 servings

⅔ cup uncooked jasmine rice

1 cup water

4 cloves garlic or ½ teaspoon garlic powder

2 medium bell peppers (red, yellow, orange or mixture)

1 medium onion

1 tablespoon vegetable oil

1 tablespoon curry powder

1 bag (12 oz) frozen shelled edamame (green) soybeans

½ teaspoon salt

¼ cup water

1 can (14 oz) unsweetened coconut milk (not cream of coconut)

Chopped fresh cilantro or parsley, if desired

½ cup salted roasted cashews

1 In a 2-quart saucepan, heat the rice and 1 cup water to boiling over high heat. Reduce heat to medium. Cover with lid; simmer 15 to 20 minutes or until the water has been absorbed and the rice is tender. (Keep the lid on the pan until the rice has cooked 15 minutes before checking if the water has been absorbed. The steam of the simmering water is necessary for the rice to cook.)

2 Meanwhile, peel and finely chop the garlic. Cut each bell pepper in half lengthwise, and cut out seeds and membrane. Cut each half into ½-inch strips, then cut the strips crosswise in half to measure 3 cups.

3 Peel the onion, and cut in half lengthwise. Place each half, cut side down, on cutting board; cut lengthwise into thirds, then cut crosswise into thirds to make about 1-inch chunks.

4 In a 12-inch nonstick skillet, heat the oil over medium-high heat. Add the curry powder; cook 1 minute, stirring constantly to prevent scorching and to develop the flavor. Stir in the garlic, bell peppers, onion, edamame, salt and ¼ cup water (add water last so it doesn't spatter). Cook 2 minutes, stirring frequently and scraping bottom of skillet to mix curry powder with vegetables. Cover with lid; cook about 4 minutes longer or until vegetables are tender.

5 Open the can of coconut milk, and stir the milk with a fork or wire whisk until it is smooth and creamy. Measure 1 cup coconut milk, and stir into vegetable mixture. Reduce heat to medium-low. Simmer uncovered about 2 minutes, stirring occasionally, until hot. Pour remaining coconut milk into storage container; cover and refrigerate for another use.

6 Serve over rice and sprinkle with cilantro and cashews.

1 Serving: Calories 550; Total Fat 27g; Cholesterol 0mg; Sodium 50mg; Total Carbohydrate 57g (Dietary Fiber 8g); Protein 19g **Carbohydrate Choices:** 4

Curried Peppers and Peas: Substitute 1 box (9 ounces) frozen green peas for the edamame.

Cook's Tips

It is best to use regular coconut milk, rather than reduced-fat (lite), because the sauce will be tastier and creamier. Look for canned coconut milk in the Asian foods aisle.

Edamame is the Japanese name for green, or unripened, soybeans. These bright green beans are rich in protein. You'll find bags of frozen shelled edamame in the frozen vegetable section.

Cutting Bell Pepper Pieces
Cut bell pepper lengthwise into
½-inch strips, then cut strips
crosswise in half.

Cutting Onion into Pieces
Place onion half, cut side down,
on cutting board. Cut lengthwise
and crosswise into 9 pieces.
Separate each piece into individual pieces.

Risotto

PREP TIME: 30 Minutes • **START TO FINISH:** 30 Minutes • 4 servings

1 small onion

3 cups chicken broth (from a 32-oz carton) or vegetable broth

1 tablespoon butter or margarine

2 tablespoons olive or vegetable oil

1 tablespoon chopped fresh parsley, if desired

1 cup uncooked Arborio or regular long-grain white rice

½ cup dry white wine or chicken or vegetable broth

½ cup freshly grated or shredded Parmesan cheese

¼ teaspoon coarse ground black pepper

1 Peel and thinly slice the onion; set aside. In a 2-quart saucepan, heat the broth over medium heat.

2 In a 10-inch skillet or 3-quart saucepan, heat the butter and oil over medium-high heat until the butter is melted. Add the onion and parsley; cook about 5 minutes, stirring frequently, until onion is tender.

3 Stir in the rice. Cook, stirring occasionally, until the edges of the rice kernels are translucent. Stir in the wine. Cook about 3 minutes, stirring constantly, until the wine is absorbed.

4 Reduce heat to medium. Stir in 1 cup of the warm broth; cook uncovered about 5 minutes, stirring frequently, until broth is absorbed. Add another 1 cup of broth; cook about 5 minutes, stirring frequently, until broth is absorbed. Stir in remaining 1 cup broth; cook about 8 minutes, stirring frequently, until rice is just tender and mixture is creamy. Stir in cheese and pepper.

1 Serving: Calories 360; Total Fat 15g; Cholesterol 15mg; Sodium 1020mg; Total Carbohydrate 43g (Dietary Fiber 0g); Protein 13g **Carbohydrate Choices:** 3

Risotto with Mushrooms: Add 2½ cups sliced mushrooms (8 ounces) with the onion in step 2.

Risotto with Peas: Cook and drain 1 box (9 or 10 ounces) frozen green peas as directed on the box. Stir peas into risotto just before serving.

Cooking Rice Kernels: Cook, stirring occasionally, until edges of kernels are translucent.

Checking Risotto Doneness: Cook until slightly thickened and mixture is creamy.

Cook's Tips

Using Arborio rice, a short-grain rice with a high starch, and slowly adding the hot broth gives risotto its creaminess. Adding the cheese at the end will thicken the risotto slightly so be sure it is creamy after the last addition of broth.

Arborio rice, a specialty of Italy, creates the creamiest risotto, but you can substitute any short-grain white rice in this recipe.

4 GREAT for GRILLING

Grilled Chicken Breasts

PREP TIME: 25 Minutes • **START TO FINISH:** 25 Minutes • 4 servings

Vegetable oil or cooking spray

4 boneless skinless (1¼ lb) or bone-in skinless (2 lb) chicken breasts

Purchased barbecue or teriyaki sauce, if desired

1 Carefully brush vegetable oil over the grill rack, or spray it with cooking spray. Prepare the coals or a gas grill for direct heat (page 264). Heat to medium heat, which will take about 40 minutes for charcoal or about 10 minutes for a gas grill.

2 Cut excess fat from chicken with kitchen scissors or knife and discard.

3 Place the chicken on the grill rack over medium heat. Cover the grill; cook boneless 15 to 20 minutes or bone-in 20 to 25 minutes, turning chicken over once with tongs about halfway through cooking. Brush chicken with the barbecue or teriyaki sauce during the last 10 minutes of cooking. Cook until juice of chicken is clear when you cut into the center of the thickest part for boneless (or thickest part is cut to the bone for bone-in) and an instant-read meat thermometer inserted into the thickest part reads 170°F.

1 **Serving:** Calories 180; Total Fat 6g; Cholesterol 85mg; Sodium 75mg; Total Carbohydrate 0g (Dietary Fiber 0g); Protein 31g **Carbohydrate Choices:** 0

Cook's Tips

For more flavor, chicken breasts can be marinated before cooking. Allow ¼ to ½ cup marinade for each 1 to 2 pounds of chicken. Marinate chicken covered in the refrigerator for 15 minutes to 2 hours.

If the chicken is frozen, place it in the refrigerator the night before you plan to use it or for at least 12 hours to thaw.

Cutting Fat from Chicken: Using kitchen scissors or a sharp knife, cut the excess fat from the chicken.

Broiled Boneless Chicken Breasts: You may need to move the oven rack so it is 4 to 6 inches below the heating unit. Set the oven control to broil. Brush the broiler pan rack with vegetable oil or spray with cooking spray. (For easy cleanup, line the bottom of the broiler pan with foil before placing chicken on rack.) Place chicken on broiler pan rack. Broil 15 to 20 minutes or until juice of chicken is clear when you cut into the center of the thickest part and an instant-read meat thermometer inserted into the thickest part reads 170°F. Brush chicken with barbecue or teriyaki sauce during the last 10 minutes of broiling.

Panfried Boneless Chicken Breasts: In a 10- or nonstick skillet, heat 1 tablespoon vegetable oil or olive oil over medium heat until hot. Add the chicken. Cook uncovered 10 to 15 minutes, turning chicken over once with tongs, until juice of chicken is clear when you cut into the center of the thickest part and an instant-read meat thermometer inserted into the thickest part reads 170°F. If desired, sprinkle with salt, pepper and paprika.

Contact-Grill Boneless Chicken Breasts: Heat closed medium-size contact grill for 5 minutes. Place chicken on grill. Close grill. Cook 4 to 6 minutes or until juice of chicken is clear when you cut into the center of the thickest part and an instant-read meat thermometer inserted into the thickest part reads 170°F. If desired, sprinkle with salt and pepper.

Mediterranean Chicken Packets

PREP TIME: 45 Minutes • **START TO FINISH:** 45 Minutes • 4 servings

4 boneless skinless chicken
breasts (about 1¼ lb)

4 plum (Roma) tomatoes

1 small red onion

1 package (4 oz) crumbled tomato-
basil feta cheese (1 cup)

2 tablespoons grated lemon peel

1 teaspoon dried oregano leaves

20 pitted kalamata olives or pitted
jumbo ripe olives

Cook's Tips

You can use a package of crumbled plain feta cheese instead of the flavored feta.

Foil packets should be opened very carefully, keeping the opening away from you. Steam collects inside the packets during cooking so you may want to use tongs to lift the foil back after cutting the X on top.

1 Prepare the coals or a gas grill for direct heat (page 267). Heat to medium heat, which will take about 40 minutes for charcoal or about 10 minutes for a gas grill.

2 Cut 4 (18 × 12-inch) sheets of heavy-duty foil. Cut fat from the chicken breasts with kitchen scissors or a knife and discard. Cut each tomato into 3 slices. Peel and finely chop the onion to measure 1 cup.

3 In a small bowl, mix the cheese, lemon peel and oregano. On center of each foil sheet, place 1 chicken breast, 3 tomato slices, ¼ cup onion and 5 olives. Spoon ¼ of the cheese mixture over chicken and vegetables on each foil piece.

4 Bring up 2 sides of foil over chicken and vegetables so edges meet. Seal edges, making a tight ½-inch fold; fold again, allowing space for heat circulation and expansion. Fold other sides to seal.

5 Place the packets on the grill rack over medium heat. Cover the grill; cook 20 to 25 minutes, rotating the packets ½ turn after 10 minutes, until juice of chicken is clear when you cut into the center of the thickest part and an instant-read meat thermometer inserted into the thickest part reads 170°F. Place each packet on a plate. To serve, cut a large X across the top of each packet with kitchen scissors; carefully fold back the foil to allow steam to escape.

1 Serving: Calories 290; Total Fat 13g; Cholesterol 110mg; Sodium 570mg; Total Carbohydrate 7g (Dietary Fiber 2g); Protein 36g **Carbohydrate Choices:** ½

Folding the Foil Packet: Bring up 2 sides of foil over chicken and vegetables so edges meet.

Sealing the Foil Packet: Make a tight ½-inch fold and fold again. Fold other sides to seal.

Cutting X on Foil Packet: To serve, cut a large X across top of packet with kitchen scissors and fold back the foil.

Grilled Juicy Burgers

PREP TIME: 25 Minutes • **START TO FINISH:** 25 Minutes • 4 burgers

1 lb lean (at least 80%) ground beef

3 tablespoons water

½ teaspoon salt

¼ teaspoon pepper

4 hamburger buns, if desired

1 Prepare the coals or a gas grill for direct heat (page 267). Heat to medium heat, which will take about 40 minutes for charcoal or about 10 minutes for a gas grill.

2 In a medium bowl, mix the beef, water, salt and pepper. Shape the mixture into 4 uniform, flat patties, each about ¾ inch thick. Handle the patties as little as possible; the more the beef is handled, the less juicy the burgers will be.

3 Place the patties on the grill rack over medium heat. Cover the grill; cook 10 to 12 minutes, turning once halfway through cooking, until an instant-read meat thermometer inserted in center of patties reads 160°F and patties are no longer pink in center. Loosen patties gently with a turner to prevent crumbling. Add buns, cut sides down, for last 4 minutes of cooking or until toasted. Serve burgers on buns.

1 Burger: Calories 190; Total Fat 13g; Cholesterol 70mg; Sodium 350mg; Total Carbohydrate 0g (Dietary Fiber 0g); Protein 20g **Carbohydrate Choices:** 0

Cook's Tips

For more flavor and better burgers, use lean or regular ground beef rather than extra lean. Extra-lean ground beef patties may crumble and not hold together as well during cooking.

Dampen your hands with water before forming patties so the meat mixture doesn't stick to your hands.

Shaping Burger Patties: Shape the patties to have smooth edges, which will keep them together during cooking and result in uniform doneness. Gently pinch to close any cracks in the patty.

Grilled Juicy Cheeseburgers: About 1 minute before the burgers are done, top each burger with 1 slice (1 ounce) American, Cheddar, Swiss or Monterey Jack cheese. Let stand on grill until cheese is melted.

Grilled Juicy Turkey Burgers: Use 1 pound ground turkey breast for the ground beef. Spray grill rack with cooking spray. Cook 13 to 15 minutes.

Broiled Juicy Burgers: You may need to move the oven rack so it is 5 to 6 inches below the heating unit. Set the oven control to broil. (For easy cleanup, line the bottom of the broiler pan with foil before placing patties on rack.) Place the patties on the broiler pan rack. Broil 10 to 14 minutes, turning once halfway through broiling, until an instant-read meat thermometer inserted in center of patties reads 160°F and patties are no longer pink in center.

Contact-Grill Juicy Burgers: Heat closed medium-size contact grill for 5 minutes. Place patties on grill. Close grill. Cook 4 to 6 minutes or until an instant-read meat thermometer inserted in center of patties reads 160°F and patties are no longer pink in center.

Panfried Juicy Burgers: Use a heavy 10-inch nonstick skillet, or lightly coat a regular skillet with oil or cooking spray. Heat the skillet over medium heat or until hot. Add the patties. Cook uncovered 10 to 12 minutes, turning once halfway through cooking, until an instant-read meat thermometer inserted in center of patties reads 160°F and patties are no longer pink in center.

Backyard Beer Burgers

PREP TIME: 25 Minutes • **START TO FINISH:** 25 Minutes • 6 sandwiches

1 small onion

2 cloves garlic or ¼ teaspoon garlic powder

1½ lb lean (at least 80%) ground beef

¼ cup regular or nonalcoholic beer

1 tablespoon Worcestershire sauce

½ teaspoon salt

¼ teaspoon pepper

6 rye or whole wheat hamburger buns, split

Ketchup, if desired

Pickle slices, if desired

1   Prepare the coals or a gas grill for direct heat (page 267). Heat to medium heat, which will take about 40 minutes for charcoal or about 10 minutes for a gas grill.

2   Peel and finely chop the onion to measure ¼ cup. Peel and finely chop the garlic.

3   In a medium bowl, mix the beef, onion, garlic, beer, Worcestershire sauce, salt and pepper. Shape the mixture into 6 patties, about ¾ inch thick.

4   Place the patties on the grill rack over medium heat. Cover the grill; cook 13 to 15 minutes, turning once, until an instant-read meat thermometer inserted in center of patties reads 160°F and patties are no longer pink in center. Add buns, cut sides down, for last 4 minutes of cooking or until toasted. Serve burgers in buns with ketchup and pickles.

1 Sandwich: Calories 310; Total Fat 14g; Cholesterol 70mg; Sodium 660mg; Total Carbohydrate 23g (Dietary Fiber 2g); Protein 24g **Carbohydrate Choices:** 1½

Backyard Beer Cheeseburgers: About 1 minute before burgers are done, top each with 1 slice (1 ounce) American, Cheddar, provolone or Monterey Jack cheese. Grill until cheese is melted.

Backyard Turkey Beer Burgers: Use 1½ pounds ground turkey breast for the ground beef. Spray grill rack with cooking spray. Cook 13 to 15 minutes.

Contact Grill Backyard Beer Burgers: Heat closed medium-size contact grill for 5 minutes. To toast buns, place cut sides down on hot grill, but do not cover. Toast buns uncovered about 1 minute or until golden brown. Remove buns and place patties on grill. Close grill. Cook beef patties 6 to 8 minutes or until meat thermometer inserted in center of patties reads 160°F and patties are no longer pink in center. (Cook turkey patties 6 to 8 minutes or until 165°F.)

Checking Burger Doneness:
The center of the burger should no longer be pink and should be evenly cooked throughout.

Cook's Tip

Resist the urge to press a turner down on a burger while it's cooking. You'll wind up squeezing out much of the juices and the burger will be drier and less tender.

Grilled Beef Steaks

PREP TIME: 20 Minutes • **START TO FINISH:** 20 Minutes • 4 servings

4 beef steaks, about ¾ inch thick
(porterhouse, rib eye, sirloin or
T-bone steaks) or about 1 inch
thick (tenderloin steaks)

1 teaspoon salt

¼ teaspoon pepper

Know Your Steaks

Select a steak that is bright red in color. Vacuum-packed beef will have a darker, purplish red color because the meat is not exposed to air, but it will return to a bright red when exposed when unwrapped. These cuts of steak—porterhouse, rib eye, sirloin, T-bone and tenderloin—are the most tender and are best for grilling, broiling and panfrying.

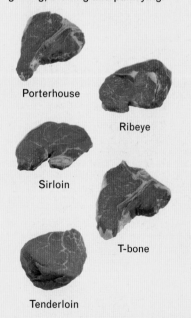

Porterhouse

Ribeye

Sirloin

T-bone

Tenderloin

1 Prepare the coals or a gas grill for direct heat (page 267). Heat to medium heat, which will take about 40 minutes for charcoal or about 10 minutes for a gas grill.

2 Cut outer edge of fat on steaks (except tenderloin steaks) diagonally at 1-inch intervals with a sharp knife. Do not cut into the meat because it will allow the juices to cook out and the beef will become dry.

3 Place the beef on the grill rack over medium heat. Cover the grill; cook 6 to 8 minutes for rib eye, 10 to 12 minutes for porterhouse and T-bone or 13 to 15 minutes for sirloin and tenderloin, turning beef once halfway through cooking, until an instant-read meat thermometer inserted in center of thickest part reads 145°F for medium-rare or 160°F for medium doneness. Sprinkle with salt and pepper.

1 Serving: Calories 210; Total Fat 9g; Cholesterol 60mg; Sodium 630mg; Total Carbohydrate 0g (Dietary Fiber 0g); Protein 31g **Carbohydrate Choices:** 0

Cutting Fat to Prevent Curling: Cut outer edge of fat diagonally at 1-inch intervals being careful not to cut into the meat.

Checking Steak Doneness: Medium doneness will be light pink in the center and brown toward the exterior.

Broiled Beef Steaks: Move the oven rack so it is 2 to 3 inches below the heating unit. Set the oven control to broil. Place beef on broiler pan rack. Broil 8 to 12 minutes for rib eye, 9 to 12 minutes for porterhouse, T-bone and sirloin or 13 to 16 minutes for tenderloin, turning beef once halfway through broiling, until an instant-read meat thermometer inserted in center of thickest part reads 145°F for medium-rare or 160°F for medium doneness. Sprinkle with salt and pepper.

Panfried Beef Steaks: Use a heavy 10- or 12-inch skillet lightly coated with vegetable oil or cooking spray or nonstick skillet. Heat the skillet over medium heat until hot. Add beef to skillet. Cook uncovered 8 to 10 minutes for rib eye, 10 to 13 minutes for tenderloin or 11 to 13 minutes for porterhouse, T-bone and sirloin, turning beef once halfway through cooking, until an instant-read meat thermometer inserted in center of thickest part reads 145°F for medium-rare or 160°F for medium doneness. Sprinkle with salt and pepper.

Contact-Grill Beef Steaks: Use only boneless beef sirloin that is ¾ inch thick. Heat closed medium-size contact grill for 5 minutes. Place steaks on grill. Close grill. Cook 6 to 8 minutes or until an instant-read meat thermometer inserted in center of thickest part reads 160°F for medium doneness. Sprinkle with salt and pepper.

Balsamic-Garlic Marinated Steak

PREP TIME: 30 Minutes • **START TO FINISH:** 8 Hours 30 Minutes • 6 servings

4 cloves garlic or ½ teaspoon garlic powder

½ cup balsamic vinegar

¼ cup chili sauce or ketchup

2 tablespoons packed brown sugar

2 tablespoons olive or vegetable oil

½ teaspoon Italian seasoning

¼ teaspoon salt

¼ teaspoon coarse ground black pepper

1 boneless beef top round steak, 1 to 1½ inches thick (1½ lb)

1 Peel and finely chop the garlic. In a shallow glass dish or resealable plastic food-storage bag, mix the garlic and remaining ingredients except beef. Add the beef; turn to coat with marinade. Cover the dish with plastic wrap or seal the bag. Refrigerate at least 8 hours but no longer than 12 hours, turning beef occasionally.

2 Prepare the coals or a gas grill for direct heat (page 267). Heat to medium heat, which will take about 40 minutes for charcoal or about 10 minutes for a gas grill. Remove the beef from the marinade, reserving the marinade.

3 Place the beef on the grill rack over medium heat. Cover the grill; cook 12 to 18 minutes for medium-rare or 17 to 21 minutes for medium doneness, turning and brushing with the marinade once or twice. Discard any remaining marinade. To serve, cut beef across grain into slices.

1 Serving: Calories 190; Total Fat 7g; Cholesterol 65mg; Sodium 220mg; Total Carbohydrate 6g (Dietary Fiber 0g); Protein 26g **Carbohydrate Choices:** ½

Cook's Tips

Always marinate food in a nonmetal dish. Acid-based marinades, such as those with vinegar, lemon juice, tomato or wine, can react with some metals and cause off-flavor in the food.

Make sure the grill is hot before adding the steak. A hot grill quickly sears the outside of the steak, sealing it so the meat stays juicy and tender.

Marinating Steak: Marinate steak in a shallow glass dish or resealable plastic food-storage bag.

Cutting Steak: For tender slices of steak, cut steak into thin slices.

Grilled Pork Chops

PREP TIME: 20 Minutes • **START TO FINISH:** 20 Minutes • 4 servings

4 pork loin or rib chops or boneless loin chops, ¾ to 1 inch thick

¾ teaspoon seasoned salt or regular salt

¼ teaspoon pepper

1 Prepare the coals or a gas grill for direct heat (page 267). Heat to medium heat, which will take about 40 minutes for charcoal or about 10 minutes for a gas grill.

2 Place pork chops on grill rack over medium heat. Cover the grill; cook 9 to 12 minutes, turning once halfway through cooking, until pork is no longer pink in center and an instant-read meat thermometer inserted in center reads 160°F. Sprinkle with seasoned salt and pepper.

1 Serving: Calories 170; Total Fat 8g; Cholesterol 70mg; Sodium 300mg; Total Carbohydrate 0g (Dietary Fiber 0g); Protein 24g **Carbohydrate Choices:** 0

Know Your Pork Chops

Fresh, lean pork should be pink with a white to grayish tint of coloring and have a fine-grained texture. Check that it is trimmed of excess fat around the edges. A little fat running through the meat, called marbling, is desirable because it adds flavor and tenderness. Look for chops that are the same thickness so they will finish cooking at the same time.

Loin or Rib Chop

Loin Chop, boneless

Cook's Tip

Pork chops are a lean cut of meat and don't have much fat throughout the muscles. They can become tough and dry if overcooked so be sure to check for doneness at the minimum cook time.

Checking Pork Chop Doneness: Cut a small slit in the pork chop. The meat should no longer be pink.

Broiled Pork Chops: You may need to move the oven rack so it is 5 to 6 inches below the heating unit. Set the oven control to broil. (For easy cleanup, line the bottom of the broiler pan with foil before placing pork on rack.) Place pork on broiler pan rack. Broil 9 to 12 minutes, turning once halfway through the broiling, until pork is no longer pink and an instant-read meat thermometer inserted in center reads 160°F. Sprinkle with seasoned salt and pepper.

Panfried Pork Chops: Use a heavy 12-inch nonstick skillet or lightly coated regular skillet with vegetable oil or nonstick cooking spray. Heat the skillet over medium heat. Add the pork chops. Cook uncovered 8 to 12 minutes, turning once halfway through cooking, until pork is brown on both sides, no longer pink in center and an instant-read meat thermometer inserted in center reads 160°F. If the pork chops have extra fat on them, fat may accumulate in the skillet; remove this fat with a spoon as it accumulates. Sprinkle pork with seasoned salt and pepper.

Contact-Grill Pork Chops: Use only boneless pork loin chops that are ¾ inch thick. Heat closed medium-size contact grill for 5 minutes. Brush 1 teaspoon vegetable or olive oil on pork; sprinkle with seasoned salt and pepper. Place pork on grill. Close grill. Cook 5 to 7 minutes or until pork is no longer pink in center and an instant-read meat thermometer inserted in center reads 160°F.

Cuban Pork Chops

PREP TIME: 15 Minutes • **START TO FINISH:** 15 Minutes • 4 servings

PORK CHOPS

4 boneless pork loin or rib chops,
about 1 inch thick (about 2 lb)

CUBAN RUB

1 clove garlic

2 tablespoons grated lime peel

1 tablespoon cracked black pepper

1 tablespoon cumin seed

2 tablespoons olive or vegetable oil

½ teaspoon salt

GARNISH, IF DESIRED

Mango slices

Rubbing Spices on Pork Chop:
Using your fingers, rub the spice
mixture evenly on both sides of
the pork chop.

1 Prepare the coals or a gas grill for direct heat (page 267). Heat to medium heat, which will take about 40 minutes for charcoal or about 10 minutes for a gas grill.

2 Remove the excess fat from the pork chops. Peel and finely chop the garlic. In a small bowl, mix the garlic and remaining rub ingredients. Rub the mixture evenly on both sides of the pork chops.

3 Place the pork chops on the grill rack over medium heat. Cover the grill; cook 8 to 10 minutes, turning pork chops frequently, until pork is no longer pink when you cut into the center and an instant-read meat thermometer inserted in the center reads 160°F. Garnish with mango slices.

1 Serving: Calories 420; Total Fat 24g; Cholesterol 140mg; Sodium 380mg; Total Carbohydrate 2g (Dietary Fiber 0g); Protein 49g **Carbohydrate Choices:** 0

Contact Grill Cuban Pork Chops: Heat closed medium-size contact grill for 5 minutes. Make Cuban Rub as directed; rub over both sides of boneless pork loin chops (do not use rib chops). Place pork on grill. Close grill. Cook 6 to 8 minutes or until pork is no longer pink when you cut into the center and a meat thermometer inserted in the center reads 160°F.

Cuban Chicken: Brush vegetable oil on the grill rack or spray with cooking spray. Heat the grill as directed. Cut fat from 4 boneless skinless chicken breasts (about 1¼ pounds) with kitchen scissors or a knife and discard. Make Cuban Rub as directed; rub over both sides of chicken breasts. Place chicken on the grill. Cover the grill; cook 15 to 20 minutes, turning chicken over once, until juice of chicken is clear when you cut into the center of the thickest part and an instant-read meat thermometer inserted into the thickest part reads 170°F.

Cook's Tip

If you don't have cumin seed
or cracked pepper on hand,
use 1 teaspoon ground cumin
for the seed and 1 teaspoon
coarsely ground pepper for the
cracked pepper.

Lemon-Pepper Pork Tenderloin

PREP TIME: 20 Minutes • **START TO FINISH:** 40 Minutes • 6 servings

1 teaspoon grated lemon peel

½ teaspoon seasoned salt

½ teaspoon coarse ground
   black pepper

½ teaspoon paprika

¼ teaspoon dried thyme leaves

2 teaspoons olive or vegetable oil

2 pork tenderloins (about ¾ lb
   each)

1   Prepare the coals or a gas grill for direct heat (page 267). Heat to medium-low heat, which will take about 40 minutes for charcoal or about 10 minutes for a gas grill.

2   In a small bowl, mix the lemon peel, seasoned salt, pepper, paprika and thyme. Brush the oil over all sides of the pork tenderloins. Rub the lemon peel mixture over pork. Some tenderloins are very narrow on one end. Tuck the narrow end under the tenderloin to make it similar thickness for even cooking.

3   Place the pork on the grill rack over medium-low heat. Cover the grill; cook 15 to 20 minutes, turning pork occasionally, until pork has slight blush of pink when you cut into the center and an instant-read meat thermometer inserted in the center reads 160°F.

4   Remove the pork from the grill; cover with foil. Let stand 5 to 10 minutes before slicing so the juices will be retained and the meat will be easier to cut.

1 Serving: Calories 160; Total Fat 6g; Cholesterol 70mg; Sodium 160mg; Total Carbohydrate 0g (Dietary Fiber 0g); Protein 26g **Carbohydrate Choices:** 0

Broiled Lemon-Pepper Pork Tenderloin: Move oven rack so pork is 4 inches from broiler heating unit. Set oven control to broil. After rubbing the lemon peel mixture over the pork, place on the rack in broiler pan. Broil 4 to 6 inches from heat following cooking time and doneness in step 3. Remove from oven, cover with foil and let stand 5 to 10 minutes.

Cook's Tip

Other dried herbs can be used for the thyme. A ¼ teaspoon dried oregano or marjoram leaves would pair nicely with the lemon flavor.

Tucking One End under Tenderloin: Fold the narrow end under so the tenderloin is similar in thickness for even cooking.

Slicing Pork Tenderloin: Using a sharp slicing knife, cut pork tenderloin crosswise into thin slices.

Ham Steak with Mustard Sauce

PREP TIME: 15 Minutes • **START TO FINISH:** 15 Minutes • 4 servings

1 cooked ham steak, ½ inch thick
  (1 lb)
1 tablespoon Dijon mustard
1 tablespoon honey
1 tablespoon apricot preserves

1 Prepare the coals or a gas grill for direct heat (page 267). Heat to medium-high heat, which will take about 40 minutes for charcoal or about 10 minutes for a gas grill.

2 Cut outer edge of fat on the ham steak diagonally at 1-inch intervals to prevent curling (do not cut into ham). In a small bowl, mix the mustard, honey and preserves.

3 Place the ham on the grill rack over medium-high heat. Cook uncovered 4 minutes. Turn ham over; brush with about half of the mustard mixture. Cook 4 minutes longer. Turn ham over again; brush with the remaining mustard mixture. Cook about 2 minutes longer or until thoroughly heated.

1 Serving: Calories 200; Total Fat 9g; Cholesterol 55mg; Sodium 1540mg; Total Carbohydrate 8g (Dietary Fiber 0g); Protein 22g **Carbohydrate Choices:** ½

Preventing Ham from Curling: Cut outer edge of fat on ham steak diagonally at 1-inch intervals to prevent curling (do not cut into the ham).

Panfried Ham Steak with Mustard Sauce: Use a heavy 12-inch nonstick skillet, or lightly coat a regular skillet with vegetable oil or cooking spray. Heat the skillet over medium heat for 5 minutes. Place ham steak in skillet. Cook 4 minutes. Turn ham over; brush with about half of the mustard mixture. Cook 2 to 4 minutes longer or until thoroughly heated. Turn ham over again; brush with the remaining mustard mixture.

Contact-Grill Ham Steak with Mustard Sauce: Heat closed medium-size contact grill for 5 minutes. Place ham steak on grill. Close grill. Cook 5 to 7 minutes or until hot. In 1-quart saucepan, heat mustard, honey and preserves over medium heat, stirring occasionally, until hot. Brush mustard mixture over ham.

Smoked Pork Chops with Mustard Sauce: Substitute 4 smoked pork chops for the ham steak and follow cooking directions in step 3.

Cook's Tips

Sweet potatoes are a tasty accompaniment. Wrap them in foil, and start grilling them before you add the ham steak. They'll cook in 30 to 35 minutes over medium-high heat.

Ham steak, sometimes labeled "ham slice," is a center-cut piece of ham that's usually fairly lean. Look for it with the other ham in the meat department.

Grilled Fish

PREP TIME: 20 Minutes • **START TO FINISH:** 20 Minutes • 4 servings

1½ lb fish steaks or 1 lb fish fillets (halibut, lake trout, mahimahi, marlin, red snapper, salmon, swordfish or tuna), about ¾ inch thick

2 tablespoons butter or margarine, melted

1 teaspoon salt

¼ teaspoon pepper

1 lemon, cut into 4 wedges

1 Brush grill rack with vegetable oil or spray with cooking spray. Prepare the coals or a gas grill for direct heat (page 264). Heat to medium heat, which will take about 40 minutes for charcoal or about 10 minutes for a gas grill.

2 Cut fish into 4 serving pieces. Brush fish with about half of the butter; sprinkle with the salt and pepper.

3 Place the fish on the grill rack (if fish fillets have skin, place skin sides down). Cover the grill; cook 10 to 14 minutes, brushing 2 or 3 times with remaining butter, until fish flakes easily with a fork. Serve with lemon wedges.

1 Serving: Calories 210; Total Fat 8g; Cholesterol 105mg; Sodium 770mg; Total Carbohydrate 1g (Dietary Fiber 0g); Protein 32g **Carbohydrate Choices:** 0

Know Your Fish

Fish is available whole, but you'll find it most often in steaks or fillets.

Fish Steak: The steak is cut from the cross section of a large fish. Steaks are ½ to ¾ inch thick. Allow ¼ to ⅓ pound per serving.

Fish Fillets: Fillets are cut lengthwise from the sides of fish. They can be purchased with or without skin.

Checking Fish Doneness:
Place a fork in the thickest part of the fish, then gently twist the fork. When the fish flakes easily, it's done.

Broiled Fish: You may need to move the oven rack so it is 4 to 6 inches from the heating unit. Set the oven control to broil. (For easy cleanup, line the bottom of the broiler pan with foil before placing fish on the rack.) Brush the broiler pan rack with vegetable oil or spray with cooking spray. Brush fish with half of the butter; sprinkle with the salt and pepper. Place fish on rack in broiler pan (if fish fillets have skin, place skin sides down). For fish steaks, broil 5 minutes. Carefully turn fish over; brush with remaining butter. Broil 4 to 6 minutes longer or until fish flakes easily with a fork. For fish fillets, broil 5 to 6 minutes or until fish flakes easily with a fork (do not turn over). Brush with remaining butter. Serve with lemon wedges.

Panfried Fish Fillets: Use 1 pound skinless lean fish fillets (flounder, halibut, mahimahi, perch, red snapper, salmon, sea bass, sole, trout or whitefish), about ¾ inch thick. If the fish fillets are large, cut into 4 servings pieces. In a shallow dish, mix ½ cup all-purpose flour, ½ teaspoon paprika, 1 teaspoon salt and ¼ teaspoon pepper. Coat both sides of fish with flour mixture. In a 10- or 12-inch skillet, heat 1 tablespoon butter or margarine and 1 tablespoon olive or vegetable oil over medium heat until hot. Add fish. Cook 6 to 10 minutes, turning once, until fish is brown and flakes easily with a fork. Serve with lemon wedges.

Salmon with Mango Salsa

PREP TIME: 20 Minutes • **START TO FINISH:** 30 Minutes • 4 servings

MANGO SALSA

1 medium mango

1 small jalapeño chile

1 small red onion

2 tablespoons finely chopped fresh or 2 teaspoons dried mint leaves

2 tablespoons lime juice

⅛ teaspoon salt

SALMON

4 salmon fillets (4 to 6 oz each)

¼ teaspoon salt

⅛ teaspoon pepper

1 Wash the mango. Cut mango lengthwise into 2 pieces, cutting as close to the seed as possible. Make lengthwise and crosswise cuts, ½ inch apart, in mango flesh to form a crisscross pattern. Turn each mango half inside out, and scrape off the pieces to measure about 1 cup.

2 Cut the stem off the jalapeño chile, cut the chile in half lengthwise and scrape out the seeds. Cut the chile into strips, then finely chop to measure 2 to 3 teaspoons. Peel and finely chop the red onion to measure ¼ cup. Wrap remaining onion with plastic wrap and refrigerate.

3 In a glass or plastic bowl, mix the mango, chile, onion, mint, lime juice and ⅛ teaspoon salt. Cover with plastic wrap; refrigerate 15 minutes. Meanwhile, continue with the recipe.

4 Prepare the coals or a gas grill for direct heat (page 267). Heat to medium heat, which will take about 40 minutes for charcoal or about 10 minutes for a gas grill.

5 Sprinkle the salmon fillets with ¼ teaspoon salt and the pepper. Place salmon, skin sides down, on the grill rack over medium heat. Cover the grill; cook 10 to 15 minutes, turning over once, until salmon flakes easily with a fork. Serve with salsa.

1 Serving: Calories 200; Total Fat 7g; Cholesterol 75mg; Sodium 290mg; Total Carbohydrate 11g (Dietary Fiber 1g); Protein 25g **Carbohydrate Choices:** 1

Contact Grill Salmon with Mango Salsa: Make Mango Salsa as directed. Heat closed medium-size contact grill for 5 minutes. Brush 1 teaspoon vegetable oil over both sides of salmon; sprinkle with salt and pepper. Place salmon, skin sides down, on grill. Close grill. Cook 4 to 5 minutes or until salmon flakes easily with a fork.

Cutting Mango Pieces: Make lengthwise and crosswise cuts, ½ inch apart, to form a criss-cross pattern.

Removing Mango Pieces: Turn mango half inside out and remove pieces with tip of knife.

Cook's Tips

If only large salmon fillets are available, purchase a 1- to 1½-pound fillet and cut it crosswise into 4 serving pieces.

The Mango Salsa can be prepared 2 days ahead and refrigerated. If fresh mangoes aren't in season, use canned mango, papaya or peaches cut into ½-inch pieces to measure 1 cup.

Lemon-Pesto Shrimp and Scallops

PREP TIME: 25 Minutes • **START TO FINISH:** 25 Minutes • 6 servings

SPECIAL EQUIPMENT
grill wok (grill basket)

1 lb uncooked deveined peeled
    large shrimp, thawed if frozen

1 lb uncooked sea scallops

¼ cup refrigerated basil pesto
    (from 7-oz container)

1 teaspoon grated lemon peel

¼ teaspoon salt

¼ teaspoon coarse ground
    black pepper

Lemon-Pesto Scallops: Omit the shrimp. Increase the scallops to 2 pounds.

Lemon-Pesto Shrimp: Omit the scallops. Increase the shrimp to 2 pounds.

1   Prepare the coals or a gas grill for direct heat (page 267). Heat to medium heat, which will take about 40 minutes for charcoal or about 10 minutes for a gas grill.

2   Rinse the shrimp with cool water, and pat dry with paper towels (if the shrimp have tails, remove the tails if desired). If the scallops are larger than 2 inches in diameter, cut each in half. Rinse with cool water, and pat dry with paper towels.

3   In a large bowl, mix the shrimp, scallops and remaining ingredients. Place seafood mixture in a grill wok or grill basket.

4   Place the grill wok on the grill rack over medium heat. Cover the grill; cook 10 to 12 minutes, stirring the seafood mixture occasionally, or turning grill basket over, until shrimp are pink and scallops are white and opaque.

1 Serving: Calories 150; Total Fat 7g; Cholesterol 130mg; Sodium 410mg; Total Carbohydrate 0g (Dietary Fiber 0g); Protein 21g **Carbohydrate Choices:** 0

Cook's Tips

If you don't have a grill basket, use a foil baking pan or double a sheet of heavy-duty foil and poke several holes in the bottom.

Scallops are classified as either sea scallops, which can be up to 2 inches in diameter, and bay scallops, which average about ½ inch in diameter. Use sea scallops for this recipe because they will be done the same time as the shrimp.

Using a Grill Wok: Place seafood mixture in a grill wok and stir the seafood mixture occasionally for even cooking.

Grating Lemon Peel: Rub the lemon across the small holes of a grater. Grate only the yellow peel because the white pith is bitter.

Sage Potato Packet

PREP TIME: 1 Hour 5 Minutes • **START TO FINISH:** 1 Hour 5 Minutes • 8 servings

Cooking spray for greasing foil

4 small (new) red potatoes

2 large baking potatoes (russet or Idaho) about 8 oz each

2 tablespoons firm butter or margarine

½ teaspoon dried sage leaves

½ teaspoon paprika

½ teaspoon seasoned salt

2 tablespoons chopped fresh chives

1 Prepare the coals or a gas grill for direct heat (page 267). Heat to medium heat, which will take about 40 minutes for charcoal or about 10 minutes for a gas grill. Cut 1 (18 × 12-inch) sheet of heavy-duty foil; spray foil with the cooking spray.

2 Scrub the potatoes thoroughly with a vegetable brush and water to remove any dirt, but do not peel. Cut red potatoes into quarters. Cut baking potatoes into 1-inch chunks to measure about 2 cups.

3 Place red and russet potatoes on center of foil sheet. Cut the butter into small pieces; sprinkle over potatoes. Sprinkle with the sage, paprika and seasoned salt.

4 Bring up 2 sides of foil over potatoes so edges meet. Seal edges, making a tight ½-inch fold; fold again, allowing space for heat circulation and expansion. Fold other sides to seal. (See page 123.)

5 Place the packet on the grill rack over medium heat. Cover the grill; cook 40 to 50 minutes, rotating the packet ½ turn after about 20 minutes, until potatoes are tender when pierced with a fork.

6 To serve, cut a large X across the top of the packet with kitchen scissors; carefully fold back the foil to allow steam to escape. Sprinkle with chives.

1 Serving: Calories 130; Total Fat 3g; Cholesterol 10mg; Sodium 115mg; Total Carbohydrate 23g (Dietary Fiber 3g); Protein 2g **Carbohydrate Choices:** 1½

Cook's Tips

Using two types of potatoes creates a nice color and texture contrast. If you don't want to use two types, use one type of potato, cutting into pieces as indicated.

For a change of flavor, use dried thyme, marjoram or basil instead of the sage.

Cutting Red and Baking Potatoes: Cut unpeeled red potatoes into quarters and unpeeled baking potatoes into 1-inch chunks.

Chopping Chives: Place chives together on a cutting board and cut across into small pieces.

Easy Italian Veggies

PREP TIME: 35 Minutes • **START TO FINISH:** 35 Minutes • 4 servings

2 large bell peppers (any color)

1 large white or red potato, about 6 oz

1 medium yellow summer squash

1 medium zucchini

1 medium onion

¼ cup butter or margarine (½ stick), room temperature

2 tablespoons lemon-pepper seasoning

¼ cup Italian dressing

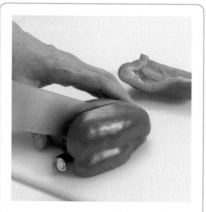

Cutting Bell Pepper into Quarters: Cut bell pepper lengthwise into quarters and cut out seeds and membrane.

1 Prepare the coals or a gas grill for direct heat (page 267). Heat to medium heat, which will take about 40 minutes for charcoal or about 10 minutes for a gas grill.

2 Cut the bell peppers lengthwise into quarters, and cut out seeds and membrane. Scrub the potato thoroughly with a vegetable brush and water to remove any dirt, but do not peel. Cut the potato lengthwise into quarters. Cut the yellow summer squash lengthwise in half. Cut the zucchini lengthwise in half. Peel the onion and cut into ½-inch slices.

3 In a small bowl, mix the butter and lemon-pepper seasoning. Brush butter mixture on the vegetables.

4 Place the vegetables directly on the grill rack over medium heat. Cover the grill; cook 10 to 20 minutes, turning vegetables frequently, until tender when pierced with a fork. As vegetables become done, remove from the grill to a platter. Cover with foil to keep warm.

5 Drizzle the dressing over the vegetables. Serve warm.

1 Serving: Calories 260; Total Fat 14g; Cholesterol 30mg; Sodium 750mg; Total Carbohydrate 28g (Dietary Fiber 5g); Protein 4g **Carbohydrate Choices:** 2

Lighten Up Easy Italian Veggies: Omit the butter. Spray the vegetables with butter-flavored cooking spray, then sprinkle with lemon-pepper seasoning. Use fat-free Italian dressing for 1 gram of fat and 120 calories per serving.

Cook's Tips

Checking for doneness is important so start checking at 10 minutes because some vegetables may be tender sooner than others. As soon as a vegetable is tender, remove it from the grill.

No lemon-pepper seasoning? Mix 1 tablespoon pepper, 1½ teaspoons salt, ¼ teaspoon garlic powder and 1 teaspoon grated lemon peel.

GRILLING FRESH VEGETABLES

Veggies on the grill can't be beat! Not only is grilling easy, it also gives a distinctive and delicious flavor to the vegetables.

Wash the vegetables and either leave them whole or cut into the size pieces suggested in the chart below. Toss the vegetables with about 2 tablespoons of melted butter or margarine, olive oil or your favorite Italian dressing until they are evenly coated. (The exception is corn on the cob, which you brush with butter, margarine, olive oil or dressing after removing the husk and before wrapping in foil.)

You will need a little extra butter, margarine, olive oil or dressing to brush on the veggies during grilling to help prevent them from sticking to the rack, cook faster and more evenly and to add flavor. If the veggies are large enough pieces, you can place them directly on the grill rack or in a grill basket or grill wok if you have one.

Prepare the coals or a gas grill for direct heat (page 264). Heat to medium heat, which will take about 40 minutes for charcoal or about 10 minutes for a gas grill.

A grill basket or wok is great for grilling fish , seafood or cut-up pieces of vegetables because you don't have to carefully turn each piece over during cooking. It also eliminates smaller pieces of food falling through the grill rack.

Place the vegetables on the grill rack. Cover the grill. Cook, turning the vegetables occasionally and brushing with additional butter, margarine, olive oil or dressing, until the vegetables are crisp-tender. If using a grill basket, turn the basket over occasionally. If using a wok, stir the veggies, turning them over, so they cook evenly. Use the chart below as an easy guide for approximate grilling times. (Types of grills and weather conditions vary and will affect the time.) Sprinkle cooked vegetables with salt and pepper.

Fresh Vegetable Grilling Chart

VEGETABLE	FORM	MINUTES
Asparagus spears	Whole	8 to 10
Bell peppers	Cut into ½-inch strips	5 to 10
Broccoli spears	Cut lengthwise in half	15 to 20
Carrots, baby-cut	Whole	20 to 25
Cauliflower florets	Cut lengthwise in half	10 to 15
Cherry tomatoes	Whole	5 to 10
Corn on the cob, husked and wrapped in foil	Whole	20 to 25
Green beans	Whole	10 to 15
Mushrooms, white	Whole with stems removed	8 to 10
Mushrooms, portabella	Caps with stems removed	8 to 10
Onions	Cut into ½-inch slices	10 to 15
Potatoes, russet or Idaho	Cut lengthwise into quarters	15 to 20
Potatoes, small red	Cut into quarters	10 to 15
Zucchini, small	Cut lengthwise in half	10 to 15

Grill Basket and Wok

Grill Basket

A hinged grill basket can be easily flipped to turn everything over at once and ensure even cooking. It is good for grilling fish, chicken pieces, burgers, sausages and cut-up pieces of vegetables. Most common shapes are square, rectangular or long and oval to resemble a fish shape. There are also specialty shapes for corn on the cob and hot dogs.

Grill Wok

This open pan, with holes on the bottom and sides, is also known as a vegetable basket or stir-fry pan. This is good for grilling cut-up pieces of vegetables, chicken or meat and seafood such as shrimp or scallops. The food can easily be turned over using a turner or stirred several times during cooking to ensure even cooking. It is available square or round.

5 SIDE SALADS and VEGGIES

Caesar Salad

PREP TIME: 20 Minutes • **START TO FINISH:** 20 Minutes • 6 servings

1 large bunch or 2 small bunches romaine lettuce

1 clove garlic

8 flat anchovy fillets (from 2-oz can), if desired

⅓ cup olive or vegetable oil

3 tablespoons lemon juice

1 teaspoon Worcestershire sauce

¼ teaspoon salt

¼ teaspoon ground mustard

Freshly ground black pepper

1 cup garlic-flavored croutons

⅓ cup grated Parmesan cheese

Cook's Tips

To save time, purchase romaine already washed, torn and ready to use. You will need 10 cups, which is about 14 ounces.

To get a head start, wash and dry romaine and seal in a food-storage plastic bag or airtight container. It will keep up to a week in the refrigerator.

1 Remove any limp outer leaves from the romaine and discard. Break remaining leaves off the core; rinse with cool water. Shake off excess water and blot to dry, or roll up the leaves in paper towels or a clean kitchen towel to dry. Tear the leaves into bite-size pieces. You will need about 10 cups of romaine pieces.

2 Peel the garlic and cut the clove in half. Rub the inside of a large salad bowl—a wooden salad bowl works best—with the cut sides of the garlic. Allow a few small pieces of garlic to remain in the bowl if desired.

3 Cut up the anchovies and place in the bowl. Add the oil, lemon juice, Worcestershire sauce, salt, mustard and pepper. Mix well with a fork or wire whisk.

4 Add the romaine and toss with 2 large spoons or salad tongs until coated with the dressing. Sprinkle with the croutons and cheese. To keep salad crisp, serve immediately.

1 Serving: Calories 190; Total Fat 15g; Cholesterol 5mg; Sodium 290mg; Total Carbohydrate 9g (Dietary Fiber 2g); Protein 4g **Carbohydrate Choices:** ½

Lighten Up Caesar Salad: Decrease oil to 3 tablespoons, increase lemon juice to ¼ cup, add 2 tablespoons water to anchovy mixture and decrease cheese to 3 tablespoons for 10 grams of fat and 140 calories per serving.

Chicken Caesar Salad: Grill 6 boneless skinless chicken breasts as directed for grilling on a contact grill (page 267). Cut each breast crosswise into ½-inch slices. Arrange a sliced breast on each Caesar salad.

Drying Romaine: Shake off excess water and blot to dry, or roll up the leaves in a paper towel to dry.

Cutting Up Anchovies: Cut the anchovies into about ¼-inch pieces so they are easier to mix into the dressing.

Greek Salad

PREP TIME: 25 Minutes • **START TO FINISH:** 25 Minutes • 4 servings

LEMON DRESSING

2 tablespoons vegetable oil

1 tablespoon lemon juice

1 teaspoon Dijon mustard

¼ teaspoon granulated sugar

⅛ teaspoon salt

Dash of pepper

SALAD

1 small bunch spinach (¼ lb)

½ head Boston or Bibb lettuce

2 small green onions with tops

1 small cucumber

2 medium plum (Roma) tomatoes

12 pitted whole ripe olives
   (from 6-oz can)

⅓ cup crumbled feta cheese
   (1½ oz)

1   In a tightly covered jar or container, shake all the dressing ingredients.

2   Remove and discard the stems of the spinach. Rinse the leaves in cool water. Shake off excess water and blot to dry, or roll up the leaves in a clean kitchen towel or paper towel to dry. Tear any large leaves into bite-size pieces. Place spinach in a large salad bowl. You will need about 5 cups of spinach pieces.

3   Separate the leaves from the head of lettuce. Rinse the leaves in cool water. Shake off excess water and blot to dry. Tear the leaves into bite-size pieces and add to the bowl.

4   Peel and slice the green onions. Peel the cucumber if it has a wax coating. Slice the cucumber. Cut the tomatoes into wedges. Add these vegetables and the olives to the bowl.

5   Break up any large pieces of the cheese with a fork and add cheese to the bowl.

6   Shake the dressing again to mix ingredients. Pour the dressing over the salad ingredients, and toss with 2 large spoons or salad tongs. To keep salad crisp, serve immediately.

1 Serving: Calories 140; Total Fat 11g; Cholesterol 10mg; Sodium 390mg; Total Carbohydrate 6g (Dietary Fiber 2g); Protein 4g **Carbohydrate Choices:** ½

Cook's Tips

Although the spinach you purchase may be labeled as being washed, you should wash it again because it may still contain some sand and dirt.

A fresh lemon will give you about 2 to 3 tablespoons of juice. To get the most juice out of a lemon, it should be at room temperature. Before squeezing, roll the lemon back and forth on the counter several times with firm pressure, which helps to burst the cells holding the lemon juice.

Washing Spinach: Place leaves in a sink or bowl filled with cool water. Swish with your hands to rinse off the dirt. Lift up the leaves to drain off excess water. Repeat until no dirt remains.

Preparing Boston Lettuce: Separate the leaves from the head of lettuce. Rinse thoroughly and blot to dry.

Spinach-Strawberry Salad

PREP TIME: 20 Minutes • **START TO FINISH:** 20 Minutes • 4 servings

HONEY-DIJON DRESSING

2 tablespoons vegetable oil

2 tablespoons honey

2 tablespoons orange juice

1 tablespoon cider vinegar or white vinegar

1 teaspoon poppy seed, if desired

2 teaspoons Dijon mustard

SALAD

1 small jicama

2 kiwifruit

½ pint (1 cup) fresh strawberries

8 cups ready-to-eat spinach (from 9- or 10-oz bag)

1 In a tightly covered jar, shake all the dressing ingredients.

2 Peel the jicama, removing the brown skin and a thin layer of the flesh just under the skin. The skin can sometimes be slightly tough. Cut about half of the jicama into about 1 × ¼-inch sticks to measure about ¾ cup. Wrap remaining jicama and refrigerate for another use.

3 Peel the kiwifruit. Cut lengthwise in half, then cut into slices. Rinse the strawberries with cool water and pat dry. Remove the leaves and cut the berries lengthwise into slices.

4 Remove and discard the stems from the spinach leaves. Rinse the leaves in cool water. Shake off excess water and blot to dry with paper towels. Tear any large leaves into bite-size pieces.

5 In a large salad bowl, place the spinach, strawberries, jicama sticks and kiwifruit slices. Shake the dressing again to mix ingredients. Pour the dressing over the salad ingredients, and toss with 2 large spoons or salad tongs. To keep salad crisp, serve immediately.

1 Serving: Calories 190; Total Fat 8g; Cholesterol 0mg; Sodium 115mg; Total Carbohydrate 28g (Dietary Fiber 7g); Protein 3g **Carbohydrate Choices:** 2

Cook's Tips

Packaged mixed salad greens that are already cleaned and ready to use are available in the produce section of the supermarket and can be used instead of the spinach. A 10-ounce bag is about 7 cups of greens. The Italian variety is especially pretty.

Leftover jicama can be cut into sticks and served with other raw vegetables for a snack or appetizer.

Cutting Jicama: Peel jicama, and cut into ¼-inch slices. Cut slices into 1-inch sticks.

Peeling Kiwifruit: Cut the fuzzy brown skin from the fruit with a paring knife.

Dill Potato and Green Bean Salad

PREP TIME: 30 Minutes • **START TO FINISH:** 1 Hour 30 Minutes • 8 servings

SPECIAL EQUIPMENT

2-quart microwavable casserole with lid

DILL DRESSING

1 clove garlic or ⅛ teaspoon garlic powder

¼ cup olive or vegetable oil

2 tablespoons chopped fresh or 2 teaspoons dried dill weed

2 tablespoons white vinegar

1 teaspoon granulated sugar

1 teaspoon ground mustard

¾ teaspoon salt

¼ teaspoon coarse ground black pepper

SALAD

¾ lb green beans

12 small (new) red or white potatoes (about 1½ lb)

1 small red onion

1 small yellow bell pepper

¼ cup water

1 Peel and finely chop the garlic. In a tightly covered jar or container, shake the garlic and remaining dressing ingredients.

2 Cut off the ends of the green beans and discard. Cut beans in half. Scrub the potatoes thoroughly with a vegetable brush and water to remove any dirt, but do not peel. Cut the potatoes into quarters.

3 In a 2-quart microwavable casserole, place the beans, potatoes and water. Cover with lid; microwave on High 10 to 12 minutes, rotating casserole ½ turn every 4 minutes, until potatoes are tender when pierced with a fork. Drain vegetables in a strainer.

4 Meanwhile, peel and chop the red onion to measure ¼ cup. Cut the bell pepper in half lengthwise, and cut out seeds and membrane. Coarsely chop the bell pepper to measure ½ cup.

5 In a large salad bowl, place the beans and potatoes. Shake the dressing and pour over the vegetables, toss with 2 large spoons. Add the onion and bell pepper; toss again. Cover with plastic wrap; refrigerate 1 to 2 hours or until chilled.

1 Serving: Calories 150; Total Fat 7g; Cholesterol 0mg; Sodium 230mg; Total Carbohydrate 20g (Dietary Fiber 3g); Protein 2g **Carbohydrate Choices:** 1

Dill Potato Salad: Omit the green beans, and double the amount of potatoes.

Cook's Tips

Be sure not to overcook the potatoes, or they will fall apart in the salad. When the potatoes are done, you should be able to just pierce them with a fork.

Tarragon, with its mild anise flavor, is a nice change from dill weed in this salad. Use 1 tablespoon fresh tarragon or 2 teaspoons dried tarragon leaves for the dill.

Garlic Bulb or Clove? The garlic bulb, or "head," is made up of many sections called "cloves."

Potatoes for Salad: Choose small red or white potatoes, which hold their shape when cooked.

SALAD GREENS BASICS

There are many types of greens and they vary in taste, shape and color. Some are slightly bitter and others have a mild flavor. There are light green leaves and those with rich reddish tones. Some are tender and others have a firmer texture. Have fun experimenting with a variety of greens to create a salad that is full of flavor, color and texture. Here are some of the more popular types of greens.

MILD-FLAVORED GREENS

Boston Lettuce (or Butterhead, Bibb)

Small rounded heads of soft, tender leaves and a delicate flavor. Bibb is smaller in size but has the same flavor.

Iceberg Lettuce (or Crisphead)

Solid, compact heads with tight leaves that range from medium green on the outside to pale green inside and has a bland, mild flavor.

Leaf Lettuce (or Green, Red, Oak Leaf)

Tender but crisp leaves that do not form tight heads. These leafy bunches have a mild flavor.

Mesclun (or Field, Wild Greens)

Mixture of young, small greens with a variety of textures and colors.

Chinese Cabbage (or Napa, Celery)

Asian variety of cabbage with long, crisp leaves that vary from pale green to white. It has a mild flavor.

Romaine (or Cos)

Narrow, elongated dark green leaves sometimes tinged with red on the tips. This mild-flavored crisp leaf has a broad white center rib, which is crunchy.

Salad in a Bag

Look for bags of mixed salad greens in the produce section of the supermarket. The bag can include one type of green or a mixture of several varieties, which can add color, flavor and texture to your salads. Some also come with a packet of salad dressing and other items to add to the salad. Although the bag may say "washed and ready to use" it is best to wash the greens under cold water and pat dry before using.

Storing and Handling Salad Greens

Be sure to purchase fresh, crisp greens. Avoid limp, bruised and discolored greens and those with rust spots. To keep greens fresh and crisp, line a plastic bag or tightly covered container with damp (not wet) paper towels. Place the unwashed greens in the bag and refrigerate up to 5 days. Iceberg lettuce should have the core removed and be rinsed under cold running water before storing.

Rinse greens under cold water just before using. Dry the greens in a salad spinner or place on a clean kitchen towel or layers of paper towels and pat gently to dry. Once greens are dry, they can be gently rolled up in a towel or paper towels and placed in a plastic bag and stored in the refrigerator up to 8 hours.

BITTER GREENS

Arugula (or Rocket)
Small, slender, dark green leaves similar to radish leaves with a slightly bitter peppery mustard flavor. Choose smaller leaves for a milder flavor.

Belgian Endive (or French)
Closed, narrow, pale green leaves with a distinct bitter flavor.

Cabbage
Green or red are most popular. Look for compact heads with tightly wrapped leaves. The flavor of cabbage can range from strong to slightly sweet.

Curly Endive
Frilly, narrow, somewhat prickly leaves with a slightly bitter taste.

Escarole
Broad, wavy, medium green leaves and slightly bitter flavor.

Frisée
Slender, curly leaves ranging in color from yellow-white to yellow-green and a slightly bitter taste.

Greens (Beet, Chard, Collard, Dandelion, Mustard)
Strong and biting flavor. When young greens are tender and milder in flavor they are a nice addition to tossed salads. Older green are too bitter for salads and should be cooked for the best flavor.

Radicchio
Resembles a small, loose-leaf cabbage with smooth, tender leaves. The most familiar variety is usually rose-colored and may have a slightly bitter taste.

Spinach
Smooth, tapered, dark green leaves, sometimes with crumpling at the edges with a slightly bitter flavor. Larger leaves may be stronger in flavor.

Watercress
Small, crisp dark-green leaves with a strong peppery slightly bitter flavor.

Italian Pasta Salad

PREP TIME: 30 Minutes • **START TO FINISH:** 1 Hour • 6 servings

GARLIC VINAIGRETTE DRESSING

1 clove garlic or ⅛ teaspoon
garlic powder

¼ cup cider vinegar or balsamic
vinegar

2 tablespoons olive or vegetable oil

½ teaspoon salt

SALAD

¼ teaspoon salt (for cooking
pasta), if desired

2 cups uncooked rotini or rotelle
(spiral) pasta (6 oz)

1 large tomato

½ of a medium cucumber

3 or 4 medium green onions
with tops

1 small red or green bell pepper

¼ cup chopped ripe olives
(from 4¼-oz can), if desired

1 Peel and finely chop the garlic. In a tightly covered jar or container, shake the garlic and remaining dressing ingredients.

2 Fill a 4-quart Dutch oven about half full of water. Add ¼ teaspoon salt if desired. Cover with lid and heat over high heat until the water is boiling rapidly. Add the pasta. Heat to boiling again. Boil uncovered 8 to 10 minutes for rotini (or 9 to 11 minutes for rotelle), stirring frequently, until tender.

3 While the water is heating and pasta is cooking, chop the tomato and cucumber, and peel and chop the onions. Place the vegetables in a large bowl.

4 Cut the bell pepper in half lengthwise, and cut out seeds and membrane. Cut bell pepper into pieces, and add to vegetables in bowl.

5 Place a strainer or colander in the sink. Pour the pasta in the strainer to drain. Rinse with cold water; drain. Add pasta to vegetables in bowl. Add the olives.

6 Shake the dressing again to mix ingredients. Pour the dressing over the vegetables and pasta, and mix thoroughly. Cover with plastic wrap; refrigerate about 30 minutes or until chilled.

1 Serving: Calories 230; Total Fat 6g; Cholesterol 0mg; Sodium 250mg; Total Carbohydrate 37g (Dietary Fiber 3g); Protein 7g **Carbohydrate Choices:** 2½

Ranch Pasta Salad: Use about ½ cup purchased ranch dressing from the supermarket instead of the Garlic Vinaigrette Dressing.

Italian Pepperoni-Pasta Salad: Add one 3.5-ounce package of sliced pepperoni (cut slices in half) and ½ cup shredded mozzarella or pizza blend cheese to the vegetables in the bowl.

Cook's Tips

You can use ½ cup purchased Italian dressing instead of making the Garlic Vinaigrette Dressing.

The water being heated for cooking the pasta will boil sooner if it is covered with a lid.

Cutting Bell Pepper: Cut bell pepper in half lengthwise; cut out seeds and membrane. Cut pepper into strips; cut strips into pieces.

165

Acorn Squash

1½ to 2 pounds is enough for 4 servings

Buy: Look for hard, tough rinds with no soft spots. The squash should feel heavy for its size.

Prepare: Wash squash. Cut in half lengthwise. You will need to do this on a cutting board and using your biggest chef's knife because the shell is quite tough. Place a paper towel under the squash to keep it from slipping while cutting. Scrape out the seeds and fibers with a soup spoon.

Bake: Heat the oven to 400°F. Place squash, cut sides up, in a baking dish. Sprinkle cut sides with salt and pepper. Place small dabs of butter or margarine over cut surface and in cavity, using about 1 tablespoon butter for each squash. Pour water into baking dish until it is about ¼ inch deep. Cover with foil. The squash will probably be taller than the baking dish, so the foil may touch the squash.

Bake 30 to 40 minutes or until tender when pierced with a fork. When removing the foil to test for doneness, open a side of the foil away from you to allow steam to escape. Lift the squash from the baking dish with a large spoon or spatula. Scrape the cooked squash out of the shell and into a serving dish.

Microwave: Pierce whole squash with tip of sharp knife in several places to allow steam to escape. Place on microwavable paper towel. Microwave on High 4 to 6 minutes or until squash is hot and rind is firm but easy to cut; cool slightly. Carefully cut in half; remove seeds. Arrange halves, cut sides down, on 10-inch microwavable plate. Cover with microwavable plastic wrap, folding back one edge ¼ inch to release steam. Microwave on High 5 to 8 minutes or until squash is tender when pierced with a knife.

1 Serving: Calories 90; Total Fat 0g; Cholesterol 0mg; Sodium 5mg; Total Carbohydrate 22g (Dietary Fiber 6g); Protein 2g **Carbohydrate Choices:** 1½

Cutting Acorn Squash: Cut squash lengthwise in half on a cutting board using a large chef's knife. Scrape out the seeds and fibers with a soup spoon.

Asparagus

1½ pounds is enough for 4 servings

Buy: Look for smooth, firm, medium-size spears with tightly closed tips. Wrap stem ends with damp paper towel and place unwashed in a plastic bag. Store in the refrigerator up to 4 days.

Prepare: Break off and discard the tough ends of the asparagus stalks where they snap easily. Wash asparagus thoroughly, including the tips, to remove any sandy soil. Remove the scales if sandy or tough. If stalk ends are quite large, peel about 2 inches of the end with a vegetable peeler so they will be more tender after cooking.

Boil: Add 1 inch of water (and ¼ teaspoon salt if desired) to a large skillet (about 10-inch size). Cover with lid; heat to boiling over high heat. Add asparagus spears. Cover; heat to boiling again. Once water is boiling, reduce heat just enough so water bubbles gently. Cook covered 4 to 5 minutes or until crisp-tender when pierced with a fork. Thinner young asparagus will cook more quickly than the more mature thicker stalks. Lift asparagus from water with tongs, allowing extra water to drip off.

Steam: Place a steamer basket in ½ inch of water in a skillet or saucepan. The water should not touch the bottom of the basket. Place asparagus spears in basket. Cover tightly with lid; heat to boiling over high heat. Once water is boiling, reduce heat to low. Steam covered 6 to 8 minutes or until crisp-tender when pierced with a fork.

Microwave: Place asparagus spears and ¼ cup water in an 8-inch square microwavable dish. Cover with microwavable plastic wrap, folding back one edge ¼ inch to release steam. Microwave on High 4 to 6 minutes, rotating dish ½ turn after 3 minutes, until crisp-tender when pierced with a fork. Let stand covered 2 minutes; drain in a strainer.

Storing Asparagus: Cover stem ends with damp paper towel and place unwashed in a plastic bag. Store in refrigerator up to 4 days.

Preparing Asparagus for Cooking: Break off tough ends of asparagus stalks where they snap easily. Discard ends.

1 Serving: Calories 25; Total Fat 0g; Cholesterol 0mg; Sodium 0mg; Total Carbohydrate 4g (Dietary Fiber 2g); Protein 2g **Carbohydrate Choices:** 0

Green Beans and Yellow Wax Beans

1 pound is enough for **4 servings**

Buy: The wax bean is a pale yellow variety of green bean. For green or yellow beans, look for long, smooth, crisp pods with fresh-looking tips and bright green or waxy yellow color. Place unwashed in a plastic bag and store in the refrigerator up to 5 days.

Prepare: Wash beans and cut off ends. Leave whole, or cut crosswise into about 1-inch pieces. To save time when cutting, place 3 to 4 beans side by side on a cutting board and cut off all the ends at one time.

Boil: Add 1 inch of water (and ¼ teaspoon salt if desired) to a medium saucepan (about 2-quart size). Add the beans. Cover with lid; heat to boiling over high heat. Once water is boiling, remove lid and reduce heat just enough so water bubbles gently. Cook uncovered 6 to 8 minutes or until crisp-tender when pierced with a fork; drain in a strainer.

Steam: Place a steamer basket in ½ inch of water in a skillet or saucepan. The water should not touch the bottom of the basket. Place beans in basket. Cover tightly with lid; heat to boiling over high heat. Once water is boiling, reduce heat to low. Steam covered 10 to 12 minutes or until crisp-tender when pierced with a fork.

Microwave: Place beans and 1 cup water in a 1-quart microwavable casserole. Cover with microwavable plastic wrap, folding back one edge ¼ inch to release steam. Microwave on High 10 to 12 minutes, stirring every 5 minutes, until crisp-tender when pierced with a fork. Let stand covered 5 minutes; drain in a strainer.

1 Serving: Calories 35; Total Fat 0g; Cholesterol 0mg; Sodium 5mg; Total Carbohydrate 7g (Dietary Fiber 3g); Protein 2g **Carbohydrate Choices:** ½

Purchasing Beans: Look for long, smooth, crisp pods with fresh-looking tips and bright green or waxy yellow color.

Cutting Beans: Lay 3 or 4 beans side by side on cutting board; cut off all the ends at one time. Cut crosswise into 1-inch pieces.

Broccoli

1½ pounds is enough for **4 servings**

Buy: Look for firm, compact dark green clusters, and avoid thick, tough stems. Place unwashed broccoli in a plastic bag and store in the refrigerator up to 5 days.

Prepare: Trim the large leaves, and cut off any tough ends of lower stems. Rinse with cool water. For spears, cut lengthwise into ½-inch-wide stalks. For pieces, cut into ½-inch-wide stalks, then cut crosswise into 1-inch pieces. If desired, cut florets into bite-size pieces.

Boil: Add 1 inch of water (and ¼ teaspoon salt if desired) to a medium saucepan (about 3-quart size). Add the broccoli spears or pieces. Cover with lid; heat to boiling over high heat. Once water is boiling, remove lid and reduce heat just enough so water bubbles gently. Cook uncovered 5 to 7 minutes or until crisp-tender when pierced with a fork; drain in a strainer.

Steam: Place a steamer basket in ½ inch of water in a skillet or saucepan. The water should not touch the bottom of the basket. Place broccoli spears or pieces in basket. Cover tightly with lid; heat to boiling over high heat. Once water is boiling, reduce heat to low. Steam covered 10 to 11 minutes or until stems are crisp-tender when pierced with a fork.

Microwave: Place **broccoli spears** with just the water that clings to the spears in an 8-inch square microwavable dish, arranging in a spoke pattern with florets in the center. Cover with microwavable plastic wrap, folding back one edge ¼ inch to release steam. Microwave on High 6 to 8 minutes, rotating dish ¼ turn after 4 minutes, until tender when pierced with a fork. Let stand covered 2 minutes; drain.

Place **broccoli pieces** with just the water that clings to the pieces in a 2-quart microwavable casserole. Cover with microwavable plastic wrap, folding back one edge ¼ inch to release steam. Microwave on High 5 to 7 minutes, stirring once, until tender when pierced with a fork. Let stand covered 2 minutes; drain.

Cutting Broccoli Spears: To make spears, cut lengthwise into ½-inch stalks. For pieces, cut the ½-inch stalks crosswise into 1-inch pieces.

Arranging Broccoli Spears for Microwaving: Place broccoli in an 8-inch square microwavable dish, arranging in a spoke pattern with florets in the center.

1 Serving: Calories 45; Total Fat 0g; Cholesterol 0mg; Sodium 35mg; Total Carbohydrate 7g (Dietary Fiber 2g); Protein 3g **Carbohydrate Choices:** ½

Carrots

1 pound (6 or 7 medium carrots) or 1 pound baby-cut carrots is enough for **4 servings**

Buy: Look for firm, smooth carrots with good color. Avoid carrots with cracks or any that have become soft or limp. Place unwashed carrots in a plastic bag and store in the refrigerator up to 2 weeks.

Prepare: Peel carrots with a vegetable peeler and cut off ends. Cut carrots crosswise into ¼-inch slices. Wash baby-cut carrots and leave whole.

Boil: Add 1 inch of water (and ¼ teaspoon salt if desired) to a medium saucepan (about 2-quart size). Cover with lid; heat to boiling over high heat. Add the carrots. Cover; heat to boiling again. Once water is boiling, reduce heat just enough so water bubbles gently. Cook carrot slices covered 6 to 10 minutes (baby-cut carrots 7 to 10 minutes) or until tender when pierced with a fork; drain in a strainer.

Steam: Place a steamer basket in ½ inch of water in a skillet or saucepan. The water should not touch the bottom of the basket. Place carrots in basket. Cover tightly with lid; heat to boiling over high heat. Once water is boiling, reduce heat to low. Steam carrot slices covered 6 to 9 minutes (baby-cut carrots 8 to 10 minutes) or until tender when pierced with a fork.

Microwave: Place carrot slices and ¼ cup water (or baby-cut carrots and 2 tablespoons water) in a 1-quart microwavable casserole. Cover with microwavable plastic wrap, folding back one edge ¼ inch to release steam. Microwave on High 6 to 8 minutes, stirring after 4 minutes, until tender when pierced with a fork. Let stand covered 5 minutes; drain in a strainer.

Purchasing Carrots: Look for firm, smooth carrots with good color. Avoid carrots with cracks or any that have become soft or limp.

Slicing Carrots: Peel carrots with a vegetable peeler and cut off ends. Cut carrots crosswise into ¼-inch slices.

1 Serving: Calories 45; Total Fat 0g; Cholesterol 0mg; Sodium 70mg; Total Carbohydrate 10g (Dietary Fiber 3g); Protein 0g **Carbohydrate Choices:** ½

Cauliflower

1 medium head (2 pounds) is enough for **4 servings**

Buy: Look for a creamy white, firm cauliflower with compact flower clusters (the white portion) and bright green, fresh, firmly attached leaves. Place unwashed in plastic bag and store in the refrigerator up to 1 week.

Prepare: Remove outer leaves, and cut off the core, or stem, close to the head. Cut any discoloration off of the flower clusters. Wash cauliflower. Cut the flower clusters (florets) off the core, and discard the core.

Boil: Add 1 inch of water (and ¼ teaspoon salt if desired) to a medium saucepan (about 3-quart size). Cover with lid; heat to boiling over high heat. Add the florets. Cover and heat to boiling again. Once water is boiling, remove lid and reduce heat just enough so water bubbles gently. Cook uncovered 5 to 7 minutes or until tender when pierced with a fork; drain in a strainer.

Steam: Place a steamer basket in ½ inch of water in a skillet or saucepan. The water should not touch the bottom of the basket. Place florets in basket. Cover tightly with lid; heat to boiling over high heat. Once water is boiling, reduce heat to low. Steam covered 6 to 8 minutes or until tender when pierced with a fork.

Microwave: Place florets and 2 tablespoons water in a 2-quart microwavable casserole. Cover with microwavable plastic wrap, folding back one edge ¼ inch to release steam. Microwave on High 8 to 10 minutes, stirring after 6 minutes, until tender when pierced with a fork. Let stand covered 2 minutes; drain in a strainer.

1 Serving: Calories 35; Total Fat 0g; Cholesterol 0mg; Sodium 35mg; Total Carbohydrate 7g (Dietary Fiber 3g); Protein 2g **Carbohydrate Choices:** ½

Preparing Cauliflower: Remove outer leaves and cut off the end of the core, or stem, close to the head.

Cutting Florets: Cut florets (flower clusters) off the core; discard the core.

Corn

4 ears of corn is enough for **4 servings**

Buy: Look for bright green husks, tight-fitting fresh-looking silk and kernels that are plump but not too large. Corn tastes best if it is purchased and cooked the same day that it was picked. If that's not possible, wrap unhusked ears in damp paper towels and store in refrigerator up to 2 days.

Prepare: Pull the green husks off the ears and remove the silk just before cooking. Do not put the corn husks or silk in your garbage disposal. If there are any bad spots on the ears, cut them out. Break off any long stems so the corn will fit easily into the pan. If any ears are too long for your pan, cut or break them in half.

Boil: Fill a 4-quart Dutch oven about half full of water; add 1 tablespoon sugar. Do not add any salt because that will make the corn tough. Cover with lid; heat to boiling over high heat. Once water is boiling, carefully add the corn and return to boiling. Boil uncovered 5 to 7 minutes or until tender when pierced with a fork. Lift corn from water with tongs, allowing extra water to drip off. Serve immediately with butter or margarine, salt and pepper.

Steam: Place a steamer basket in ½ inch of water in a skillet. The water should not touch the bottom of the basket. Place corn in basket. Cover tightly with lid; heat to boiling over high heat. Once water is boiling, reduce heat to low. Steam covered 5 to 7 minutes or until tender when pierced with a fork.

Microwave: Wrap each ear of corn in microwavable plastic wrap. Microwave on High for times below, turning once with tongs, until tender when pierced with a fork. Let stand covered 2 minutes.

1 ear: 2 to 3 minutes
2 ears: 3 to 4 minutes
4 ears: 6 to 8 minutes

1 Serving: Calories 110; Total Fat 1g; Cholesterol 0mg; Sodium 15mg; Total Carbohydrate 22g (Dietary Fiber 3g); Protein 3g **Carbohydrate Choices:** 1½

Purchasing Corn: Look for bright green husks, tight-fitting fresh-looking silk and kernels that are plump but not too large.

Husking Corn: Pull the green husks off the ears and remove silk just before cooking. Do not put the corn husks or silk in your garbage disposal.

Mushrooms

1 pound is enough for 4 servings

Buy: Look for creamy white to light brown caps that are tightly closed around the stems. If the caps are slightly open, the "gills" (or underside) should be light pink or tan. If the caps are completely open and show the gills, the mushrooms may not be fresh. To store, do not wash. Wrap in paper towels and place in a plastic or paper bag. Refrigerate up to 4 days.

Prepare: Wipe clean with damp paper towel or, if necessary, rinse with cool water. Do not soak them in water because they will absorb water and become mushy. Dry thoroughly. Do not peel. Cut off and discard the end of each stem. Cut each mushroom lengthwise into ¼-inch slices.

Sauté: Heat ¼ cup butter or margarine in a large skillet (about 12-inch size) over medium-high heat until butter begins to bubble. Add mushroom slices. Cook uncovered 4 to 6 minutes, lifting and stirring constantly with a turner or large spoon, until tender when pierced with a fork. If using a nonstick skillet, you can use just 2 tablespoons butter.

Steam: Place a steamer basket in ½ inch of water in a skillet or saucepan. The water should not touch the bottom of the basket. Place mushroom slices in basket. Cover tightly with lid; heat to boiling over high heat. Once water is boiling, reduce heat to low. Steam covered 4 to 5 minutes or until tender when pierced with a fork.

Microwave: Place mushroom slices and 1 tablespoon butter, margarine or vegetable oil in a 1-quart microwavable casserole. Cover with microwavable paper towel. Microwave on High 3 to 4 minutes or until tender when pierced with a fork.

1 **Serving:** Calories 30; Total Fat 0g; Cholesterol 0mg; Sodium 5mg; Total Carbohydrate 4g (Dietary Fiber 1g); Protein 3g **Carbohydrate Choices:** 0

Cleaning Mushrooms: Wipe with a damp paper towel or rinse with cold water to remove dirt and then wipe with paper towel.

Slicing Mushrooms: Cut mushrooms lengthwise into ¼-inch slices by placing them on a cutting board with the stems up.

Potatoes, Small (New) Red or White

10 to 12 (1½ pounds) is enough for **4 servings**

Buy: Look for nicely shaped, smooth, firm potatoes with unblemished skins. The skin on new potatoes is not fully mature so the skin may be "feathering" or "skinning," which is normal. Avoid potatoes that are wrinkled, have a green tinge to the skin or have large skinned and discolored areas. Choose potatoes of similar size, about 1½ inches in diameter. Store unwashed potatoes in a cool (45°F–60°F), dry, dark place with good ventilation up to 2 weeks.

Prepare: Gently scrub potatoes with a vegetable brush or cellulose sponge. The skin is tender so there is no need to peel the potatoes before cooking.

Boil: Place potatoes in a medium saucepan (about 2-quart size). Add enough water just to cover the potatoes. Cover with lid; heat to boiling over high heat. Once water is boiling, reduce heat just enough so water bubbles gently. Cook covered 20 to 30 minutes or until tender when pierced with a fork; drain in a strainer.

Steam: Place a steamer basket in ½ inch of water in a skillet or saucepan. The water should not touch the bottom of the basket. Place potatoes in basket. Cover tightly with lid; heat to boiling over high heat. Once water is boiling, reduce heat to low. Steam covered 18 to 22 minutes or until tender when pierced with a fork.

Microwave: Place potatoes and ¼ cup water in a 1½-quart microwavable casserole. Cover with microwavable plastic wrap, folding back one edge ¼ inch to release steam. Microwave on High 9 to 11 minutes, stirring once, until tender when pierced with a fork. Let stand covered 5 minutes; drain in a strainer.

Purchasing Small (New) Potatoes: Look for nicely shaped, smooth, firm potatoes with unblemished skins. The skin is not fully mature so it may be "feathering" or look very thin.

Scrubbing Small (New) Potatoes: Scrub potatoes thoroughly with a vegetable brush and water to remove any dirt.

1 Serving: Calories 130; Total Fat 0g; Cholesterol 0mg; Sodium 10mg; Total Carbohydrate 30g (Dietary Fiber 4g); Protein 3g **Carbohydrate Choices:** 2

Potatoes, Red or White

6 medium (2 pounds) is enough for **4 servings**

Buy: Look for nicely shaped, smooth, firm potatoes with unblemished skins. Avoid potatoes that are wrinkled or have a green tinge to the skin. Store unwashed potatoes in a cool (45°F–60°F), dry, dark place with good ventilation up to 2 weeks.

Prepare: Gently scrub potatoes with a vegetable brush or cellulose sponge. Leave skins on or peel thinly with a vegetable peeler, and remove large eyes. Cut into large pieces, 2 to 2½ inches.

Boil: Place potatoes in a medium saucepan (about 2-quart size). Add enough water just to cover the potatoes. Cover with lid; heat to boiling over high heat. Once water is boiling, reduce heat just enough so water bubbles gently. Cook covered 20 to 30 minutes or until tender when pierced with a fork; drain in a strainer.

Steam: Place a steamer basket in ½ inch of water in a skillet or saucepan. The water should not touch the bottom of the basket. Place potatoes in basket. Cover tightly with lid; heat to boiling over high heat. Once water is boiling, reduce heat to low. Steam covered 30 to 35 minutes or until tender when pierced with a fork.

1 Serving: Calories 180; Total Fat 0g; Cholesterol 0mg; Sodium 15mg; Total Carbohydrate 40g (Dietary Fiber 5g); Protein 4g **Carbohydrate Choices:** 2½

Note: For russet or Idaho baking potatoes, see Baked Potatoes on page 182.

Purchasing Red or White Potatoes: Look for nicely shaped, smooth, firm potatoes with unblemished skins and no green tinge to the skin.

Removing Potato Eyes: Leave skins on or peel thinly with a vegetable peeler or paring knife. Remove large eyes using the tip of a paring knife.

Asparagus-Pepper Stir-Fry

PREP TIME: 25 Minutes • **START TO FINISH:** 25 Minutes • 4 servings

1 bunch (1 lb) asparagus

1 medium bell pepper (any color)

2 cloves garlic or ¼ teaspoon garlic powder

1 tablespoon orange juice

1 tablespoon soy sauce

½ teaspoon grated gingerroot or ¼ teaspoon ground ginger

1 teaspoon vegetable or olive oil

1 Break off the tough ends of the asparagus stalks where they snap easily. Wash asparagus; cut into 1-inch pieces. Cut the bell pepper in half lengthwise, and cut out seeds and membrane. Cut bell pepper into ¾-inch pieces. Peel and finely chop the garlic.

2 In a small bowl, mix the orange juice, soy sauce and ginger; set aside.

3 In a 10-inch nonstick skillet or wok, heat the oil over medium heat. Add the asparagus, bell pepper and garlic. Stir-fry with a turner or large spoon 3 to 4 minutes, lifting and stirring constantly, until vegetables are crisp-tender when pierced with a fork.

4 Stir in the juice mixture. Cook and stir 15 to 30 seconds or until vegetables are coated.

1 Serving: Calories 40; Total Fat 1.5g; Cholesterol 0mg; Sodium 230mg; Total Carbohydrate 5g (Dietary Fiber 2g); Protein 2g **Carbohydrate Choices:** ½

Cook's Tip

Stir-frying asparagus is one of the best ways to bring out its fresh spring flavor. Choose thinner spears for the most tender texture.

Cutting Asparagus: Wash asparagus and then cut into 1-inch pieces.

Grating Gingerroot: Rub peeled gingerroot across the small holes of a grater.

Dilled Carrots and Pea Pods

PREP TIME: 15 Minutes • **START TO FINISH:** 15 Minutes • 4 servings

1½ cups fresh snow (Chinese) pea pods (about 5 oz)

1½ cups ready-to-eat baby-cut carrots (about 8 oz)

1 tablespoon butter or margarine

2 teaspoons chopped fresh or ½ teaspoon dried dill weed

⅛ teaspoon salt

1 Wash the pea pods and snap off the stem end of each one. To remove the strings from the pea pods, start at the stem end and pull the string along the straight edge of the each pea pod.

2 Add 1 inch of water to a 2-quart saucepan. Cover with lid; heat the water to boiling over high heat. Add the carrots. Cover; heat to boiling again. Once water is boiling, reduce heat just enough so water bubbles gently. Cook covered about 4 minutes or until carrots are crisp-tender when pierced with a fork. Do not drain water.

3 Add the pea pods to the carrots in saucepan. Heat uncovered until water is boiling again; continue boiling uncovered 2 to 3 minutes, stirring occasionally, until pea pods are crisp-tender. Pea pods cook very quickly, so be careful not to overcook them. Drain carrots and pea pods in a strainer, then return to saucepan.

4 Stir the butter, dill weed and salt into carrots and pea pods until butter is melted.

1 Serving: Calories 60; Total Fat 3g; Cholesterol 10mg; Sodium 130mg; Total Carbohydrate 7g (Dietary Fiber 2g); Protein 1g **Carbohydrate Choices:** ½

Cook's Tips

Snow pea pods are very similar to snap pea pods, and they can be used interchangeably. Both are edible pea pods with tender, sweet peas inside.

One 6-ounce package of frozen snow (Chinese) pea pods can be substituted for the fresh pea pods. Thaw them before cooking in step 3.

Removing Strings from Pea Pods: Snap off the stem end of pea pod, and pull the string along the straight edge of the pea pod to remove it.

Chopping Fresh Dill: With kitchen scissors, snip the dill leaves from the stem into a small bowl or measuring cup. Snip leaves into very small pieces. Discard the stems.

Roasted Autumn Vegetables

PREP TIME: 20 Minutes • **START TO FINISH:** 1 Hour 5 Minutes • 8 servings

SPECIAL EQUIPMENT

15 × 10 × 1-inch pan

1 small butternut squash
(about 1½ lb)

2 medium unpeeled Yukon gold
or red potatoes

1 medium red onion

1 dark-orange sweet potato or yam
(about 6 oz)

1 clove garlic or ⅛ teaspoon garlic
powder

Cooking spray for greasing pan

1 cup ready-to-eat baby-cut carrots

2 tablespoons olive or vegetable oil

1 tablespoon chopped fresh or
1 teaspoon dried sage leaves

1 tablespoon chopped fresh or
1 teaspoon crushed dried
rosemary leaves

½ teaspoon salt

1 Wash the squash. Using a chef's knife, carefully cut off the bottom and stem ends of the squash. Cut the narrow part (neck) from the rounded bottom part of the squash; cut the rounded bottom in half. Using a spoon, scoop out the seeds and fibers from the bottom halves and discard. Using a sharp vegetable peeler, remove the peel from the neck and 2 bottom halves. Cut squash into 1-inch pieces.

2 Scrub the potatoes thoroughly with a vegetable brush and water to remove any dirt, but do not peel. Cut each potato into eighths. Peel the onion; cut into 16 wedges and separate pieces. Peel the sweet potato and cut into 1-inch pieces. Peel and finely chop the garlic.

3 Heat the oven to 425°F. Spray a 15 × 10 × 1-inch pan with the cooking spray. Place the squash, potatoes, onion, sweet potato and carrots in the pan. Pour the oil over the vegetables. Sprinkle with the garlic, sage, rosemary and salt. Stir to coat vegetables.

4 Roast uncovered 35 to 45 minutes, stirring occasionally, until vegetables are crisp-tender when pierced with a fork.

1 Serving: Calories 150; Total Fat 3.5g; Cholesterol 0mg; Sodium 200mg; Total Carbohydrate 26g (Dietary Fiber 4g); Protein 3g **Carbohydrate Choices:** 2

Lighten Up Roasted Autumn Vegetables: Omit the olive oil and instead spray the pan and vegetables with olive oil–flavored cooking spray to reduce the calories to 90 and the fat to 0 grams per serving.

Cutting Butternut Squash:
Cut off bottom and stem ends of squash. Cut the narrow part (neck) off and cut the rounded bottom in half.

Removing Seeds and Fibers from Butternut Squash: Using a tableware soup spoon, scoop out the seeds and fibers from bottom halves and discard.

Baked Potatoes

PREP TIME: 5 Minutes • **START TO FINISH:** 1 Hour 20 Minutes • 1 potato for each serving

1 or more large baking potatoes (russet or Idaho), about 8 oz each and all about the same size

Butter or margarine, if desired

Sour cream or plain yogurt, if desired

1   Heat the oven to 375°F. Scrub the potatoes thoroughly with a vegetable brush and water to remove any dirt, but do not peel.

2   Pierce the potatoes on all sides with a fork to allow steam to escape during baking. Place potatoes directly on the oven rack. (If potatoes are wrapped in foil, the steam cannot escape, so the potatoes will be more moist and slightly gummy instead of fluffy.)

3   Bake 1 hour to 1 hour 15 minutes or until potatoes feel tender when squeezed gently. Be sure to use a pot holder because potatoes will be very hot to the touch.

4   To serve, cut an X in the top of each potato. Gently squeeze potato from the bottom to open. Serve with butter or sour cream.

1 Serving: Calories 170; Total Fat 0g; Cholesterol 0mg; Sodium 15mg; Total Carbohydrate 37g (Dietary Fiber 4g); Protein 4g **Carbohydrate Choices:** 2½

Microwave Baked Potatoes: Scrub the potatoes thoroughly with a vegetable brush, but do not peel. Pierce potatoes on all sides with a fork. Place potatoes on a microwavable paper towel in microwave oven. Microwave uncovered on High for the times below, turning over once, until tender when gently squeezed using a pot holder. Cover with clean kitchen towel and let stand 5 minutes.

1 potato: 4 to 5 minutes;
2 potatoes: 6 to 7 minutes;
3 potatoes (arranged in a spoke pattern with narrow ends in center): 8 to 10 minutes;
4 potatoes (arranged in a spoke pattern with narrow ends in center): 12 to 14 minutes

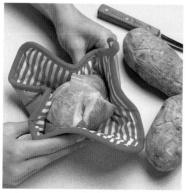

Purchasing Baking Potatoes: Russet potatoes are best for baking because they are high in starch and low in moisture which yields a light, fluffy potato. Idaho have a medium starch content and are good for baking and mashed potatoes but not potato salads.

Cutting X in Baked Potato: Cut an X in the top of each potato, then gently squeeze from the bottom to force the potato open.

182   Side Salads and Veggies

Cook's Tip

The bake time and oven temperature for baking potatoes can be adjusted so that other foods can bake at the same time. Bake potatoes in a 350°F oven 1 hour 15 minutes to 1 hour 30 minutes, in a 325°F oven about 1 hour 30 minutes.

Roasted Red Potatoes

PREP TIME: 15 Minutes • **START TO FINISH:** 1 Hour 30 Minutes • 4 servings

12 small (new) red potatoes
(about 1½ lb)

2 medium green onions with tops

2 tablespoons olive or vegetable oil

2 tablespoons chopped fresh or
2 teaspoons dried rosemary
leaves, crushed

1 Heat the oven to 350°F. Scrub the potatoes thoroughly with a vegetable brush and water to remove any dirt, but do not peel. Peel and slice the green onions to measure 2 tablespoons.

2 Place the potatoes in an ungreased 8-inch or 9-inch square pan or 13 × 9-inch pan. Drizzle the oil over the potatoes, and turn potatoes so all sides are coated.

3 Sprinkle the onions and rosemary over the potatoes, and stir the potatoes.

4 Roast uncovered about 1 hour 15 minutes, stirring occasionally, until potatoes are tender when pierced with a fork.

1 Serving: Calories 200; Total Fat 7g; Cholesterol 0mg; Sodium 10mg; Total Carbohydrate 31g (Dietary Fiber 4g); Protein 3g **Carbohydrate Choices:** 2

Cook's Tips

Most small red potatoes are about 2 inches in diameter. If they are much bigger, cut them in half so they will roast more quickly.

Leftover roasted potatoes make great fried potatoes. Cut potatoes into about ¼-inch slices. In a skillet, heat a small amount of vegetable oil over medium heat; add potato slices. Cook, turning potatoes over with a turner occasionally, until golden brown and hot.

Coating Potatoes with Oil:
Place potatoes in pan. Drizzle the oil over the potatoes, and turn potatoes so all sides are coated.

Baked Potato Wedges

PREP TIME: 15 Minutes • **START TO FINISH:** 45 Minutes • 4 servings

¾ teaspoon salt

½ teaspoon granulated sugar

½ teaspoon paprika

¼ teaspoon ground mustard

¼ teaspoon garlic powder,
if desired

3 large baking potatoes (russet or
Idaho), about 8 oz each

Cooking spray

1   Heat the oven to 425°F. In a small bowl or measuring cup, mix the salt, sugar, paprika, mustard and garlic powder.

2   Scrub the potatoes thoroughly with a vegetable brush and water to remove any dirt, but do not peel. Cut each potato in half lengthwise. Turn potatoes cut sides down, and cut each half lengthwise into 4 wedges. In a 13 × 9-inch pan, arrange the potato wedges with skin sides down.

3   Spray the potato wedges with the cooking spray until lightly coated. Sprinkle with the salt mixture.

4   Bake uncovered 25 to 30 minutes or until potatoes are tender when pierced with a fork. The baking time will vary depending on the size and type of the potato used.

1 Serving: Calories 140; Total Fat 1g; Cholesterol 0mg; Sodium 460mg; Total Carbohydrate 28g (Dietary Fiber 3g); Protein 3g **Carbohydrate Choices:** 2

Cook's Tips

Cut potatoes into wedges just before using, or the cut sides will turn brown.

Use russet or Idaho potatoes because they are best for baking.

Cutting Potato Wedges: Cut each potato in half lengthwise. Turn potatoes cut sides down, and cut each half lengthwise into 4 wedges.

Garlic Smashed Potatoes

PREP TIME: 15 Minutes • **START TO FINISH:** 35 Minutes • 8 servings (½ cup each)

4 medium red or white potatoes (about 1⅓ lb)

6 cloves garlic

⅓ cup chopped fresh flat-leaf or curly-leaf parsley

½ teaspoon salt

Pepper, if desired

¼ cup sour cream

1 Scrub the potatoes with a vegetable brush and water to remove any dirt, but do not peel. Cut the potatoes into 1-inch pieces. Peel the garlic cloves and leave whole.

2 In a 3-quart saucepan, place the potatoes and garlic; add enough water to cover potatoes. Heat to boiling over high heat. Once water is boiling, reduce heat just enough so water bubbles gently. Cover with lid; cook 15 to 20 minutes or until potatoes are tender when pierced with a fork. Place a strainer over a large bowl in the sink. Drain potatoes and garlic in the strainer, reserving cooking liquid.

3 Return potatoes and garlic to saucepan. Add parsley, salt and pepper. Mash with potato masher just until lumpy. Gradually add about ¼ cup cooking liquid, mashing until combined but still lumpy. Stir in sour cream. Discard remaining cooking liquid.

1 Serving: Calories 80; Total Fat 1.5g; Cholesterol 0mg; Sodium 160mg; Total Carbohydrate 15g (Dietary Fiber 2g); Protein 2g **Carbohydrate Choices:** 1

Cook's Tips

Red or white potatoes are good for smashed potatoes because they hold their shape and aren't as soft and fluffy as an Idaho or Russet potato. Leaving the peel on the potatoes adds texture.

You can mash the potatoes in the saucepan if you used an unlined stainless steel or glass saucepan. If you used a nonstick saucepan or one that isn't shiny inside, mash the potatoes in a bowl.

Chopping Fresh Parsley: With kitchen scissors, snip the leaves from the stems into a measuring cup or small bowl. Snip the leaves into very small pieces with the kitchen scissors. Discard the stems.

Smashing Cooked Potatoes: Mash the drained cooked potatoes with potato masher just until lumpy.

6 SNACKS and SWEET TREATS

Baked Buffalo Wings

PREP TIME: 30 Minutes • **START TO FINISH:** 1 Hour 15 Minutes • 12 servings (2 pieces and 1 tablespoon sauce each)

SPECIAL EQUIPMENT

15 × 10 × 1 inch pan

BLUE CHEESE SAUCE

⅓ cup plain yogurt

1 tablespoon mayonnaise or salad dressing

1 tablespoon finely crumbled blue cheese

WINGS

12 chicken wings (about 2 lb)

2 tablespoons honey

2 tablespoons ketchup

2 tablespoons red pepper sauce

1 tablespoon Worcestershire sauce

Paprika

Celery sticks, if desired

1   In a small bowl, mix the sauce ingredients. Cover with plastic wrap; refrigerate at least 1 hour to blend flavors. Meanwhile, continue with the recipe.

2   Using kitchen scissors or a sharp knife, cut each chicken wing at the joints to make 3 pieces. Discard the tips.

3   In a resealable food-storage plastic bag, mix the honey, ketchup, pepper sauce and Worcestershire sauce. Add the chicken. Seal the bag; refrigerate at least 15 minutes but no longer than 24 hours, turning occasionally, to marinate.

4   Heat the oven to 350°F. Line a 15 × 10 × 1-inch pan with foil. Place the chicken on the foil in the pan; sprinkle with the paprika.

5   Bake 45 to 50 minutes, brush with pan juices after 30 minutes, or until wings are golden brown and juice of chicken is clear when the thickest part is cut to the bone (180°F). Serve chicken with celery sticks and sauce.

1 Serving: Calories 110; Total Fat 7g; Cholesterol 25mg; Sodium 100mg; Total Carbohydrate 4g (Dietary Fiber 0g); Protein 8g **Carbohydrate Choices:** 0

Cook's Tips

To save time, purchase 2 pounds chicken drummettes (about 24) for the chicken wings. Skip step 2, and continue as directed in step 3.

Your favorite purchased blue cheese dressing can be used instead of the Blue Cheese Sauce. You'll need about 1 cup dressing.

Cutting Chicken Wing: Using kitchen scissors or a sharp knife, cut each chicken wing at joints to make 3 pieces. Discard tip.

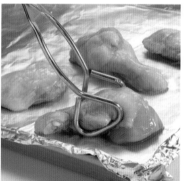

Placing Chicken in Pan: Place chicken pieces in a single layer on the foil in the pan. Sprinkle with paprika.

Roasted Red Bell Pepper Bruschetta

PREP TIME: 15 Minutes • **START TO FINISH:** 15 Minutes • 16 appetizers

16 diagonal slices baguette French
bread, ½ inch thick

About ¼ cup olive oil

8 to 10 large cloves garlic

1 jar (7.5 oz) roasted red bell
peppers

2 tablespoons chopped flat-leaf
(Italian) parsley or 1 teaspoon
parsley flakes

2 tablespoons shredded Parmesan
cheese

1 tablespoon olive oil

¼ teaspoon salt

¼ teaspoon pepper

1 Heat the oven to 375°F. Place the bread slices on an ungreased cookie sheet. Drizzle about 1 teaspoon olive oil (of the ¼ cup olive oil) on each bread slice. Bake about 4 minutes or until golden brown. Turn bread over; bake about 4 minutes longer or until golden brown.

2 Cut each garlic clove in half; rub cut sides over tops and sides of toasted bread slices. Discard garlic.

3 Drain the red peppers in a strainer in the sink. Cut the peppers into ½-inch strips. In a medium bowl, mix the peppers, parsley, Parmesan cheese, 1 tablespoon olive oil, the salt and pepper. Spoon onto toast.

1 Appetizer: Calories 70; Total Fat 5g; Cholesterol 0mg; Sodium 110mg; Total Carbohydrate 6g (Dietary Fiber 0g); Protein 1g **Carbohydrate Choices:** ½

Fresh Tomato Bruschetta: Use 1 cup chopped tomato (about 1 large) instead of the roasted red bell peppers. If you like, stir in 2 tablespoons drained small capers.

Cook's Tips

Flat-leaf parsley, also known as Italian parsley, is becoming more popular. It has a stronger "peppery" flavor than the better-known curly-leaf parsley. Either will work in this recipe.

You can toast the bread slices up to 1 day ahead. Cool, then store in an airtight container at room temperature.

Slicing French Bread: scalloped-edge or sharp bread knife, cut the baguette diagonally into ½-inch slices using a back-and-forth motion.

Rubbing Garlic on Toast: Rub garlic clove half, cut side down, over top and side of toasted bread slice.

Cheese Quesadillas

PREP TIME: 20 Minutes   •   **START TO FINISH:** 25 Minutes   •   6 servings (3 wedges each)

SPECIAL EQUIPMENT

cookie sheet or large shallow
baking pan (about 15 × 10 inches)

---

1 small tomato

3 medium green onions with tops

6 flour tortillas (8 to 10 inch)

2 cups shredded Colby or Cheddar
cheese (8 oz)

2 tablespoons chopped green
chiles (from 4.5-oz can)

Chopped fresh cilantro or parsley,
if desired

1   Heat the oven to 350°F. Chop the tomato. Peel and chop the green onions.

2   Place the tortillas on a clean counter or on waxed paper. Sprinkle ⅓ cup of the cheese evenly over half of each tortilla. Top cheese with the tomato, onions, chiles and cilantro, dividing ingredients so each tortilla has an equal amount.

3   Fold each tortilla in half over filling, and place on an ungreased cookie sheet.

4   Bake about 5 minutes or just until cheese is melted. Cut each quesadilla into 3 wedges, beginning cuts from the center of the folded side.

1 Serving: Calories 300; Total Fat 16g; Cholesterol 40mg; Sodium 570mg; Total Carbohydrate 26g (Dietary Fiber 1g); Protein 13g **Carbohydrate Choices:** 2

Lighten Up Cheese Quesadillas: For 3 grams of fat and 230 calories per serving, use reduced-fat cheese and reduced-fat tortillas.

Chicken Quesadillas: Sprinkle 2 cups finely chopped or shredded cooked chicken over cheese, dividing equally among tortillas, before adding tomato, onions, chiles and cilantro.

Cook's Tips

Tortillas are available in a variety of flavors. Look for regular, whole wheat, fat-free and flavored varieties such as spinach or tomato.

If all 3 quesadillas will not fit on your cookie sheet, bake just 1 at a time. Bake more as you need them, so they'll always be hot.

Chopping a Tomato: Cut tomato in half; place cut side down. Cut into about ½-inch slices. Cut slices into small pieces.

Cutting Quesadillas: Using kitchen scissors or a sharp knife, cut each quesadilla into 3 wedges, beginning on folded side.

Guacamole

PREP TIME: 10 Minutes • **START TO FINISH:** 10 Minutes • 16 servings (2 tablespoons dip and 3 chips each)

2 large ripe avocados

1 plum (Roma) tomato

1 tablespoon lime juice

1 tablespoon chopped fresh
    cilantro, if desired

¼ teaspoon salt

Dash ground red pepper (cayenne)

Tortilla chips

1 Cut each avocado in half lengthwise around the pit. Twist the halves in opposite directions to separate them. Place the avocado half with the pit on a countertop. Hit the pit with the sharp edge of a knife. Grasp the avocado half, then twist the knife to loosen and remove the pit. Scoop the avocado flesh with a spoon into a medium bowl. Coarsely mash the avocados with a fork.

2 Chop the tomato. Stir the lime juice, tomato, cilantro, salt and red pepper into the avocados.

3 Serve guacamole with tortilla chips.

1 **Serving:** Calories 90; Total Fat 6g; Cholesterol 0mg; Sodium 95mg; Total Carbohydrate 8g (Dietary Fiber 2g); Protein 1g **Carbohydrate Choices:** ½

Cook's Tips

If only very firm, unripe avocados are available in the supermarket, let the avocado ripen at room temperature until it yields to gentle pressure but is still firm.

The lime juice not only adds flavor but helps keep the mashed avocados from darkening. Add it to the mashed avocados as soon as possible. If you don't have any lime juice, you can use lemon juice.

Removing Avocado Pit: Hit the pit with the sharp edge of a knife. Grasp the avocado half, then twist the knife to remove the pit.

Scooping Out Avocado: Scoop the avocado flesh with a spoon into a medium bowl.

Hot Artichoke Dip

PREP TIME: 10 Minutes • **START TO FINISH:** 35 Minutes • 12 servings (2 tablespoons dip and 3 crackers each)

SPECIAL EQUIPMENT

1-quart casserole or small ovenproof serving dish

---

4 medium green onions with tops

1 can (14 oz) artichoke hearts in water

½ cup mayonnaise or salad dressing

½ cup grated Parmesan cheese

Crackers or cocktail rye bread

1 Heat the oven to 350°F. Peel and chop the onions.

2 Drain the artichoke hearts in a strainer. Chop the artichoke hearts into small pieces.

3 In a 1-quart casserole or small ovenproof serving dish, mix the onions, artichoke hearts, mayonnaise and cheese.

4 Cover with lid or foil; bake 20 to 25 minutes or until hot. Serve dip with crackers.

1 Serving: Calories 150; Total Fat 11g; Cholesterol 5mg; Sodium 260mg; Total Carbohydrate 9g (Dietary Fiber 1g); Protein 3g **Carbohydrate Choices:** ½

Lighten Up Artichoke Dip: For 5 grams of fat and 90 calories per serving, use ⅓ cup plain fat-free yogurt and 3 tablespoons reduced-fat mayonnaise for the ½ cup mayonnaise.

Cook's Tips

To save time, mix ingredients in a microwavable casserole. Cover with microwavable plastic wrap, folding back the corner 2 inches to vent steam. Microwave on Medium-High (70%) 4 to 5 minutes, stirring after 2 minutes.

Prepare this dip ahead of time, and refrigerate up to 24 hours. Heat when you are ready to serve it, adding about 5 minutes to the bake time.

Chopping Artichoke Hearts: Chop the artichoke hearts into small pieces.

Fresh Tomato Salsa

PREP TIME: 15 Minutes • **START TO FINISH:** 1 Hour 15 Minutes • About 3½ cups salsa

3 large tomatoes

1 small green bell pepper

6 medium green onions with tops

3 cloves garlic

1 medium jalapeño chile

2 tablespoons chopped fresh
cilantro, if desired

2 tablespoons lime juice

½ teaspoon salt

Flour tortillas or tortilla chips,
if desired

1 Place a large glass or plastic bowl near your cutting board. After cutting or chopping each ingredient, add each one to the bowl. Cut each tomato in half crosswise. Gently squeeze each half, cut side down, to remove the seeds. Chop the tomatoes.

2 Cut the bell pepper lengthwise in half, and cut out seeds and membrane. Chop the bell pepper.

3 Peel and slice the green onions. Peel and finely chop the garlic.

4 Cut the stem off the jalapeño chile, cut the chile lengthwise in half and scrape out the seeds. Cut the chile into strips, and then finely chop.

5 Add the cilantro, lime juice and salt. Mix all the ingredients. Cover with plastic wrap; refrigerate at least 1 hour to blend flavors but no longer than 7 days.

6 Serve salsa with flour tortillas or tortilla chips or as an accompaniment to chicken, fish and other main dishes.

1 Tablespoon: Calories 0; Total Fat 0g; Cholesterol 0mg; Sodium 20mg; Total Carbohydrate 0g (Dietary Fiber 0g); Protein 0g **Carbohydrate Choices:** 0

Cook's Tips

If you desire a hotter salsa, leave the seeds and membrane in the jalapeño chile.

The seeds and membrane of chiles contain irritating, burning oils. You may want to wear plastic gloves when handling chiles and be especially careful not to rub your face or eyes until the oils have been washed away.

Seeding a Tomato: Cut the tomato in half crosswise. Gently squeeze each half, cut side down, to remove the seeds.

Seeding a Jalapeño Chile: Cut the stem off the jalapeño chile, cut the chile lengthwise in half and scrape out the seeds and membrane.

Roasted Garlic

PREP TIME: 10 Minutes • **START TO FINISH:** 1 Hour • 8 servings

4 garlic bulbs

8 teaspoons olive or vegetable oil

Salt and pepper to taste

½ loaf baguette French bread
(8 inches), cut into 16 (½-inch)
slices

1 Heat the oven to 350°F.

2 Carefully peel the paperlike skin from around each bulb of garlic, leaving just enough to hold the cloves together. Cut a ¼- to ½-inch slice from the top of each bulb to expose the cloves. Place bulb, cut side up, on a 12-inch square of foil.

3 Drizzle 2 teaspoons oil over each bulb. Sprinkle with salt and pepper. Wrap foil securely around the bulb. Place in a baking pan or pie plate.

4 Bake 45 to 50 minutes or until garlic is tender when pierced with a toothpick or fork. Cool slightly. To serve, gently squeeze one end of each clove to release the roasted garlic. Spread on slices of bread.

1 Serving: Calories 120; Total Fat 6g; Cholesterol 0mg; Sodium 200mg; Total Carbohydrate 16g (Dietary Fiber 0g); Protein 3g **Carbohydrate Choices:** 1

Cook's Tips

Garlic bulbs, sometimes called "heads" of garlic, are made up of as many as 15 sections called "cloves," each of which is covered with a thin skin. You can find garlic bulbs in the produce section of the supermarket.

Roasting garlic results in a mellow, mild flavor that's wonderful on French bread, in mashed or baked potatoes, in dips or added to melted butter to toss with vegetables.

Preparing Garlic for Roasting: Carefully peel paperlike skin from around each garlic bulb, leaving just enough to hold the cloves together. Cut a ¼- to ½-inch slice from top of each bulb to expose cloves.

Wrapping Garlic in Foil: Place bulb, cut side up, on 12-inch square of foil. Drizzle 2 teaspoons oil over each bulb. Sprinkle with salt and pepper. Wrap foil securely.

Strawberry Smoothies

PREP TIME: 10 Minutes • **START TO FINISH:** 10 Minutes • 4 servings (about 1 cup each)

SPECIAL EQUIPMENT

blender or food processor

1 pint (2 cups) fresh strawberries

1 cup milk

2 containers (6 oz each) strawberry low-fat yogurt

1 Serving: Calories 140; Total Fat 2.5g; Cholesterol 10mg; Sodium 75mg; Total Carbohydrate 25g (Dietary Fiber 1g); Protein 6g **Carbohydrate Choices:** 1½

Cook's Tip

You can use other flavored yogurts such as banana cream pie, mixed berry or key lime pie for a flavor change.

1 Place the strawberries in a strainer and rinse under cold running water. Gently pat dry with paper towels. Reserve 4 strawberries for the garnish. Cut out the hull, or "cap," from the remaining strawberries with a paring knife.

2 In a blender or food processor, place the strawberries, milk and yogurt.

3 Cover; blend on high speed about 30 seconds or until smooth. Pour into glasses. Garnish each with a strawberry.

Lighten Up Strawberry Smoothies: For 90 calories and no fat per serving, use fat-free (skim) milk and fat-free strawberry yogurt.

Removing Hull from Strawberry: Cut out the hull, or "cap," with the point of a paring knife.

Peachy Chai Smoothies

PREP TIME: 10 Minutes • **START TO FINISH:** 10 Minutes • 3 servings (1 cup each)

SPECIAL EQUIPMENT

blender or food processor

2 ripe fresh medium peaches

2 containers (6 oz each) vanilla thick & creamy low-fat yogurt

⅓ cup chai tea latte mix (from 10-oz package)

½ cup milk

Ground nutmeg, if desired

1 Serving: Calories 210; Total Fat 3.5g; Cholesterol 10mg; Sodium 200mg; Total Carbohydrate 36g (Dietary Fiber 0g); Protein 9g **Carbohydrate Choices:** 2½

1 Cut each peach in half around the pit and pull the halves apart. Remove the pit with the tip of a spoon. Peel the halves, then slice; you will need about 1⅓ cups.

2 In a blender or food processor, place the peach slices, yogurt, dry chai mix and milk.

3 Cover; blend on high speed about 1 minute or until smooth and creamy. Pour into glasses. Sprinkle with a dash of nutmeg.

Cutting Peach Slices: Peel the peach halves and cut into slices.

Cook's Tips

Chai tea latte mix is a blend of black tea, honey, vanilla and spices. You will find it by the tea and coffee in the super-market.

Use very ripe peaches for the best peach flavor. If fresh peaches aren't available, use about 1½ cups frozen sliced peaches, slightly thawed.

Outrageous Double Chocolate-White Chocolate Chunk Cookies

PREP TIME: 1 Hour 25 Minutes • **START TO FINISH:** 1 Hour 25 Minutes • About 2 dozen cookies

SPECIAL EQUIPMENT

electric mixer; cooling rack

1 bag (24 oz) semisweet chocolate chips (4 cups)

1 package (6 oz) white chocolate baking bars

1 cup butter or margarine (2 sticks), room temperature

1 cup packed brown sugar

1 teaspoon vanilla

2 large eggs

2½ cups all-purpose flour

1½ teaspoons baking soda

½ teaspoon salt

1 cup pecan or walnut halves

1 Heat the oven to 350°F. In a 1-quart saucepan, heat 1½ cups of the chocolate chips over low heat, stirring constantly, until melted. Cool to room temperature, about 15 minutes, but do not allow chocolate to become firm. Meanwhile, cut the white chocolate baking bars into ¼- to ½-inch chunks; set aside.

2 In a large bowl, beat the butter, brown sugar and vanilla with an electric mixer on medium speed until light and fluffy. Beat in the eggs and melted chocolate until light and fluffy. With a wooden spoon, stir in the flour, baking soda and salt. Stir in the remaining 2½ cups chocolate chips, the white chocolate chunks and pecan halves.

3 For each cookie, spoon dough into a ¼-cup dry-ingredient measuring cup and level off with a knife. On an ungreased cookie sheet, drop the dough about 2 inches apart.

4 Bake 12 to 14 minutes or until set (centers will appear soft and moist). Cool on cookie sheet 2 minutes, then remove from cookie sheet to a cooling rack, using a turner. Cool cookie sheets between batches.

1 Cookie: Calories 380; Total Fat 22g; Cholesterol 40mg; Sodium 200mg; Total Carbohydrate 41g (Dietary Fiber 2g); Protein 4g **Carbohydrate Choices:** 3

Outrageous Double-Chocolate Chunk Cookies: Use 1 package (5 ounces) milk chocolate candy bar, cut into ¼- to ½-inch chunks, instead of the white chocolate baking bars.

Chopping White Chocolate Baking Bar: Place the baking bar on a cutting board. Using a chef's knife, chop the bar into ¼- to ½-inch chunks.

Measuring Cookie Dough: Spoon dough into a ¼-cup dry-ingredient measuring cup and level off with a knife.

Cook's Tip

To save time, use 1 cup white vanilla baking chips (from a 12-ounce bag) instead of chopping the white chocolate baking bars.

Banana Bread

PREP TIME: 15 Minutes • **START TO FINISH:** 3 Hours 30 Minutes • 1 loaf (24 slices)

SPECIAL EQUIPMENT

loaf pan (8 × 4 inches); cooling rack

Cooking spray for greasing pan

3 very ripe medium bananas

1¼ cups granulated sugar

½ cup butter or margarine (1 stick), room temperature

2 large eggs

½ cup buttermilk

1 teaspoon vanilla

2 ½ cups all-purpose flour

1 teaspoon baking soda

1 teaspoon salt

1 cup chopped nuts, if desired

1 Move the oven rack to a low position so the tops of the pans will be in the center of the oven. Heat the oven to 350°F. Spray just the bottom of two 8 × 4-inch loaf pans with the cooking spray.

2 In a medium bowl, mash the bananas with a potato masher or fork to measure 1½ cups.

3 In a large bowl, stir together the sugar and butter. Stir in the eggs until well mixed. Stir in the bananas, buttermilk and vanilla until smooth. Stir in the flour, baking soda and salt just until moistened. Stir in the nuts. Divide batter evenly between the pans.

4 Bake about 1 hour or until golden brown and toothpick inserted in center comes out clean.

5 Cool in pan 10 minutes. Run a knife along the sides of the pan to loosen the bread; remove bread from pan to a cooling rack. Cool completely, about 2 hours, before slicing.

1 Slice: Calories 140; Total Fat 4.5g; Cholesterol 30mg; Sodium 140mg; Total Carbohydrate 22g (Dietary Fiber 0g); Protein 2g **Carbohydrate Choices:** 1½

Banana-Cranberry Bread: Stir ½ cup sweetened dried cranberries in with the nuts.

Cook's Tip

Put overripe bananas in the freezer, unpeeled, for later use. When you're ready to use them, just thaw them, cut off one end and squeeze the banana into a measuring cup. The banana will be very mushy and not look great but will work just fine.

Very Ripe Banana: The banana skin should be turning brown with black spots and soft to the touch.

Mashing Bananas: Mash the bananas with a potato masher or fork until moist with some lumps.

Apple Crisp

PREP TIME: 20 Minutes • **START TO FINISH:** 1 Hour • 6 servings

6 medium tart cooking apples, such as Greening, Rome or Granny Smith

¾ cup packed brown sugar

½ cup all-purpose flour

½ cup quick-cooking or old-fashioned oats

¾ teaspoon ground cinnamon

¾ teaspoon ground nutmeg

⅓ cup butter or margarine, room temperature

Ice cream or half-and-half, if desired

1   Heat the oven to 375°F. Peel the apples if desired. Cut the apples into quarters. Cut the core and remove seeds from the center of each quarter. Cut each quarter into slices. You will need about 6 cups of apple slices. Spread the slices in an ungreased 8-inch square pan.

2   In a medium bowl, mix the brown sugar, flour, oats, cinnamon and nutmeg. Cut in the butter by pulling 2 table knives through ingredients in opposite directions or toss with fork until mixture is crumbly. Sprinkle mixture evenly over apples.

3   Bake 35 to 40 minutes or until the topping is golden brown and the apples are tender when pierced with a fork. Serve warm with ice cream or half-and-half.

1 Serving: Calories 350; Total Fat 11g; Cholesterol 25mg; Sodium 85mg; Total Carbohydrate 59g (Dietary Fiber 5g); Protein 3g **Carbohydrate Choices:** 4

Blueberry Crisp: Substitute 6 cups of fresh or frozen blueberries for the apples. If using frozen blueberries, thaw and drain them first.

Rhubarb Crisp: Substitute 6 cups cut-up fresh rhubarb for the apples. Sprinkle ½ cup granulated sugar over rhubarb; stir to combine. Continue as directed in step 2. If rhubarb is frozen, thaw and drain.

Cook's Tips

Some other apples good for baking are Braeburn, Cortland, Haralson, Honeycrisp, Jonathan, Northern Spy and Golden Delicious. You may want to check your farmers' markets to see if there are local varieties too.

Use a vegetable peeler to peel apples. Doing so is quick, and the peeler removes just a thin skin.

Cutting Apples Slices: Peel apples if desired. Cut the apple into quarters and cut core and seeds from each quarter. Cut each quarter into slices.

Sprinkling Oatmeal Topping: Sprinkle the oatmeal crumb mixture evenly over the apples.

Strawberry Shortcakes

PREP TIME: 30 Minutes • **START TO FINISH:** 1 Hour 45 Minutes • 6 servings

SPECIAL EQUIPMENT

electric mixer

STRAWBERRIES

1 quart (4 cups) fresh strawberries

½ cup granulated sugar

SHORTCAKES

2 cups all-purpose flour

2 tablespoons granulated sugar

3 teaspoons baking powder

1 teaspoon salt

⅓ cup shortening

¾ cup milk

SWEETENED WHIPPED CREAM

¾ cup whipping cream

2 tablespoons granulated or powdered sugar

Cook's Tips

Shortcake dough should be soft and slightly sticky. Try not to overmix the dough because it will become tough and the shortcakes will not be as flaky.

When whipping cream, soft peaks are formed when the beaters are lifted from the cream and the tip of the peak curls over slightly. Overbeating the cream will make it too stiff and have a curdled appearance but it will still taste good.

1   Place strawberries in a strainer and rinse under cold running water. Gently pat dry with paper towels. Cut out the hull, or "cap," with the point of a paring knife (see page 206). Cut the strawberries lengthwise into slices. In a large bowl, mix sliced strawberries and ½ cup sugar. Let stand 1 hour.

2   Meanwhile, place a medium bowl and the beaters of electric mixer in refrigerator to chill. These will be used later to beat the whipping cream, which beats better in a cold bowl.

3   Heat the oven to 450°F. In a medium bowl, mix the flour, 2 tablespoons sugar, the baking powder and salt. Cut in the shortening by pulling 2 table knives through ingredients in opposite directions until the mixture looks like fine crumbs.

4   Stir the milk into the crumb mixture just until blended and a dough forms. If the crumb mixture is not completely moistened, stir in an additional 1 to 3 teaspoons milk. On an ungreased cookie sheet, drop the dough by 6 spoonfuls 3 inches apart.

5   Bake 10 to 12 minutes or until golden brown. While shortcakes are baking, continue with the next step.

6   Pour the whipping cream into the chilled bowl, and add 2 tablespoons sugar. Insert the chilled beaters in the electric mixer. Beat on high speed until soft peaks form.

7   Remove shortcakes from the cookie sheet to a cooling rack. Split warm or cool shortcakes horizontally. Spoon about ¾ of the whipped cream and strawberries over bottoms of shortcakes. Top with tops of shortcakes and remaining whipped cream and strawberries.

1 Serving: Calories 490; Total Fat 22g; Cholesterol 35mg; Sodium 660mg; Total Carbohydrate 67g (Dietary Fiber 3g); Protein 7g **Carbohydrate Choices:** 4½

Lighten Up Strawberry Shortcakes: For 420 calories and 13 grams of fat per serving, substitute 1½ cups frozen (thawed) fat-free whipped topping for the Sweetened Whipped Cream.

Making Shortcake Dough: Stir the milk into the crumb mixture just until blended and a dough forms.

Dropping Shortcake Dough onto Cookie Sheet: Drop dough by 6 spoonfuls onto ungreased cookie sheet.

Frozen Chocolate Mousse

PREP TIME: 10 Minutes • **START TO FINISH:** 4 Hours 30 Minutes • 8 servings

SPECIAL EQUIPMENT

electric mixer or hand beater

2 cups whipping cream

¼ cup almond-, chocolate- or coffee-flavored liqueur*

½ cup chocolate-flavor syrup

Fresh raspberries, crushed cookies or chopped nuts, if desired

1   Pour the whipping cream into a large bowl, and place in the refrigerator about 20 minutes to chill. The cream will beat better in a cold bowl. Beat the whipping cream with an electric mixer on high speed until stiff peaks form. Be careful not to overbeat because the cream will begin to curdle and separate.

2   Gently pour the liqueur and chocolate syrup over the whipped cream. To fold ingredients together, use a rubber spatula to cut down vertically through the whipped cream, then slide the spatula across the bottom of the bowl and up the side, turning the whipped cream over. Rotate the bowl ¼ turn, and repeat this down-across-up motion. Continue mixing in this way just until ingredients are blended.

3   In an ungreased 9-inch square pan, spread the whipped cream mixture.

4   Cover pan with foil or plastic wrap; freeze at least 4 hours but no longer than 2 months. For serving pieces, cut mousse into 4 rows by 2 rows. Garnish with fresh raspberries. Serve immediately. Store any remaining mousse covered in the freezer.

*If you'd prefer to omit the liqueur, increase the amount of chocolate-flavor syrup to ¾ cup.

1 Serving: Calories 230; Total Fat 19g; Cholesterol 65mg; Sodium 25mg; Total Carbohydrate 11g (Dietary Fiber 0g); Protein 2g **Carbohydrate Choices:** 1

Chocolate Mousse: After folding the liqueur, chocolate syrup and whipped cream together, spoon the mousse into 8 serving dishes or wine glasses. Serve immediately or refrigerate to serve later.

Cook's Tips

When whipping cream, stiff peaks are formed when the beaters are lifted and the peak stands straight up.

The liqueur keeps this dessert from freezing totally solid. That's why the mousse can be served immediately after taking it from the freezer.

Folding Chocolate Syrup into Whipped Cream: Using a rubber spatula, cut down through the whipped cream, then slide the spatula across the bottom of the bowl and up the side, turning the whipped cream over.

7 THREE GET-TOGETHER MENUS

THANKSGIVING
TURKEY DINNER

Thanksgiving is one of the most celebrated holidays. Impress your family and invite them to Thanksgiving dinner—one that you prepared! Or invite some friends who are unable to be with their families and enjoy a great meal together.

Menu

For 8

Roast Turkey with Bread Stuffing

Turkey Gravy

Mashed Potatoes

Green Beans with Walnuts

Cranberry Sauce

Dinner Rolls with Butter

Pumpkin Pie

Coffee and Tea

Wine, if desired

Shopping List

NONPERISHABLES

Produce
- ☐ Garlic
- ☐ White potatoes
- ☐ Onion
- ☐ 1 bag (12 oz) cranberries, fresh or frozen

Groceries
- ☐ 1 can (15 oz) pumpkin (not pumpkin pie mix)
- ☐ 1 can (12 oz) evaporated milk
- ☐ 1 bag (22 oz) frozen whole green beans
- ☐ Dried thyme leaves
- ☐ Ground sage
- ☐ Ground cinnamon
- ☐ Ground ginger
- ☐ Ground cloves
- ☐ Seasoned salt, if desired
- ☐ Salt
- ☐ Pepper
- ☐ Browning sauce, if desired
- ☐ All-purpose flour
- ☐ Granulated sugar
- ☐ Vegetable oil
- ☐ Cooking spray
- ☐ Foil
- ☐ Walnuts or walnut pieces
- ☐ Coffee
- ☐ Tea
- ☐ Bottled water and sodas
- ☐ Wine, if desired

OTHER GROCERIES

Produce
- ☐ Celery
- ☐ Fresh thyme, if desired
- ☐ Red bell pepper

Dairy
- ☐ Butter or margarine
- ☐ Milk
- ☐ Whipping cream
- ☐ Eggs

Poultry and Meat
- ☐ 12- to 15-lb whole turkey, frozen or fresh

Bakery
- ☐ Bread

The Game Plan

Up to 2 weeks ahead:

- [ ] Buy any nonperishable groceries
- [ ] Gather table cloths or placemats, napkins, serving dishes and chairs

3 days ahead:

- [ ] Buy remaining groceries
- [ ] Wrap dinner rolls in foil and freeze
- [ ] Prepare, cover and refrigerate Cranberry Sauce (page 229)
- [ ] Select serving dishes

2 days ahead:

- [ ] Thaw turkey, if frozen, in refrigerator

1 day ahead:

- [ ] Prepare, cover and refrigerate bread stuffing, Roast Turkey with Bread Stuffing (page 223; step 3)
- [ ] Prepare Pumpkin Pie (page 227); cool, cover and refrigerator
- [ ] Prep for Green Beans with Walnuts (page 228)
  - [ ] Cut red pepper into thin strips, place in resealable plastic bag and refrigerate
  - [ ] Chop garlic, place in small resealable plastic bag and refrigerate
  - [ ] Chop the walnuts, place in resealable plastic bag and store at room temperature
- [ ] Chill the wine
- [ ] Set the table

5 hours ahead:

- [ ] Heat oven to 325°F. Wash turkey and pat dry with paper towels.
- [ ] Stuff turkey with bread stuffing, place on rack in shallow pan
- [ ] Place stuffed turkey immediately in oven to roast

1 hour ahead:

- [ ] Peel potatoes for Mashed Potatoes (page 226), cover with cold water in saucepan to keep them from turning brown before cooking
- [ ] Place butter and Cranberry Sauce on the table

45 minutes ahead:

- [ ] Begin to cook potatoes
- [ ] Prepare coffee
- [ ] Whip cream for Pumpkin Pie, cover and refrigerate

30 minutes ahead:

- [ ] Remove turkey from oven, place on carving board or platter and cover with foil to keep warm
- [ ] Place rolls in foil in oven to heat
- [ ] Remove stuffing from turkey, place in serving bowl and cover with foil to keep warm
- [ ] Prepare Turkey Gravy (page 225)
- [ ] Prepare the Green Beans with Walnuts (page 228)
- [ ] Carve turkey and arrange on platter. Cover with foil to keep warm and serve within 10 minutes.
- [ ] Mash potatoes and cover to keep warm. They can hold about 5 minutes but no longer than 10 minutes.

10 minutes ahead:

- [ ] Fill water glasses
- [ ] Make tea
- [ ] Remove rolls from oven and place in serving basket
- [ ] Place green beans, gravy and mashed potatoes in serving bowls. Place food on the table.
- [ ] Serve the wine

After dinner:

- [ ] Serve pumpkin pie with whipped cream
- [ ] Serve coffee and tea

Roast Turkey with Bread Stuffing

PREP TIME: 30 Minutes • **START TO FINISH:** 4 Hours 30 Minutes • 12 servings

SPECIAL EQUIPMENT

metal skewer; shallow roasting pan with rack

TURKEY

1 whole turkey (12 to 15 lb), thawed if frozen

3 tablespoons butter or margarine, melted

BREAD STUFFING

15 slices bread

2 large celery stalks with leaves

1 medium onion

¾ cup butter or margarine (1½ sticks)

1½ teaspoons chopped fresh or ½ teaspoon dried thyme leaves

1 teaspoon salt

½ teaspoon ground sage

¼ teaspoon pepper

TURKEY GRAVY (PAGE 225)

Cook's Tip

If the turkey is frozen remember to allow extra time to thaw it. To thaw a 12- to 15-pound whole turkey, place turkey (in its original wrap) in a baking pan on the bottom shelf in the refrigerator for 2 to 3 days.

1 Heat the oven to 325°F. From the body cavity of the turkey, remove the bag of giblets and neck (if included in the turkey you purchased); discard. Rinse the cavity; pat dry with paper towels. Set turkey aside while making stuffing.

2 Stack 3 slices of the bread and cut into ½-inch pieces; repeat with remaining bread to measure 10 cups. Chop the celery, including the leaves. Peel and chop the onion.

3 In a 4-quart Dutch oven, melt ¾ cup butter over medium-high heat. Add the celery and onion; cook 6 to 8 minutes, stirring occasionally, until tender. Remove the Dutch oven from the heat. Gently toss the celery mixture with the bread cubes, thyme, salt, sage and pepper, using a spoon, until bread cubes are evenly coated.

4 Stuff the turkey just before roasting, not ahead of time. Turn the turkey so the breast side is down. Fill the neck cavity lightly with the stuffing; fasten neck skin to back of turkey with a skewer.

5 Turn the turkey so the breast side is up. Fold the wings across the back of the turkey so the tips are touching. Fill the body cavity lightly with stuffing. (Do not pack stuffing because it will expand during roasting.) Place any remaining stuffing in a 1- or 2-quart casserole that has been sprayed with cooking spray; cover and refrigerate. Heat stuffing in casserole with turkey for the last 35 to 40 minutes of roasting or until thoroughly heated.

6 Tuck the legs under the band of skin at the tail (if present), or tie together with heavy string, then tie to tail if desired. On the rack in a shallow roasting pan, place the turkey with the breast side up. Brush melted 3 tablespoons butter over turkey. Insert ovenproof meat thermometer so the tip is in the thickest part of inside thigh and does not touch bone. (Do not add water or cover turkey.)

7 Roast uncovered 3 hours to 3 hours 45 minutes. After roasting about 2 hours, place a tent of foil loosely over turkey when it begins to turn golden, and cut band of skin or remove tie holding legs to allow inside of thighs to cook through. **(CONTINUES ON NEXT PAGE)**

Lighten Up Roast Turkey with Bread Stuffing: Decrease butter to ¼ cup. In step 3, heat butter and ½ cup chicken broth to boiling in Dutch oven over medium-high heat. Cook celery and onion in broth mixture.

Cornbread Stuffing: Substitute 1 bag (16 ounces) seasoned cornbread stuffing for the Bread Stuffing. Prepare and stuff turkey as directed on the bag.

8 Turkey is done when thermometer reads 180°F and legs move easily when lifted or twisted. Thermometer placed in center of stuffing will read 165°F when done. If a meat thermometer is not used, begin testing for doneness after about 2 hours 30 minutes. When turkey is done, place on a warmed platter or cutting board; cover with foil to keep warm. Let stand about 15 minutes for easiest carving. Meanwhile, make Turkey Gravy (page 225). Spoon stuffing from the turkey to a serving dish. See Carving Roast Chicken and Turkey (page 257).

9 Remove leftover turkey and stuffing from the turkey and place in separate containers. Cover and refrigerate leftovers.

1 Serving: Calories 590; Total Fat 34g; Cholesterol 190mg; Sodium 670mg; Total Carbohydrate 20g (Dietary Fiber 1g); Protein 50g **Carbohydrate Choices:** 1

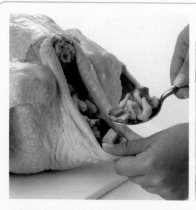

Fill the neck cavity lightly with stuffing, with breast side up.

Fasten neck skin to back of turkey with metal skewer.

Fold turkey wings under and across back of turkey so tips are touching.

Fill turkey body cavity lightly with stuffing.

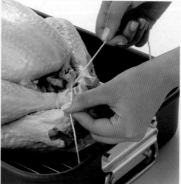

Tuck legs under band of skin at tail or tie together with heavy string.

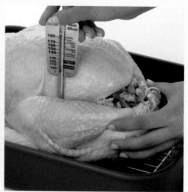

Insert ovenproof thermometer so tip is in thickest part of inside thigh and does not touch bone.

Turkey Gravy

PREP TIME: 20 Minutes • **START TO FINISH:** 20 Minutes •
8 servings (¼ cup each)

¼ cup fat from turkey drippings

Vegetable oil

¼ cup all-purpose flour

2 cups liquid (turkey juices, canned
    chicken broth or water)

Browning sauce, if desired

Salt and pepper, if desired

1 Pan and drippings will be hot, so be careful when handling. Pour drippings (turkey juices and fat) from roasting pan into a glass measuring cup, leaving the brown particles in the pan. With a spoon, skim fat from drippings. Return ¼ cup of the fat to the roasting pan. (If there isn't enough fat, add oil to measure ¼ cup.) Measuring accurately is important because too little fat makes the gravy lumpy and too much fat makes the gravy greasy.

2 Stir the flour into the fat in the pan, using a wire whisk. Cook over low heat, stirring constantly, until the mixture is smooth and bubbly. Remove the pan from the heat.

3 Add enough chicken broth or water to remaining drippings to measure 2 cups. Stir into pan. Heat to boiling over high heat, stirring constantly. Continue boiling 1 minute, stirring constantly. Stir in a few drops of browning sauce for a richer, deeper color. Taste the gravy, and add salt and pepper, if desired.

1 Serving: Calories 70; Total Fat 6g; Cholesterol 5mg; Sodium 0mg; Total Carbohydrate 3g (Dietary Fiber 0g); Protein 0g **Carbohydrate Choices:** 0

Cook's Tip

This recipe can easily be doubled or tripled if there are enough drippings. Taste the gravy before adding additional salt and pepper because they may not need to be doubled or tripled.

Skimming Fat: Using a spoon, remove the layer of fat on top of the drippings.

Thickening Gravy: Heat to boiling, stirring constantly. Continue boiling 1 minute, stirring constantly.

SPECIAL EQUIPMENT

potato masher or electric mixer

8 medium white or red potatoes
(about 2½ lb)

⅓ cup butter or margarine,
room temperature

½ to ⅔ cup milk

½ teaspoon salt

Dash of pepper

Mashed Potatoes

PREP TIME: 10 Minutes • **START TO FINISH:** 50 Minutes • 8 servings

1   Wash and peel the potatoes; cut into about 2- to 2½-inch pieces. Remove the butter from the refrigerator so it can soften while the potatoes cook.

2   In a 2-quart saucepan, place the potatoes and just enough water to cover them. Cover with lid; heat to boiling over high heat. Once water is boiling, reduce heat just enough so water bubbles gently. Cook covered 20 to 30 minutes or until potatoes are tender when pierced with a fork. Drain the potatoes in a strainer.

3   Return the drained potatoes to the saucepan; cook over low heat about 1 minute to dry them, shaking the pan to keep the potatoes from sticking. Drying the potatoes will help make them fluffier when mashed. Place the milk in a microwavable measuring cup and microwave uncovered on HIGH 40 seconds or just until warm. Or, in a 1-quart saucepan, heat the milk just until warm.

4   Place the potatoes in a medium bowl to be mashed. You can mash them in the same saucepan they were cooked in if the saucepan will not be damaged by the potato masher or electric mixer.

5   Mash the potatoes with a potato masher or electric mixer until no lumps remain. Add the warm milk in small amounts, beating after each addition. You may not use all the milk because the amount needed to make potatoes smooth and fluffy depends on the type of potato used. Add the butter, salt and pepper. Mash vigorously until potatoes are light and fluffy.

1 Serving: Calories 190; Total Fat 8g; Cholesterol 20mg; Sodium 210mg; Total Carbohydrate 26g (Dietary Fiber 2g); Protein 3g **Carbohydrate Choices:** 2

Horseradish Mashed Potatoes: Add 2 tablespoons prepared mild or hot horseradish with the butter, salt and pepper in step 5.

Garlic Mashed Potatoes: Peel 8 cloves of garlic, and cook them with the potatoes. Mash the garlic cloves with the potatoes.

Cook's Tip

Warming the milk and having the butter at room temperature before adding to the potatoes will make the mashed potatoes smoother and keep them warm longer.

Peeling Potatoes: With a vegetable peeler or paring knife, carefully remove the peel.

Green Beans with Walnuts

PREP TIME: 20 Minutes • **START TO FINISH:** 20 Minutes •
8 servings (¾ cup each)

1 small red bell pepper

2 cloves garlic

1 bag (22 oz) frozen whole green
   beans

2 tablespoons butter or margarine

½ cup chopped walnuts or walnut
   pieces

¾ teaspoon seasoned salt or
   regular salt

1 Cut the bell pepper in half lengthwise, and cut out seeds and membrane. Cut the bell pepper into very thin strips. Peel and finely chop the garlic.

2 Cook the green beans on the stove-top or in the microwave as directed on the bag until tender when pierced with a fork. Drain in a strainer; cover to keep warm.

3 While the beans are cooking, in a 12-inch nonstick skillet, melt the butter over medium heat. Add the bell pepper and garlic; cook 2 to 4 minutes, stirring constantly, until bell pepper is crisp-tender when pierced with a fork. Stir in the walnuts; cook and stir until hot.

4 Add the green beans; sprinkle with the seasoned salt. Cook and stir just until thoroughly heated.

1 Serving: Calories 110; Total Fat 8g; Cholesterol 10mg; Sodium 160mg; Total Carbohydrate 6g (Dietary Fiber 3g); Protein 2g **Carbohydrate Choices:** ½

Cook's Tips

For a flavor change, use ½ cup chopped pecans or almonds instead of the walnuts.

Here's a twist to this recipe you might want to try. Use a 7-ounce jar of roasted red bell peppers, drained and cut into thin strips, for the bell pepper and ½ cup roasted salted cashews for the walnuts. Reduce the seasoned salt to ½ teaspoon.

Cutting Bell Pepper into Thin Strips After removing the seeds and membrane from the bell pepper halves, cut each half into very thin strips, about ¼-inch wide.

Cranberry Sauce

PREP TIME: 30 Minutes • **START TO FINISH:** 3 Hours 30 Minutes •
16 servings (about ¼ cup each)

1 bag (12 oz) fresh or frozen
    cranberries (about 3½ cups)

2 cups water

2 cups granulated sugar

1   Rinse the cranberries in a strainer with cool water, and remove any stems or blemished berries.

2   In a 3-quart saucepan, heat the water and sugar to boiling over medium heat, stirring occasionally. Continue boiling 5 minutes longer, stirring occasionally.

3   Stir in the cranberries. Heat to boiling over medium heat, stirring occasionally. Continue boiling about 5 minutes longer, stirring occasionally, until cranberries begin to pop.

4   Remove the saucepan from the heat, and pour the sauce into a bowl or container. Refrigerate about 3 hours or until chilled. Store any leftover cranberry sauce covered in the refrigerator.

1 Serving: Calories 110; Total Fat 0g; Cholesterol 0mg; Sodium 0mg; Total Carbohydrate 28g (Dietary Fiber 0g); Protein 0g **Carbohydrate Choices:** 2

Cranberry-Orange Sauce: Make sauce as directed except add 2 teaspoons grated orange peel with the cranberries.

Cook's Tip

Be sure to cook the cranberries until they pop in order to release the natural pectin, which thickens the sauce.

Cooking Cranberries Boil cranberries until the cranberries begin to pop open.

Grating Orange Peel Rub the orange across the small rough holes of a flat grater.

Pumpkin Pie

PREP TIME: 30 Minutes • **START TO FINISH:** 6 Hours • 8 servings

SPECIAL EQUIPMENT

electric mixer or hand beater

NO ROLL PASTRY

1⅓ cups all-purpose flour

⅓ cup vegetable oil

½ teaspoon salt

2 tablespoons cold water

FILLING

2 large eggs

½ cup granulated sugar

½ teaspoon salt

1 teaspoon ground cinnamon

½ teaspoon ground ginger

⅛ teaspoon ground cloves

1 can (15 oz) pumpkin (not pumpkin pie mix)

1 can (12 oz) evaporated milk

SWEETENED WHIPPED CREAM

½ cup whipping cream

1 tablespoon granulated or powdered sugar

Cook's Tip

Be sure to purchase canned pumpkin, not pumpkin pie mix. The pie mix has sugar and spices already in it. But if you did purchase pumpkin pie mix by mistake, use it and follow the directions on the label.

1   Heat the oven to 425°F. In a medium bowl, mix the flour, oil and ½ teaspoon salt with a fork until all flour is moistened. Sprinkle with the cold water, 1 tablespoon at a time, tossing with fork until all water is absorbed. Shape pastry into a ball, using your hands. Press pastry in the bottom and up the side of a 9-inch glass pie plate.

2   In a large bowl, beat the eggs slightly with a wire whisk or hand beater. Beat in ½ cup sugar, ½ teaspoon salt, the cinnamon, ginger, cloves, pumpkin and milk.

3   To prevent spilling, place the pastry-lined pie plate on the oven rack before adding the filling. Carefully pour the pumpkin filling into the pie plate. Bake 15 minutes.

4   Reduce the oven temperature to 350°F. Bake about 45 minutes or until a knife inserted in the center comes out clean. Cool pie on a cooling rack 30 minutes. Refrigerate about 4 hours or until chilled.

5   Place a medium bowl and the beaters of electric mixer in refrigerator about 20 minutes to chill. Pour the whipping cream into the chilled bowl, and add 1 tablespoon sugar. Insert the chilled beaters in the electric mixer. Beat on high speed until soft peaks form. Serve immediately with the pie. Cover; refrigerate any remaining pie up to 3 days.

1 Serving: Calories 340; Total Fat 17g; Cholesterol 75mg; Sodium 370mg; Total Carbohydrate 40g (Dietary Fiber 2g); Protein 8g **Carbohydrate Choices:** 2½

No Roll Pastry: Press pastry in the bottom and up the side of the pie plate.

CASUAL LASAGNA DINNER

Enjoy the weekend and invite a few friends over for lasagna. Everything can be made ahead or assembled quickly at the last minute so you will have time to spend with your friends. If they offer to bring something, ask them to bring some appetizers to nibble on or beverages.

Menu

For 8

Make-Ahead Lasagna

Italian Romaine Salad

Garlic Bread

Tiramisu

Coffee and Tea

Wine, if desired

Shopping List

NONPERISHABLES

Produce
- Garlic
- Onion
- Red onion

Groceries
- 1 can (14.5 oz) diced tomatoes
- 1 can (10¾ oz) condensed tomato soup
- 1 can (6 oz) tomato paste
- 1 jar (6 oz) marinated artichoke hearts
- Lasagna noodles
- Garlic powder
- Salt
- Pepper
- Granulated sugar
- Powdered sugar
- Unsweetened baking cocoa
- Seasoned croutons
- Vegetable oil, if desired
- Cooking spray
- Olive oil, if desired
- Foil
- Coffee
- Espresso coffee, if desired
- Tea
- Light rum or rum extract
- Bottled water and sodas
- Wine, if desired

OTHER GROCERIES

Produce
- Fresh parsley
- Fresh basil or dried basil leaves
- Lemons
- Romaine lettuce

Dairy
- Shredded Parmesan cheese
- Shredded mozzarella cheese
- 1 container (12 oz) small curd cottage cheese
- Butter or margarine
- 1 package (8 oz) cream cheese
- Whipping cream

Poultry and Meat
- 1 lb lean (at least 80%) ground beef

Groceries
- Kalamata or jumbo ripe olives

Bakery
- 1 package (3 oz) ladyfingers
- 1 loaf (1 lb) French bread

The Game Plan

Up to 2 weeks ahead:

☐ Buy any nonperishable groceries

☐ Gather table cloths or placemats, napkins, serving dishes and chairs

2 days ahead:

☐ Buy remaining groceries

☐ Prepare, cover and refrigerate Lemon Vinaigrette for Italian Romaine Salad (page 234; step 1)

☐ Select serving dishes

1 day ahead:

☐ Prepare, cover and refrigerate Make-Ahead Lasagna (page 233)

☐ Prepare, cover and refrigerate Tiramisu (page 236)

☐ Prep for Italian Romaine Salad (page 234)

   ☐ Wash, dry and tear romaine leaves into bite-size pieces (step 2). Place in resealable plastic bag and refrigerate.

   ☐ Slice onion (step 3), place in resealable plastic bag and refrigerate

☐ Chill the wine

☐ Set the table

2 hours ahead:

☐ Heat oven to 350°F. Remove foil and plastic wrap from lasagna. Replace foil and place lasagna in oven to bake.

☐ Prepare Garlic Bread (page 235), wrap in foil and leave at room temperature

20 minutes ahead:

☐ Remove lasagna from oven; let stand 15 minutes

☐ Increase oven temperature to 400°F. Place bread in foil in oven to heat.

☐ Prepare Italian Romaine Salad (page 234) and place in serving bowl

10 minutes ahead:

☐ Fill water glasses

☐ Make tea

☐ Remove bread from oven and place in serving basket or plate.

☐ Place lasagna, salad and bread on the table.

☐ Serve the wine

After dinner:

☐ Serve tiramisu

☐ Serve coffee and tea

Make-Ahead Lasagna

PREP TIME: 40 Minutes • **START TO FINISH:** 4 Hours 5 Minutes • 8 servings

1 medium onion

1 lb lean (at least 80%) ground beef

⅓ cup chopped fresh parsley

2 tablespoons chopped fresh or 1½ teaspoons dried basil leaves

1 tablespoon granulated sugar

1 teaspoon salt

⅛ teaspoon garlic powder

1 can (14.5 oz) diced tomatoes, undrained

1 can (10¾ oz) condensed tomato soup

1 can (6 oz) tomato paste

2½ cups water

12 uncooked lasagna noodles

1 container (12 oz) small-curd cottage cheese

2 cups shredded mozzarella cheese (8 oz)

¼ cup shredded Parmesan cheese

1 Serving: Calories 430; Total Fat 15g; Cholesterol 55mg; Sodium 1030mg; Total Carbohydrate 43g (Dietary Fiber 3g); Protein 31g **Carbohydrate Choices: 3**

1 Peel and chop the onion to measure ½ cup.

2 In a 4-quart Dutch oven, cook the beef and onion over medium-high heat 5 to 7 minutes, stirring occasionally, until beef is thoroughly cooked. Place a strainer or colander in a large bowl; line strainer with a double thickness of paper towels. Pour the beef mixture into the strainer to drain. Return beef mixture to Dutch oven; discard paper towels and any juices in the bowl.

3 Into the beef, stir the parsley, basil, sugar, seasoned salt, garlic, tomatoes (with liquid), soup, tomato paste and water. Heat to boiling over high heat, stirring occasionally. Once mixture is boiling, reduce heat just enough so mixture bubbles gently. Cook uncovered 20 minutes.

4 In an ungreased 13 × 9-inch glass baking dish, spread 2 cups of the sauce. Top with 4 uncooked noodles. Spread half of the cottage cheese over noodles; spread with 2 cups sauce. Sprinkle with 1 cup mozzarella cheese. Repeat with 4 noodles, remaining cottage cheese, 2 cups sauce and remaining mozzarella cheese. Top with remaining noodles and sauce; sprinkle with Parmesan cheese. Cover with foil; refrigerate 2 hours but no longer than 24 hours.

5 Heat oven to 350°F. Bake covered 30 minutes. Remove foil; bake 30 to 40 minutes until hot in center. Let stand 15 minutes before cutting.

Cook's Tip

To save time, you can use 6½ cups of your favorite prepared spaghetti sauce for the 8 sauce ingredients (chopped parsley through water). Stir the prepared sauce into the drained beef mixture. Continue as directed in step 4.

Spreading Beef Sauce in Pan: Spread 2 cups of the sauce in the bottom of a baking dish.

Topping with Lasagna Noodles: Arrange the 4 uncooked lasagna noodles on top of the cheese.

Italian Romaine Salad

PREP TIME: 20 Minutes • **START TO FINISH:** 20 Minutes • 8 servings

LEMON VINAIGRETTE

1 or 2 medium lemons

2 cloves garlic or ¼ teaspoon garlic powder

2 tablespoons olive or vegetable oil

¼ teaspoon salt

¼ teaspoon pepper

SALAD

1 large bunch or 2 small bunches romaine lettuce

1 small red onion

1 cup pitted kalamata olives or pitted jumbo ripe olives

1 jar (6 oz) marinated artichoke hearts, undrained

½ cup seasoned croutons

⅓ cup shredded Parmesan cheese

1 Roll each lemon on the countertop with the palm of your hand, using gentle pressure (this will help release the juices). Cut 1 lemon in half; squeeze juice from each half. Use enough lemons until you have ¼ cup lemon juice. Peel and finely chop the garlic. In a tightly covered jar or container, shake lemon juice, garlic, oil, salt and pepper.

2 Remove any limp outer leaves from the romaine and discard. Break remaining leaves off the core; rinse with cool water. Shake off excess water and blot to dry, or roll up the leaves in a clean kitchen towel or paper towel to dry. Tear the leaves into bite-size pieces. You will need about 10 cups of romaine pieces.

3 Peel the onion; slice onion and separate into rings.

4 In a large glass or plastic bowl, place the romaine, onion, olives and artichoke hearts (with liquid). Shake the vinaigrette again to mix ingredients. Pour vinaigrette over the salad ingredients, and toss with 2 large spoons or salad tongs until evenly coated.

5 Sprinkle the croutons and cheese over the salad. Serve immediately.

1 Serving: Calories 140; Total Fat 10g; Cholesterol 0mg; Sodium 410mg; Total Carbohydrate 8g (Dietary Fiber 2g); Protein 3g **Carbohydrate Choices:** ½

Cook's Tips

To save time, purchase ready-to-use romaine that is washed and torn into bite-size pieces. You will need 10 cups, which is about 14 ounces.

You can toss the salad in a large resealable food-safe plastic bag. Place all the ingredients in the bag, seal and shake until evenly distributed. Pour the tossed salad into the serving bowl.

Squeezing Lemon Juice: Squeeze and measure juice by placing juicer over a measuring cup.

Tossing Romaine Salad: Pour vinaigrette over the salad in a large glass bowl. Toss with 2 large spoons until evenly coated.

SPECIAL EQUIPMENT

heavy-duty foil

1 clove garlic or ¼ teaspoon
   garlic powder

⅓ cup butter or margarine,
   room temperature

1 loaf (1 lb) French bread

Garlic Bread

PREP TIME: 15 Minutes • **START TO FINISH:** 35 Minutes •
1 loaf (18 slices)

1 Heat the oven to 400°F. Peel and finely chop the garlic. In a small bowl, mix the garlic and butter.

2 Cut the bread crosswise into 1-inch slices. Spread the butter mixture over 1 side of each bread slice. Reassemble the loaf, and wrap securely in heavy-duty foil.

3 Place foil-wrapped loaf on oven rack. Bake 15 to 20 minutes or until hot.

1 Slice: Calories 100; Total Fat 4.5g; Cholesterol 10mg; Sodium 170mg; Total Carbohydrate 13g
(Dietary Fiber 0g); Protein 2g **Carbohydrate Choices:** 1

Herb-Cheese Bread: Omit the garlic. Mix 2 teaspoons chopped fresh parsley, ½ teaspoon dried oregano leaves, 2 tablespoons grated Parmesan cheese and ⅛ teaspoon garlic salt with the butter.

Onion Bread: Omit the garlic. Mix 2 tablespoons finely chopped onion with the butter.

Cook's Tip

The garlic bread can be heated in the microwave instead of the oven. Do not wrap loaf in foil. Instead, divide the loaf in half, and place halves side by side in napkin-lined microwavable basket or on microwavable dinner plate. Cover with napkin and microwave on Medium (50%) 1 minute 30 seconds to 3 minutes, rotating basket ½ turn after 1 minute, until bread is hot.

Assembling Garlic Bread Loaf
Spread butter mixture over 1 side of each bread slice. Reassemble the loaf, and wrap securely in heavy-duty foil.

SPECIAL EQUIPMENT

heavy-duty foil

1 cup whipping cream

1 package (8 oz) cream cheese, room temperature

½ cup powdered sugar

2 tablespoons light rum or ½ teaspoon rum extract

1 package (3 oz) ladyfingers (12 ladyfingers)*

½ cup cold prepared espresso or strong coffee

2 teaspoons unsweetened baking cocoa

Tiramisu

PREP TIME: 35 Minutes • **START TO FINISH:** 4 Hours 35 Minutes • 9 servings

1 Pour the whipping cream into a medium bowl, and place in the refrigerator about 20 minutes to chill. The cream will beat better in a cold bowl.

2 In another medium bowl, beat the cream cheese and powdered sugar with an electric mixer on medium speed until smooth. On low speed, beat in the rum; set aside. Wash and dry the beaters of the electric mixer.

3 Beat the whipping cream on high speed until stiff peaks form. Gently spoon the whipped cream onto the cream cheese mixture. To fold together, use a rubber spatula to cut down vertically through the mixtures, then slide the spatula across the bottom of the bowl and up the side, turning the mixtures over. Rotate the bowl ¼ turn, and repeat this down-across-up motion. Continue mixing in this way just until ingredients are blended.

4 Split each ladyfinger in half horizontally. In the bottom of an ungreased 8-inch square or 9-inch round cake pan, arrange half of the ladyfingers, cut sides up. Drizzle ¼ cup of the cold espresso over the ladyfingers. Spread half of the cream cheese mixture over ladyfingers.

5 Arrange the remaining ladyfingers, cut sides up, over the cream cheese mixture. Drizzle with the remaining ¼ cup cold espresso, and spread with the remaining cream cheese mixture.

6 Sprinkle the cocoa over the top of the dessert. If you have a small strainer, place the cocoa in the strainer and shake it over the dessert. Otherwise, shake the cocoa from a spoon. Cover with plastic wrap; refrigerate about 4 hours or until the filling is firm. For serving pieces, cut tiramisu into 3 rows by 3 rows. Store any remaining tiramisu covered in the refrigerator.

1 Serving: Calories 250; Total Fat 18g; Cholesterol 60mg; Sodium 110mg; Total Carbohydrate 16g (Dietary Fiber 0g); Protein 3g **Carbohydrate Choices:** 1

Lighten Up Tiramisu: For 8 grams of fat and 165 calories per serving, use reduced-fat cream cheese (Neufchâtel) instead of regular cream cheese. Use 2 cups frozen (thawed) reduced-fat whipped topping for the whipping cream.

* Ladyfingers are small, oval-shaped cakes usually found in the bakery department or freezer section of the supermarket. If they are not available, substitute 1 package (10.75 oz) frozen pound cake, thawed. Cut cake into ¾-inch slices. Arrange slices to cover the bottom of the pan, cutting to fit if necessary. Drizzle the ½ cup espresso over the cake slices. Top with cream cheese mixture and sprinkle with baking cocoa.

Cook's Tip

You can use instant espresso coffee powder to make the espresso. Mix 2 measuring tablespoons coffee powder into ½ cup boiling water. Stir until powder is dissolved and refrigerate until cold.

Arranging Ladyfingers in Pan: Split ladyfingers in half horizontally. Arrange half of them, cut sides up, over bottom of pan. Drizzle with ¼ cup of the cold espresso.

Sprinkling with Cocoa: Place cocoa in a small strainer, and shake it over the tiramisu.

WEEKEND BRUNCH

A brunch is a great way to celebrate a fun occasion—baby shower, wedding shower, Dad or Mom's birthday, to mention a few. Or just have some friends over to kick off the day with good food and conversation.

Menu

For 8

Ham and Cheddar Strata

Mixed Fresh Fruit Salad

Blueberry Muffins

Coffee and Tea

Shopping List

NONPERISHABLES

Groceries
- [ ] Vegetable oil
- [ ] Honey
- [ ] Vanilla
- [ ] Salt
- [ ] Ground mustard
- [ ] Red pepper sauce
- [ ] Paprika, if desired
- [ ] Poppy seed
- [ ] Baking powder
- [ ] Granulated sugar
- [ ] All-purpose flour
- [ ] Cooking spray
- [ ] Plastic wrap
- [ ] Paper baking cups, if desired
- [ ] Foil
- [ ] Coffee
- [ ] Tea
- [ ] Bottled water and sodas
- [ ] Wine, if desired

OTHER GROCERIES

Produce
- [ ] Fresh, frozen or canned blueberries
- [ ] Medium pineapple
- [ ] Medium orange
- [ ] Seedless green grapes
- [ ] Large apple
- [ ] Lemon or frozen lemon juice
- [ ] Green onions

Dairy
- [ ] Butter or margarine
- [ ] Milk
- [ ] Shredded Cheddar cheese
- [ ] Eggs

Poultry and Meat
- [ ] Cooked smoked ham (about 10 oz)

Bakery
- [ ] Bread

The Game Plan

Up to 2 weeks ahead:

☐ Buy any nonperishable groceries

☐ Gather table cloths or placemats, napkins, serving dishes and chairs

2 days ahead:

☐ Buy remaining groceries

☐ Select serving dishes

1 day ahead:

☐ Prepare, cover and refrigerate Ham and Cheddar Strata (page 241)

☐ Prep for Mixed Fresh Fruit Salad (page 242)

   ☐ Prepare Honey-Poppy Seed Dressing (step 1), cover and refrigerate

   ☐ Cut pineapple into 1-inch chunks, cover and refrigerate

   ☐ Wash and cut grapes, cover and refrigerate

☐ Set the table

2 hours 30 minutes ahead:

☐ Heat oven to 400°F. Prepare and bake Blueberry Muffins (page 243).

1 hour 30 minutes ahead:

☐ Heat oven to 300°F. Uncover and bake Ham and Cheddar Strata (page 241).

30 minutes ahead:

☐ Prepare Mixed Fresh Fruit Salad (page 242), cover and refrigerate

☐ Make coffee

10 minutes ahead:

☐ Remove strata from oven and let stand

☐ Make tea

☐ Fill water glasses

☐ Place muffins in serving basket or bowl. Spoon salad into serving bowl.

☐ Place strata, muffins and salad on the table

☐ Serve coffee and tea

Ham and Cheddar Strata

PREP TIME: 15 Minutes   •   **START TO FINISH:** 1 Hour 35 Minutes   •   8 servings

Cooking spray for greasing pan

8 medium green onions with tops

12 slices bread

2 cups cut-up cooked smoked ham (about 10 oz)

2 cups shredded Cheddar cheese (8 oz)

6 large eggs

2 cups milk

1 teaspoon ground mustard

¼ teaspoon red pepper sauce

Paprika, if desired

1   Spray a 13 × 9-inch (3-quart) glass baking dish with the cooking spray. Peel and thinly slice the green onions; you will need about ½ cup. Trim crusts from the bread.

2   Arrange 6 bread slices in baking dish. Layer the ham, cheese and onions on bread in dish. Cut remaining bread slices diagonally in half; arrange on onions.

3   In a medium bowl, beat the eggs, milk, mustard and pepper sauce with a fork or wire whisk; pour evenly over bread. Cover with plastic wrap or foil and refrigerate up to 24 hours.

4   Heat the oven to 300°F. Uncover strata and sprinkle with paprika. Bake uncovered 1 hour to 1 hour 10 minutes or until center is set and bread is golden brown. Let stand 10 minutes before cutting into serving pieces.

1 Serving: Calories 360; Total Fat 19g; Cholesterol 215mg; Sodium 1010mg; Total Carbohydrate 24g (Dietary Fiber 1g); Protein 25g **Carbohydrate Choices:** 1½

Cook's Tips

The strata can be assembled and baked without refrigerating. After pouring the egg mixture over the bread, sprinkle with paprika and bake as directed in step 4.

Slices of whole grain or whole wheat bread also make a good strata. And for a real flavor change, use slices of raisin-cinnamon bread.

Arranging Bread on Strata: Cut 6 slices bread diagonally in half. Arrange on top of onions, overlapping the slices slightly.

Lighten Up Ham and Cheese Strata: Use reduced-fat ham, reduced-fat Cheddar cheese and fat-free (skim) milk for 9 grams of fat and 280 calories per serving.

Ham and Swiss Strata: Use 2 cups shredded Swiss cheese for the Cheddar cheese.

SPECIAL EQUIPMENT

large salad or mixing bowl

HONEY–POPPY SEED DRESSING

¼ cup vegetable oil
3 tablespoons honey
2 tablespoons lemon juice
1½ teaspoons poppy seed

SALAD

1 medium pineapple
1 medium orange
1 small bunch seedless green
   grapes
1 large unpeeled apple

Mixed Fresh Fruit Salad

PREP TIME: 30 Minutes • **START TO FINISH:** 30 Minutes • 6 servings

1 In a tightly covered jar or container, shake the dressing ingredients.

2 Cut the pineapple lengthwise into quarters. Cut off the rind and the core, removing any "eyes" or spots left from the rind. Cut the pineapple into about 1-inch chunks to make 4 cups.

3 Peel the orange, using a paring knife. Cut along the membrane of both sides of one orange section. Remove that section, and continue with the rest of the orange.

4 Wash the grapes, and cut in half.

5 Cut the unpeeled apple into quarters, and remove the core and seeds. Cut each quarter into 1-inch pieces.

6 Shake the dressing again to mix ingredients. In a large glass or plastic bowl, mix the fruits and the dressing. Cover; refrigerate until ready to serve. Store any remaining salad covered in the refrigerator.

1 **Serving:** Calories 210; Total Fat 10g; Cholesterol 0mg; Sodium 0mg; Total Carbohydrate 31g (Dietary Fiber 2g); Protein 1g **Carbohydrate Choices:** 2

Cook's Tips

For a creamy fruit salad, substitute ½ cup frozen (thawed) whipped topping and ½ teaspoon grated lemon peel for the Honey-Poppy Seed Dressing. Stir into fruit just before serving.

Rather than cutting up a pineapple, use purchased pineapple chunks. If pieces are large, cut into about 1-inch chunks.

Two cups strawberries, cut in half, can be substituted for half of the pineapple.

Cutting an Orange into Sections: Cut along the membrane of both sides of one orange section. Remove that section, and continue with the rest of the orange.

Peeling and Cutting up Pineapple: Cut pineapple lengthwise into quarters. Cut off the rind and the core, removing any "eyes" or spots left from the rind. Cut pineapple into about 1-inch chunks.

Blueberry Muffins

PREP TIME: 15 Minutes • **START TO FINISH:** 45 Minutes • 12 muffins

1   Heat the oven to 400°F. Spray just the bottoms of 12 regular-size muffin cups with the cooking spray, or line each cup with a paper baking cup.

2   If using canned blueberries, drain them in a strainer. Rinse fresh or canned blueberries with cool water, and discard any crushed ones. Do not thaw frozen blueberries. Pull off any stems from blueberries.

3   In a large bowl, beat the milk, oil, vanilla and egg with a fork or wire whisk until well mixed. Stir in the flour, sugar, baking powder and salt all at once just until the flour is moistened. The batter will be lumpy. If the batter is mixed too much, the muffins will have high peaks instead of being rounded.

4   Carefully stir in the blueberries. Spoon the batter into the muffin cups, dividing batter evenly.

5   Bake 20 to 25 minutes or until golden brown. If baked in a sprayed pan, let stand about 5 minutes in the pan, then remove muffins from pan to a cooling rack. If baked in paper baking cups, immediately remove muffins from the pan to a cooling rack. Serve warm or cool.

1 Muffin: Calories 160; Total Fat 6g; Cholesterol 20mg; Sodium 230mg; Total Carbohydrate 25g (Dietary Fiber 0g); Protein 3g **Carbohydrate Choices:** 1½

SPECIAL EQUIPMENT

muffin pan with 12 regular-size muffin cups; paper baking cups if desired; cooling rack

---

Cooking spray to grease muffin cups or 12 paper baking cups

1 cup fresh, frozen or canned blueberries

1 cup milk

¼ cup vegetable oil

½ teaspoon vanilla

1 large egg

2 cups all-purpose flour

⅓ cup granulated sugar

3 teaspoons baking powder

½ teaspoon salt

Cook's Tips

For nicely shaped muffins that have no rim around the edge, grease only the bottoms of the muffin cups, using cooking spray.

The secret to making tender muffins is to not overmix the batter. Just stir until all of the flour looks moistened and there are some lumps, then gently fold in the blueberries.

Stirring Blueberries into Muffin Batter: Carefully stir blueberries into the muffin batter.

Filling Muffin Cups: Using an ice cream scoop is an easy way to fill muffin cups.

BEYOND the BASICS

Ingredient Glossary

Understanding ingredients is one step to successful cooking. Check this list to find ingredients used in recipes in this cookbook, as well as other common ingredients.

BAKING POWDER: leavening mixture made from baking soda, an acid and a moisture absorber. Do not substitute baking powder for baking soda because acid proportions in the recipe may be unbalanced.

BAKING SODA: leavening known as bicarbonate of soda. Must be mixed with an acid ingredient (such as lemon juice, buttermilk or molasses) to release carbon dioxide gas bubbles.

CAPERS: unopened flower buds of a Mediterranean plant. Available pickled in a vinegar brine.

CHEESE: There are four cheese categories: natural, processed, pasteurized process and artisan.

Natural cheeses: are either unripened or ripened. Unripened cheeses are made by coagulating milk proteins with acid and are soft cheeses such as cottage cheese, cream cheese, and Brie. Ripened cheeses are made by coagulating milk proteins with enzymes and culture acids. Examples of semisoft varieties are feta, Monterey Jack and mozzarella. Hard cheeses are Cheddar, Edam and Swiss. Parmesan and Asiago are very hard cheeses.

Processed cheeses: are made by heating one or more natural cheeses and adding emulsifying salts. Processed cheeses contain more moisture than natural cheeses and are usually sold in tubes or jars.

Pasteurized process cheeses: are usually a blend of one or more varieties of natural cheese that have been ground, blended and heated. This process stops the ripening of the cheese. The very popular American cheese is a good example of this type of cheese.

Artisan cheeses: are handcrafted in small batches by artisan cheese makers in individually owned or small regional creameries.

CHILES: they are available in many colors, sizes and degrees of heat. Chiles range in length from ¼ inch to 12 inches with the smaller chiles being hotter. The seeds of chiles contain most of the heat-containing oils which can irritate and burn your eyes, nose and skin so always wear plastic gloves when handling chiles. Wash your hands with warm, soapy water after handling chiles. If you prefer a hotter dish, leave the seeds and ribs in the chile when chopping.

Anaheim chiles: available fresh or dried, these slim chiles come in various shades of green, are between 5 and 8 inches long and are mildly hot. They are sold in cans as "mild green chiles."

Chipotle chiles: smoked, dried jalapeño chiles. Can be purchased loose in the dried form, pickled or canned in adobo sauce.

Jalapeño chiles: jade green or red chile, 2 to 3 inches long, that packs a heat wallop. The smallest ones are the hottest. Called escabeche when pickled, chipotle when dried and smoked.

Serrano chiles: among the hottest chiles; range in color from bright green to scarlet. Look for them fresh, canned, dried, pickled and packed in oil.

Thai chiles: narrow, thin chiles ranging in color from bright lime green to orange and bright red. Their intense heat adds kick to Thai dishes.

CHOCOLATE: cocoa beans are shelled, roasted and ground to make a thick paste called chocolate liquor. Cocoa butter is the fat or oil from the cocoa bean. Chocolate liquor is processed to make:

Baking cocoa: dried chocolate liquor, with the cocoa butter removed, is ground into unsweetened cocoa. Cocoa drink mixes contain milk powder and sugar and are not a direct substitution for baking cocoa.

Semisweet, bittersweet, sweet and milk chocolate: contain from 10 to 35 percent chocolate liquor, varying amounts of cocoa butter, sugar and, for some, milk and flavorings. Available in bars and chips for baking or eating.

Unsweetened chocolate: contains 50 to 58 percent cocoa butter. Bitter in flavor, it's used primarily in baking.

"White" chocolate: is not true chocolate because it doesn't contain chocolate liquor. Made from cocoa butter, sugar, milk solids and vanilla. Often called white baking chips or vanilla baking bar.

COCONUT: the firm, creamy-white meat of the coconut fruit. Available shredded or flaked, either sweetened or unsweetened, in cans or plastic bags.

CORN SYRUP: clear, thick liquid (dark and light are interchangeable in recipes) made from corn sugar mixed with acid.

CORNSTARCH: white, powdery "flour" made from a portion of the corn kernel and is used to thicken puddings, sauces, gravies and soups and stews. To substitute for all-purpose flour, use half as much cornstarch.

CREAM: made by separating butterfat from the liquid in whole milk. It is pasteurized and processed into several forms:

Half-and-half: blend of milk and cream containing 10 to 12 percent butterfat. It won't whip, but you can use it in place of light or heavy cream in many recipes.

Sour cream: commercially cultured with lactic acid to give it a tangy flavor. Regular sour cream is 18 to 20 percent butterfat; and light sour cream is made from half-and-half and can be substituted for regular sour cream in most recipes. Fat-free sour cream has all the fat removed and may not work well in all recipes that call for regular sour cream.

Ultra-pasteurized whipping cream: has been heated briefly to kill microorganisms that cause milk products to sour. It has a longer shelf life than regular cream.

Heavy whipping cream: the richest cream and contains 36 to 40 percent butterfat. It doubles in volume when whipped.

EGGS: not only delicious as a food but are used as an ingredient as a leavener in cakes and breads, a base for dressings and mayonnaise, thickener in sauces and custards and a coating base for breaded foods. An egg with a brown or white shell has the same flavor and nutritive value. Pasteurized liquid eggs, found in cartons in the refrigeration section, mix the white and yolks and then pasteurize them at a heat level that kills any bacteria without cooking the eggs.

FATS AND OILS: add richness and flavor to food, aid in browning, help bind ingredients together, tenderize baked goods and are used for frying.

Butter: saturated fat made from cream that must be at least 80 percent butterfat by USDA standards. It is high in flavor and has a melt-in-your-mouth texture. Butter is sold in lightly salted and unsalted (also known as sweet butter) sticks, whipped in tubs and as butter-flavored granules.

Butter-margarine blends: available in sticks and tubs, blends usually are a combination of 60 percent margarine and 40 percent butter and are interchangeable with butter or margarine.

Margarine: an unsaturated butter substitute made with at least 80 percent fat by weight and flavoring from dairy products. Most margarine uses vegetable oils made from soybeans, cottonseed and corn. It's sold in sticks and as soft spreads in tubs.

Oils for cooking: liquid fats delicate to bland in flavor and treated to withstand high-temperature cooking and long storage.

- **Cooking spray:** available in regular (unflavored), butter and olive oil varieties. It can be used to spray cooking pans to prevent food from sticking. Or sprayed directly on food for low-fat cooking. Cooking spray for baking combines unflavored cooking oil with real flour and is used for spraying baking pans.

- **Olive oil:** olive oil is made from pressed olives and classified in several ways: extra virgin, virgin, olive oil and light olive oil.

- **Vegetable oil:** blend of oils from various vegetables, such as corn, cottonseed, peanut, safflower, canola and soybean.

Reduced-calorie (or light) butter or margarine: water and air have been added to these products, and they contain at least 20 percent less fat than regular butter or margarine. Do not use for baking or cooking.

Shortening: vegetable oils that are hydrogenated so they'll be solid at room temperature. Use butter-flavored and regular shortening interchangeably. Sold in sticks and cans.

Vegetable-oil spreads: margarine products with less than 80 percent fat (vegetable oil) by weight usually are labeled as vegetable oil spreads. They're sold in sticks for all-purpose use, including some baking if they contain more than 65 percent fat, so check the label. Also sold in tubs and in squeeze bottles but should not be used for baking.

FLOUR: primary ingredient in breads, cakes, cookies and quick breads, and used for making sauces and gravy and coating meats, poultry and fish.

All-purpose flour: selected wheats blended to be used for all kinds of baking. Available both bleached and unbleached.

Self-rising flour: made from a blend of hard and soft wheats that includes leavening and salt. For best results, don't substitute self-rising flour for all-purpose flour, unless directed in a recipe, because leavening and salt proportions won't be accurate.

Quick-mixing flour: enriched, all-purpose flour that's granular and processed to blend easily with liquid to make gravies and sauces.

Whole wheat flour: ground from the complete wheat kernel, whole wheat flour gives a nutty flavor and dense texture to breads and other baked goods.

GARLIC: pungent bulbs made up of individual cloves and encased in papery skin. Available in many forms: fresh, peeled and in jars, as a paste, as juice, dried, powdered and flaked. Garlic is best stored in a cool, dry place.

GINGERROOT: plump tubers with knobby branches. Grate unpeeled gingerroot, or peel and chop or slice it. Wrap tightly in plastic and store in the refrigerator.

HERBS: leaves of plants without woody stems that have distinctive fragrances and flavors—from savory to sweet—and are available fresh and dried. (See Top Herb Picks page 265.)

HONEY: natural sweetener produced by bees. Honey is safe for persons 1 year of age and older. Store honey at room temperature.

LEGUMES: term for beans, peas and lentils, which are the nutritious seeds of leguminous plants. They can be purchased dried, canned or frozen.

MAPLE SYRUP: golden brown to amber-colored sweetener made by boiling down the sap of sugar maple trees. Refrigerate after opening. Maple-flavored syrup usually is corn syrup combined with a little pure maple syrup.

MAYONNAISE/SALAD DRESSING: mixture made from egg yolks, vinegar and seasonings that's beaten to make an emulsion that keeps its creamy texture during storage. Available in jars in regular, light, low-fat and fat-free versions. Salad dressing is a similar product, but is made of starch thickener, vinegar, eggs and sweetener. Salad dressing can be substituted for mayonnaise in salads or spreads, but use only mayonnaise in hot or cooked dishes.

MILK: Refers to cow's milk in the recipes in this book.

Buttermilk: thick, smooth liquid made by culturing skim or part-skim milk with lactic acid bacteria.

Evaporated milk: whole milk with more than half of the water removed before the mixture is homogenized. Evaporated milk is a little thicker than whole milk and has a slightly "cooked" taste. Do not use it as a substitute for sweetened condensed milk in recipes.

Fat-free (skim) milk: contains virtually no fat.

1 percent low-fat milk: has 99 percent of milk fat removed.

2 percent reduced-fat milk: has 98 percent of milk fat removed.

Sweetened condensed milk: made when about half of the water is removed from whole milk and sweetener is added. Do not substitute it in recipes calling for evaporated milk.

Whole or regular milk: Has at least 3.5 percent milk fat.

MUSHROOMS: belong to the fungus family and are available fresh, dried and canned. There are many shapes, colors and flavors. To clean fresh mushrooms, cut a thin slice from the bottom of the stem. Gently wipe with a cloth or soft brush or rinse quickly with cold water; pat dry with paper towels.

Crimini: known as the Italian brown mushroom, they're darker in color and stronger in flavor than white mushrooms.

Enoki: slightly crunchy mushrooms with tiny caps and long, edible stems; grown in clusters.

Morel: a wild mushroom with a rich, earthy flavor that looks like a little cone-shaped sponge. Look for fresh morels in the produce section from April to June; dried morels, which have a stronger, smokier flavor, are available year-round.

Porcini (cèpes): these wild mushrooms are prized for their strong, woodsy flavor. Although available fresh, the dried version is more common.

Portabella (portobello): large portabella mushrooms have a flat cap and open veins. Due to their meaty texture, they're often grilled and served as a meat substitute. Baby portabella mushrooms are more tender and can be used like white mushrooms.

Shiitake: known for its meaty flavor and texture, it has a dark brown umbrella-shaped cap and tan gills. The stems are usually woody and should be discarded.

White (button): the most popular mushroom, is creamy white with a rounded cap, it ranges in size from small to jumbo for stuffing.

MUSTARD: made from seeds from the mustard plant and adds pungent flavor to foods.

Ground mustard: dried mustard seed that has been finely ground.

Mustard (yellow or American): prepared from mild white mustard seeds and mixed with sugar, vinegar and seasonings. Dijon mustard is prepared from brown mustard seeds mixed with wine, unfermented grape juice and seasonings. Many other flavors of mustards are available.

ORGANIC: foods are grown without the use of synthetic pesticides or chemical fertilizers. The USDA organic standards also prohibit the use of antibiotics, artificial (or synthetic) flavors, hormones, preservatives, synthetic colors, as well as ingredients that are irradiated or genetically engineered.

PASTA: see Pasta Basics page 68.

PEPPERCORNS: spice berry that is ground to produce black and white peppers. Available as whole berries, ground or coarsely ground. Green peppercorns are underripe berries that are packed in brine; they are available in bottles and cans.

PESTO: sauce made by blending fresh basil, pine nuts, Parmesan cheese, garlic and olive oil until smooth. Pesto can also be made using parsley, cilantro, spinach and sun-dried tomatoes to mention a few varieties. Look for it in the refrigerator case or in the pasta sauce section of your supermarket.

RED PEPPER SAUCE: condiment, often used as an ingredient, made from hot chile peppers and cured in either salt or vinegar brine. Many varieties and levels of hotness are available.

RICE: grain that is a staple in cuisines around the world.

Regular long-grain rice: milled to remove the hull, germ and most of the bran. It's available as both long and short grains. The shorter the grain, the stickier the cooked rice will be; therefore, long grain is a better all-purpose rice.

Converted (parboiled rice): steamed and pressure cooked before being milled and polished. This removes excess starch, so the grains stay separate after cooking.

Instant (precooked) rice: commercially cooked, rinsed and dried before packaging, resulting in a very short cook time. White, brown and wild rice are all available in this form.

Arborio (Italian or risotto) rice: shorter, fatter and has a higher starch content than regular short-grain rice. Originally from northern Italy, Arborio is preferred for making risotto because as it cooks, the rice releases starch to give the dish its distinctive creamy texture.

Aromatic rices: contain a natural ingredient that gives them a nutty or perfumy smell and taste. Aromatic rices include basmati, jasmine, wild pecan rice, Wehani rice and popcorn rice.

Brown rice: unpolished rice with only the outer hull removed. It has a slightly firm texture and nutlike flavor, and takes longer to cook than regular long-grain rice.

Wild rice: this isn't really a grain but the seed of a grass that grows in marshes and rivers. This very dark greenish-brown seed has a distinctive nutlike flavor and chewy texture.

ROASTED BELL PEPPERS: sweet red or other color bell peppers that have been roasted and packed in jars.

SALSA: sauce of tomatoes, onions, green chiles, vinegar and sometimes cilantro. Available fresh, canned or bottled. Green salsa, or salsa verde, is made with tomatillos. Also, any sauce of fresh chopped fruits and/or vegetables.

SCALLION: looks much like its cousin, the green onion (immature onion). True scallions are milder in flavor than green onions but can be used interchangeably.

SHALLOT: an onion with multiple cloves that looks like garlic. The papery skin that covers the bulbs should be removed. Shallots are milder in flavor and are interchangeable with onions.

SPICES: come from various parts of plants and trees: the bark, buds, fruits, roots, seeds and stems. Available grated, ground, powdered, in stick form or whole. (See Top Spice Flavors page 266.)

SOY SAUCE: brown sauce made from soybeans, wheat, yeast and salt used for main dishes and vegetables and as a condiment.

SUGAR: sweetener produced from sugar beets or cane sugar. Available in several forms:

Brown: made by mixing white sugar with molasses. Available in light and dark varieties; dark brown sugar has more molasses added and a stronger flavor. If brown sugar hardens, store it in a closed container with a slice of apple or a slice of fresh bread for 1 to 2 days to soften.

Granulated: white, granular sugar that should be used when recipes call for just "sugar." It's available in boxes and bags, as well as in cubes.

Molasses: dark thick syrup from the sugar refining process. Molasses is available in light (mild flavor) and dark (full flavor) varieties.

Powdered (confectioners'): granulated sugar that has been processed to a fine powder.

SUN-DRIED TOMATOES: ripe tomatoes that have been dried, making them chewy and sweet with an intense tomato flavor. Available dried or in jars packed in oil with or without herbs.

TORTILLA: round, flat unleavened bread made from ground wheat (flour tortilla) or corn (corn tortilla). The fresh version comes in many flavors as well as fat-free.

VINEGAR: made from fermented liquids, such as wine, beer or cider, that has been converted by a bacterial activity to a weak solution of acetic acid.

Apple cider vinegar: from fermented apple cider and is milder than white vinegar.

Balsamic vinegar: from Trebbiano grape juice and gets its dark color and pungent sweet flavor from aging in wooden barrels over a period of years.

Distilled white vinegar: made from grain-alcohol.

Herb vinegars: made by steeping herbs in vinegar such as basil, tarragon, dill.

Rice vinegar: made from fermented rice.

Wine vinegar: made from red or white wine and is pleasantly pungent.

WORCESTERSHIRE SAUCE: blend of ingredients: garlic, soy sauce, tamarind, onions, molasses, lime, anchovies, vinegar and other seasonings. White Worcestershire sauce is also available.

Cooking Terms Glossary

Cooking has a vocabulary of terms and definitions of its own. This glossary isn't a complete list, but it will help you learn the most common terms you may see in cookbooks. For other helpful cooking or food information, see Basic Preparation Techniques (page 10), Ingredient Glossary (page 245) and Common Abbreviations (page 9).

AL DENTE: doneness description for pasta cooked until tender but firm to the bite.

BAKE: cook in oven surrounded by dry heat. Bake uncovered for dry, crisp surfaces or covered for moistness.

BASTE: spoon liquid over food (pan drippings over turkey) during cooking to keep it moist.

BATTER: uncooked mixture of flour, eggs and liquid in combination with other ingredients; thin enough to be spooned or poured (muffins, pancakes).

BEAT: combine ingredients vigorously with spoon, fork, wire whisk or electric mixer until mixture is smooth and uniform.

BLANCH: plunge food into boiling water for a brief time to preserve color, texture and nutritional value or to remove skin (vegetables, fruits, nuts).

BLEND: combine ingredients with spoon, wire whisk or rubber scraper until mixture is very smooth and uniform. A blender or food processor also may be used.

BOIL: heat liquid until bubbles rise continuously and break on the surface and steam is given off. For rolling boil, the bubbles form rapidly.

BREAD: coat a food (fish, meat, vegetables) by usually first dipping into a liquid (beaten egg or milk) then into bread or cracker crumbs or cornmeal before frying or baking. *See also* Coat.

BROIL: cook directly under or above a red-hot heating unit.

BROWN: cook quickly over high heat, causing food surface to turn brown.

CARAMELIZE: melt sugar slowly over low heat until it becomes golden brown, caramel-flavored syrup. Also a term for cooking vegetables and meats until golden brown to develop the flavor.

CASSEROLE: mixture that usually contains meat, vegetables, a starch such as pasta or rice and a sauce; in some parts of the country is called a hot dish. It also refers to a deep, usually round, ovenproof baking dish made of glass or ceramic with handles and a cover that the food is cooked in.

CHILL: place food in the refrigerator until it becomes thoroughly cold.

COAT: cover food evenly with crumbs or sauce. *See also* Bread.

COOL: allow hot food to stand at room temperature for a specified amount of time. Placing hot food on a wire rack will help it cool more quickly. Stirring mixture occasionally also will help it cool more quickly and evenly.

CORE: remove the center of a fruit (apple, pear, pineapple). Cores contain small seeds (apple, pear) or have a woody texture (pineapple).

COVER: place lid, plastic wrap or foil over a container of food.

CUT IN: distribute solid fat in dry ingredients until particles are desired size by crisscrossing two knives, or cutting with a pastry blender in a rolling motion.

CRISP-TENDER: doneness of vegetables cooked until they retain some of the crisp texture of the raw food.

DASH: less than ⅛ teaspoon of an ingredient.

DEEP-FRY OR FRENCH-FRY: cook in hot fat that's deep enough to float the food. *See also* Fry, Panfry, Sauté.

DEGLAZE: remove excess fat from skillet after food has been panfried, add small amount of liquid (broth, water, wine) and stir to loosen browned bits of food in skillet. This mixture is used as base for sauce.

DIP: moisten or coat by plunging below the surface of a liquid, covering all sides (dipping onion ring into batter, dipping bread into egg mixture for French toast).

DISSOLVE: stir a dry ingredient (flavored gelatin) into a liquid ingredient (boiling water) until the dry ingredient disappears.

DOT: drop small pieces of an ingredient (butter, margarine) randomly over food (sliced apples in an apple pie).

DOUGH: mixture of flour and liquid in combination with other ingredients (often including a leavening) that is stiff but pliable. Dough can be dropped from a spoon (for cookies), rolled (for pie crust) or kneaded (for bread).

DRAIN: pour off liquid by putting a food into a strainer or colander. When liquid is to be saved, place the strainer in a bowl or other container.

DRIZZLE: pour topping in thin lines from a spoon in an uneven pattern over food (glaze over cake or cookies).

DUST: sprinkle lightly with flour, granulated sugar, powdered sugar or baking cocoa. Can use a small strainer to sprinkle sugar or baking cocoa over cakes, desserts or bars.

FLAKE: break lightly into small pieces, using fork (cooked fish).

FOLD: combine two mixtures lightly while preventing loss of air. Using a rubber spatula, cut down through mixtures. Slide spatula across bottom of bowl and up the side, turning the bottom mixture over the top mixture. Continue mixing in this way just until mixtures are blended (folding liqueur into whipped cream).

FRY: cook in hot fat over moderate or high heat. *See also* Deep-Fry, Panfry, Sauté.

GARNISH: decorate food with small amounts of other foods that have distinctive color or texture (parsley, fresh berries, carrot curls) to enhance appearance.

GLAZE: brush, spread or drizzle an ingredient or mixture of ingredients (meat stock, heated jam, melted chocolate) on hot or cold foods to give a glossy appearance or hard finish.

GREASE: spray the bottom and sides of a pan with cooking spray or cooking spray for baking to prevent food from sticking during baking (muffins, some casseroles). Shortening can be used to coat the bottom and sides of a pan using a pastry brush, waxed paper or paper towel. Butter and margarine usually contain salt and may cause hot foods to stick, so they should not be used for greasing unless specified in a recipe.

HEAT OVEN: turn the oven control(s) to the desired temperature, allowing the oven to heat thoroughly before adding food. Heating takes about 10 minutes for most ovens. Also called preheat.

HULL: remove the stem and leaves, using knife or huller (strawberries).

HUSK: remove the leaves and outer shell (corn on the cob).

KNEAD: work dough on a floured surface, using hands or an electric mixer with dough hooks, into a smooth, elastic mass. Kneading develops the gluten in flour and results in breads, biscuits and other baked goods with an even texture and a smooth, rounded top. Kneading by hand can take up to about 15 minutes.

MARINATE: let food stand, usually in refrigerator, in acidic liquid in a glass or plastic container to add flavor or to tenderize. Marinade is the savory liquid in which the food is marinated.

MELT: turn a solid (chocolate, butter) into liquid by heating.

MICROWAVE: cook, reheat or thaw food in a microwave oven.

MINCE: cut food into very fine pieces; smaller than chopped food.

MIX: combine ingredients in any way that distributes them evenly.

PANFRY: fry meat or other food starting with a cold skillet, using little or no fat and usually pouring off fat from meat as it accumulates during cooking. *See also* Deep-Fry, Fry, Sauté.

POACH: cook in simmering liquid just below the boiling point (eggs, fish).

POUND: flatten boneless cuts of chicken and meat to uniform thickness, using flat side of meat mallet or small heavy skillet.

PUREE: mash or blend food until smooth and uniform consistency, using a blender or food processor or by forcing food through a sieve.

REDUCE: boil liquid uncovered to evaporate some of the liquid and intensify flavor of remaining liquid.

REDUCE HEAT: lower heat to allow mixture to continue cooking slowly and evenly.

REFRIGERATE: place food in refrigerator until it becomes thoroughly cold or to store it.

ROAST: cook meat uncovered on rack in shallow pan in oven without adding liquid.

ROLL: flatten dough into a thin, even layer, using a rolling pin (cookies, pie crust).

ROLL UP: roll a flat food (tortilla) with a filling on it from one end until it is tube shaped (enchilada, wrap).

SAUTÉ: cook in hot fat over medium-high heat occasionally turning. *See also* Deep-Fry, Fry, Panfry.

SCALD: heat liquid to just below the boiling point. Tiny bubbles form at the edge. A thin skin will form on the top of scalded milk.

SCORE: cut surface of food about ¼ inch deep, using knife, to aid in cooking, flavoring or tenderizing or for appearance.

SEAR: brown meat quickly over high heat to seal in juices.

SEASON: add flavor, usually with salt, pepper, herbs or spices.

SIMMER: cook in liquid at just below the boiling point. Usually done after reducing heat from a boil. Bubbles will rise slowly and break just below the surface.

SKIM: remove fat or foam from surface of soup, broth, stock or stew, using a spoon or ladle.

SOFT PEAKS: whipping cream or egg whites beaten until peaks are rounded or curl when beaters are lifted from bowl. *See also* Stiff Peaks.

SOFTEN: let cold food stand at room temperature, or microwave at low power setting, until no longer hard (butter, cream cheese).

STEAM: cook food by placing on a rack or steamer basket over a small amount of boiling or simmering water in a covered pan.

STEW: cook slowly in a small amount of liquid for a long time (pot roast, stew).

STIFF PEAKS: whipping cream or egg whites beaten until peaks stand up straight when beaters are lifted from bowl. *See also* Soft Peaks.

STIR: combine ingredients with circular or figure-eight motion until uniform consistency. Stir once in a while for "stirring occasionally," stir often for "stirring frequently" and stir continuously for "stirring constantly."

STIR-FRY: cooking uniform pieces of food in small amount of hot oil over high heat, lifting and stirring constantly with a turner or large spoon.

STRAIN: pour mixture or liquid through a fine sieve or strainer to remove larger particles.

TEAR: break into pieces, using fingers (lettuce for a salad, bread slices for soft bread crumbs).

TOAST: brown lightly, using toaster, oven, broiler or skillet (bread, coconut, nuts).

TOSS: tumble ingredients lightly with a lifting motion (salads).

VINAIGRETTE: dressing of oil, vinegar, salt and pepper that can be flavored with mustard and a little Worcestershire sauce.

WHIP: beat ingredients to add air and increase volume until ingredients are light and fluffy (whipping cream, egg whites).

ZEST: outside colored layer of citrus fruit (oranges, lemons) that contains aromatic oils and flavor. Also, to remove outside colored layer of citrus fruit in fine strips, using knife, zester or vegetable peeler.

Useful Preparation Techniques

Slicing Apples: Cut the apple from stem end down into fourths. Cut the core and seeds from the center of each fourth using a paring knife. Cut each fourth into slices.

Removing Avocado Pit: Cut avocado lengthwise in half. Hit the seed of the avocado with the sharp edge of a knife. Grasp the avocado half, then twist the knife to loosen and remove the seed.

Chopping Bell Pepper: Cut bell pepper lengthwise in quarters. Cut out membrane and seeds. Cut each quarter into strips and then into pieces.

Roasting Bell Peppers or Chiles: Broil whole with tops about 5 inches from heat, turning occasionally with tongs, until about 60 percent of the skin is blistered and blackened (charred). Place in a plastic bag using tongs. Seal bag and let stand 20 minutes. The steam helps to remove the skin and continues to cook the peppers or chiles. Peel skin with fingers or using a paring knife (wear plastic gloves when peeling chiles to prevent burning fingers).

Coating Chicken or Fish: Place seasonings and flour or bread crumbs in a plastic bag. Add a few pieces of chicken or fish at a time; seal the bag and shake until each piece is evenly coated.

Seeding Chiles: Wear plastic gloves to help prevent burning hands or fingers when handling hot chiles. Cut off stem of chile and cut chile lengthwise in half. With tip of paring knife, scrape out seeds and membrane.

Crushing Crackers or Chips:
Place a few crackers or chips in a
plastic bag. Seal the bag and crush
crackers or chips into fine crumbs
with a rolling pin, flat side of mallet or
bottom of heavy saucepan.

Making Croutons: Heat oven to
400°F. Spread one side of ½-inch thick
bread slices with softened butter or
margarine. Cut the bread into ½-inch
strips; cut across the strips to make
½-inch cubes. Spread in ungreased
baking pan. Sprinkle with chopped
herbs, grated Parmesan cheese or
spices if desired. Bake uncovered,
stirring occasionally, 10 to 12 minutes or until golden brown.

Skimming Fat: Remove fat floating
on top of broth or soup by moving
a large spoon over the surface of the
broth or soup to skim the fat off the
top. Remove fat and discard, leaving
as much of the broth as possible.

Chopping Garlic: Hit garlic clove
with flat side of chef's knife blade to
crack the skin, which will then slip
off easily. Finely chop garlic using
chef's knife.

Crushing Garlic: Crush garlic using a
garlic press or press with side of chef's
knife or mallet to break into small
pieces.

Chopping Gingerroot: Peel gingerroot using a paring knife. Cut into thin
slices; cut the slices into thin strips.
Chop the strips using a chef's knife.

Grating Gingerroot: Grate gingerroot by rubbing it across the small rough holes of a grater.

Slicing Green Onions: Remove outer layer of the green onions and cut off the tip with the stringy end. Place the onions side-by-side and cut into thin slices, including some of the green part.

Chopping Herbs: Place washed herb leaves into a measuring cup or small deep bowl. Cut into small pieces using kitchen scissors. Or use a chef's knife and chop herbs on a cutting board.

Cutting Jicama: Peel jicama and cut into ¼-inch slices. Cut slices into sticks or pieces.

Peeling Kiwifruit: Cut the fuzzy brown skin from the fruit using a paring knife. (The skin is edible so you can leave it on if you like.) Cut the fruit into slices or wedges.

Juicing Lemons, Limes or Oranges: Place a juicer over a measuring cup. Cut the fruit in half. Rotate and squeeze each fruit half on the juicer and the juice will go into the measuring cup and most of the seeds and pulp will stay in the juicer.

Shredding Lettuce or Cabbage: Cut head of lettuce or cabbage into quarters. Place one quarter, cut side down, on cutting board. Cut out core. Cut lettuce or cabbage into thin slices with a chef's or carving knife. Cut slices several times to make smaller pieces.

Cutting Mango: Cut the mango lengthwise in half cutting along the flat side of the seed on one side; repeat on the other side. Discard the pit. Cut a crisscross pattern in the flesh of each mango half, being carefully not to cut through the peel. Turn each mango half inside out and cut off the mango pieces.

Cutting Meat with Grain: Cut meat with the grain into strips (the "grain" of the meat is the muscle fibers that run the length of a cut of meat). Then cut the across the grain into slices.

Shredding Cooked Meat: Using two forks, pull the forks in opposite directions to make irregular bite-size pieces of meat.

Cleaning Fresh Mushrooms: Wipe clean with a damp paper towel. If mushrooms have dirt clinging to them, quickly rinse under running water and drain. Trim off and discard stem ends. Leave mushrooms whole, or cut into slices.

Slicing Mushrooms: Wipe mushrooms with paper towels to clean. Cut off stem ends and discard. Cut mushroom caps into thin slices.

Soaking Dried Mushrooms: Soak mushrooms in enough warm water to cover about 30 minutes. Rinse well and squeeze out excess moisture. Cut off and discard the tough stems.

Sectioning Oranges or Grapefruit: After removing the peel, cut along the membrane of both sides of a section. Remove the section and continue with remaining sections.

Cutting Papaya: Cut the papaya lengthwise in half, and scoop out the seeds using a spoon. Remove peel using a sharp knife. Cut papaya into slices or pieces.

Slicing Peaches: Cut the peach lengthwise in half around the pit. Twist the peach halves in opposite directions to separate and remove the pit. Peel the peach halves, and cut into slices.

Slicing Pears: Cut the pear from stem end down into fourths. Cut the core and seeds from the center of each fourth using a paring knife. Cut each fourth into slices.

Removing Pea Pod Strings: Snap off the stem end of the pea pod, and pull the string down the length of the pea pod to remove it.

Peeling Pineapple: Twist leafy top from pineapple. Stand pineapple upright on cutting board and carefully cut into fourths. Holding one fourth securely, cut fruit from rind. Cut off core and remove "eyes" using tip of paring knife.

Peeling Shrimp: Starting at the large end of the shrimp, use your fingers to peel off the shell. Leave tail intact if you like.

Deveining Shrimp: Make a shallow cut lengthwise down the back of the shrimp, using a paring knife. Wash out the dark brown or black vein.

Hulling Strawberries: Use the tip of a paring knife to remove the green leaf, or use an inexpensive strawberry huller.

Chopping Tomatoes: Cut tomato in half; place cut side down on cutting board. Cut half into strips and cut into small pieces.

Seeding Tomatoes: Cut tomato crosswise in half. Gently squeeze halves to remove seeds.

Soaking Dried Tomatoes (Sun-Dried Tomatoes): Soak tomatoes in hot water to cover for 20 minutes or until pliable; drain and pat dry.

Carving Roast Chicken and Turkey

1. Use a sharp carving knife and meat fork for best results. While gently pulling leg away from body, cut through joint between thigh and body to separate drumstick and thigh. Serve these whole or carve them.

2. Make a deep horizontal cut into breast just above wing.

3. Insert fork in top of breast; starting halfway up breast, carve slices down to the horizontal cut from outer edge of bird to the center. Remove wings by cutting through joint between wing and body.

Selecting Knives

The right tools make cooking easier, and owning a good set of knives is essential. High-quality knives last a lifetime, making them a worthwhile investment.

Department and kitchen supply stores will carry several brands; a knowledgeable salesperson can help you pick out high-quality knives to meet your budget.

The best knives are made from high-carbon stainless-steel blades with handles that are riveted in place. High-carbon stainless steel resists corrosion and discoloration, and the blades sharpen easily. Before you buy, pick up the knife to make sure it feels balanced and comfortable in your hand.

Keep knives sharpened for the best performance and safety. Always wash knives by hand because dishwasher detergents are too harsh and may damage them over time.

Know Your Thermometers

Food thermometers are indispensable friends in the kitchen because they indicate when foods have reached a safe internal temperature and also help prevent overcooking. Here are three common thermometers that are readily available and easy to use.

Dial Oven-Safe (meat, poultry or roast thermometer): Can be used in roasts, poultry, casseroles and stuffing, staying in the oven while food is cooking. Insert it 2 to 2½ inches deep into the food to get an accurate reading (not recommended for thin foods).

Dial Instant-Read: Not designed to stay in food during cooking. Can be used for roasts, poultry, casseroles and stuffing. Insert it 2 to 2½ inches deep into thick and thin foods to get a temperature reading; it takes only 15 to 20 seconds. For thin foods, insert it into the side instead of the top.

Digital Instant-Read: Not designed to stay in food during cooking. Insert it ½ inch deep into thick and thin foods to get a temperature reading; it takes only about 10 seconds.

Equipment Wish List

Now that you are more comfortable cooking, here is a "wish list" of items you may want to add to your kitchen.

KITCHEN GADGETS

Colander: For draining pasta and other foods after cooking and for draining fresh produce after washing.

Fork, Long-Handled: Great for holding meat and poultry in place while it is being sliced or carved.

Funnel: Helps to prevent spilling when pouring liquids to a smaller container.

Garlic Press: Used to crush garlic cloves into very small pieces and is faster than chopping garlic.

Grater, Flat: Also known as a rasp grater, has rows of minute, ultra sharp holes that shred or grate food precisely and cleanly without tearing. They are available with or without handles.

Ice-Cream Scoop: Choose a sturdy scoop that will work well in frozen ice cream and yogurt. It is helpful to have a spring-release so the scoop can be used for filling muffin cups or scooping cookie dough.

Juicer: To squeeze fresh juice from oranges, lemons, limes and other citrus fruits.

Kitchen Scissors (or Shears): Good for snipping fresh herbs and for all-purpose cutting and trimming of ingredients.

Knife, Boning: A long narrow blade using for removing chicken bones from raw chicken, remove skin from raw fish fillets and for slicing soft foods.

Knife, Bread: A long serrated blade used for slicing breads and other soft food with a crust or tough skin.

Knife, Utility: A thin blade used for slicing foods such as sandwiches, fruits, cheese, cakes, bars and other soft foods.

Potato Masher: Used for mashing potatoes, bananas for bread and muffins and making applesauce.

Salad Spinner: After washing salad greens, this is a quick and easy way to dry them.

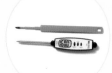

Spatula, Metal Flexible: A long metal blade that is useful when measuring dry ingredients to level off the measuring cup. Also good for frosting cakes.

Thermometer, Digital Instant-Read: Not designed to stay in food during cooking but great to test internal temperature of meat.

POTS AND PANS

Casserole Dishes: Covered or uncovered glass or ceramic cookware for baking and serving food—all in the same dish.

Grill Pan: A square skillet that has a ridged bottom so food cooks above the fat and gives food "grill lines." It is good for cooking meat, fish, chicken and hot sandwiches.

Muffin Pan: One pan with 6 or 12 individual cups for baking muffins or cupcakes. The cups range in size from small (or miniature) to jumbo.

Omelet Pan: A skillet with slopping sides so the omelet is easy to turn out of the pan.

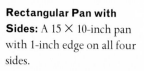

Rectangular Pan with Sides: A 15 × 10-inch pan with 1-inch edge on all four sides.

Roasting Pan with Rack: A large shallow pan with a rack to suspend the meat so it doesn't cook in its own juice or fat.

Stockpot: A large pot, usually 5 quarts or larger, used to cook soups, stews and pasta.

SMALL ELECTRICAL APPLIANCES

Blender: Can be used to blend, mix, juice or chop some ingredients, as well as to whirl smoothies and puree cooked fruits and vegetables.

Blender, Handheld (or Immersion): Used to blend small amounts of food, puree cooked vegetables, beans or fruits and frothing liquids. It can be used in a pan or bowl rather than transferring food to a blender container.

Contact Grill: An indoor-use grill that cooks the food between two grids. The grids have ridges to give the food grill marks. The food is cooked from both sides so it cooks much quicker than on a conventional outdoor grill.

Food Processor: Used primarily for shredding, chopping, or slicing vegetables and fruit. Also used for making sauces, puree fruits or vegetables and making bread and pastry doughs.

Food Processor, Mini: The small plastic work bowl has a sharp S-shaped blade that easily chops small amounts of meat, herbs, nuts, fruits and vegetables.

Griddle: Used for pancakes, grilled sandwiches, eggs and other fried foods. The thermostat control keeps the griddle temperature even during cooking.

Handheld Mixer: An easy way to whip cream and beat cakes and other desserts. It also can be used to mash potatoes.

Slow Cooker: An electric pot that cooks food very slowly. It is available in various sizes and has high and low settings. The ceramic liner may be permanent or removable for easy cleaning.

Waffle Iron: Available in both electric and range-top models in a number of shapes, such as square, rectangular, round and heart. Look for a waffle iron with nonstick grids for easy cooking and cleaning.

Wok: A round-bottom cooking pan with deep sides for stir-frying and steaming. Both electric and range-top woks are available. Most electric woks have a nonstick surface.

Top Herb Picks

Herbs are a great way to add flavor and variety to dishes. If you have time and space, you can even grow your own.

Too much of any herb can overwhelm a food or become bitter, so use small amounts and taste the dish before adding more. Dried herbs are more concentrated than fresh; so if a recipe calls for 1 tablespoon chopped fresh herbs, substitute 1 teaspoon dried herbs.

To get the most flavor from dried herbs, crumble them in the palm of you hand after measuring them. To chop fresh herbs such as parsley, thyme and rosemary, remove the leaves from the stems and place them in a measuring cup. Use kitchen scissors to cut the leaves into very small pieces.

Fresh herbs, such as basil, cilantro, parsley and rosemary can be stored in the refrigerator. Just snip off the bottom of the stems and place them in a glass in about one inch of water. Seal the glass in a plastic bag and refrigerate for up to 1 week.

Dried and ground herbs start to lose their flavor after 6 months and should be replaced after one year. It's a good idea to write the date on the bottle or box so you know when to replace them. Buy herbs in the smallest quantity possible to ensure freshness.

Basil: Fresh and dried leaves; ground **Flavor:** Sweet and spicy **Uses:** Eggs, pesto, salads, soups, pasta sauce, vegetables

Bay Leaf: Fresh and dried leaves **Flavor:** Earthy, grassy, and slightly piney **Uses:** Meats, sauces, soups, stews, vegetables

Cilantro: Fresh and dried leaves **Flavor:** Lively, pungent flavor some describe as slightly soapy **Uses:** Mexican and Asian dishes

Dill Weed: Fresh and dried **Flavor:** Fresh, peppery and tangy **Uses:** Breads, dips, fish, soups, salads, vegetables

Marjoram: Fresh and dried leaves; ground **Flavor:** Aromatic with bitter overtone **Uses:** Fish, lamb, poultry, soups, stews, stuffings

Mint: Fresh and dried leaves **Flavor:** Strong, cool, fresh and sweet **Uses:** Beverages, desserts, fish, lamb, sauces

Oregano: Fresh and dried leaves; ground **Flavor:** Aromatic with pleasant bitter overtone **Uses:** Italian dishes, fish, meats, poultry

Rosemary: Fresh and dried leaves **Flavor:** Fresh, sweet flavor **Uses:** Breads, casseroles, lamb, pork, vegetables

Sage: Fresh and dried leaves; rubbed; ground **Flavor:** Slightly bitter with subtle musty-mint flavor **Uses:** Poultry, meats, stuffing, sausage

Thyme: Fresh and dried leaves; ground **Flavor:** Aromatic, pungent **Uses:** Fish, meats, poultry, stews

Top Spice Flavors

Spices are made from the seeds, buds, fruit, bark or roots of plants, and have been used to boost the flavor in foods for hundreds of years. Store your spices in a cool, dry place. Ground spices loose some of their flavor after 6 months and whole spices after 1 year. As with herbs, if you write the purchase date on the box or jar, you'll know when to replace your spices.

Chili Powder: Ground blend **Flavor:** Blend of chile peppers and spices; from mild to hot, depending on the variety **Uses:** Casseroles, Mexican dishes, soups, stews

Cinnamon: Stick and ground **Flavor:** Aromatic, sweet and woodsy **Uses:** Cakes, cookies, desserts, pies, savory dishes

Cumin: Whole and ground **Flavor:** Strongly fragrant, slightly smoky, warm flavor **Uses:** Chilies, curries, Asian, Mediterranean, Mexican and Middle Eastern dishes

Curry Powder: Ground blend **Flavor:** Strongly fragrant, mild to hot depending on variety **Uses:** Appetizers, curries, eggs, fish, pork, poultry, seafood, sauces

Garlic: Powdered, minced, flaked, fresh, paste, juice **Flavor:** Pungent with slightly musty flavor **Uses:** Appetizers, meats, seafood, poultry, salads, sauces, soups, vegetables

Ginger: Fresh, crystallized and ground **Flavor:** Spicy-hot, sweet **Uses:** Beverages, cookies, cakes, desserts, pies, fish, tea

Italian Seasoning: Ground blend **Flavor:** Savory with overtones of oregano, basil and rosemary **Uses:** Italian dishes, pasta, pizza, meats, casseroles

Nutmeg: Whole and ground **Flavor:** Fragrant, sweet and spicy **Uses:** Beverages, cakes, cookies, desserts, sauces

Paprika: Ground **Flavor:** Slightly bitter; ranges from sweet to hot **Uses:** Casseroles, eggs, garnishes, meats

Pepper, Black: Whole, ground, cracked **Flavor:** Slightly hot with a hint of sweetness **Uses:** Savory foods of all kinds

Grilling Basics

Charcoal and gas are the two fuels typically associated with grilling, but electric grills are also an option. Deciding between the three comes down to personal preference.

Charcoal Grills

If there is a tradition in grilling, charcoal is it. Available in all types and sizes, the simplest charcoal grill consists of a firebox with a grate to hold the charcoal, a grill rack for the food and sometimes a cover or lid. They are available as square covered grill, open grill or brazier (no cover) or the popular kettle grill with a deep rounded bottom and a generous lid and come in many sizes.

Gas Grills

Convenience is the key to the popularity of gas grills. They're quick and easy to start with no charcoal required. Heat controls let you cook food more evenly and accurately. Gas is used to heat ceramic briquettes, lava rock, made from natural volcanic stone, or metal bars. Most models are fueled by refillable liquid propane (LP) gas tanks; others are directly hooked up to a natural gas line. Gas grills come in all shapes, sizes and price ranges, from tabletop models to elaborate wagon styles.

Electric Grills

If you live in an apartment or condominium building where charcoal or gas grills are prohibited, an electric outdoor grill may be your obvious choice. Mobility can be limited because these grills require a separate 110/120-volt grounded outlet with a required 1,600 to 1,800 watts of cooking power. Most electric grills include a smoking element, such as lava rock, which will give food a grilled flavor similar to that produced by charcoal and gas grills.

Indoor Contact Grill

This compact, countertop indoor grill may remind you of a waffle iron at first glance. The exterior is usually made of stainless steel or plastic. The hinged grill opens up to reveal two nonstick metal grill surfaces that allow you to cook both sides of a food simultaneously. Grooves in the grill surface channel fat away from the food you are cooking into a drip tray. Several sizes are available. For easy cleanup, unplug the grill and place a couple of wet paper towels between the cover and the base, then close for 10 minutes.

Direct and Indirect Heat Grilling

DIRECT HEAT GRILLING: Food is cooked on the grill rack directly over the heat source. This method is best for foods that cook in less than 25 minutes, like burgers.

INDIRECT HEAT GRILLING: Food is cooked on the grill rack but not directly over the heat source but instead the heat comes from the sides. This method is best for foods that take longer than 25 minutes to cook, like whole chickens, turkeys or roasts.

When Are Coals Ready?

After lighting the briquettes, leave them in the mounded shape until they are glowing red, which takes about 20 minutes, then spread them out into a single layer. In daylight, coals are ready when coated with a light gray ash; after dark, coals are ready when they have an even red glow.

Check the temperature of the coals by holding your hand, palm side down, near the grill rack and time how long you can comfortably keep it there.

To determine the number of seconds, count "one thousand one, one thousand two."

> 2 seconds = High heat
> 3 seconds = Medium-High heat
> 4 seconds = Medium heat
> 5 seconds = Low heat

Five Tips for Grilling Success

1 Before lighting coals or turning on gas, grease rack with vegetable oil, using a brush, or spray it with cooking spray. Never grease or spray the rack after the coals are lit or gas is on because it may create a fire.

2 For even cooking, place thicker foods in the center of the grill rack and smaller pieces on the edges.

3 Keep the heat as even as possible throughout the grilling period. If you're not getting a sizzle, the fire may be too cool. Regulate the heat by spreading the coals or raking them together, opening or closing the vents or adjusting the control on a gas or electric grill.

4 Use long-handled barbecue tools to allow for a safe distance between you and the intense heat of the grill.

5 Never serve cooked meat, poultry, fish or seafood on the same unwashed platter used to carry it to the grill. Bacteria can be present in juices of raw meat left on the platter and will transfer to the cooked meat.

Controlling Flare-Ups

Fats and liquids dripping through the grill rack can cause flare-ups and burn the food. Here are some tips for keeping them under control.

- Don't line the inside of the bottom of the grill with foil. This prevents grease from draining properly into the grease catch pan.

- Keep the bottom of the grill and grease catch pan clean and free of debris.

- Trim excess fat from meats.

- Move food to a different area of the grill rack.

- Brush on sugary or tomato-based sauces during the last 10 to 15 minutes to avoid burning.

- For charcoal grills, spread coals farther apart, or if necessary, remove food from the grill and spritz the flames with water from a spray bottle. When flames are gone, return the food to the grill rack.

- For gas or electric grill, turn all the burners off. Never use water to extinguish flames on a gas grill. When flames are gone, light the grill again.

- Clean the grill rack with a brass brush or piece of crumbled aluminum foil after each use.

- After cooking on a gas grill, turn the heat setting to high for 10 to 15 minutes with the lid closed. This burns off residue from the grill rack and lava rock or ceramic briquettes.

Four Steps to Food Safety

1. Keep your kitchen clean

- Wash your hands *before and after* handling food, and utensils and *after handling* raw meat, poultry, fish, shellfish and eggs.

- Cleaning Basics

   Wash all utensils and surfaces with hot, soapy water after contact with raw meat, poultry, fish or seafood.

   Use paper towels when working with-and cleaning up after-raw meat, poultry, fish or seafood.

   Clean countertops and appliances with hot, soapy water or other cleaners, like those labeled "antibacterial."

   Wash sponges and dish cloths in hot soapy water in the washing machine. For added safety, sanitize them by soaking in a mixture of ¾ cup chlorine bleach to 1 gallon water.

   Keep pets out of the kitchen and away from food.

- Cutting Board Safety

   Hard plastic or glass cutting boards are the safest for cutting raw poultry, meat, fish and seafood because they are less porous than wooden cutting boards. Disposable cutting sheets are also good.

   Wooden cutting boards are porous so should be used for such things as fresh produce, bread and nuts but not for raw poultry, meat, fish and seafood.

   When a cutting board gets deep cuts and scratches, toss it out.

   Wash with hot, soapy water after each use or if dishwasher-safe, run it through the dishwasher.

For added safety, cover the entire board with a mixture of 1 teaspoon chlorine bleach to 1 quart (4 cups) water. Let stand 2 to 3 minutes; rinse thoroughly and air-dry or pat dry with paper towels.

2. Keep hot foods hot

- Hot foods must be kept at 140°F or above.

- If hot food has been sitting at room temperature for up to 2 hours including prep time, refrigerate it or reheat it.

- Poultry, meat, fish or seafood shouldn't be partially cooked and then set aside or refrigerated to finish cooking later because this could encourage bacterial growth. Foods can be partially cooked in the microwave or parboiled only if they will be cooked immediately.

- Keep cooked food hot, or refrigerate it until ready to serve. This includes carryout foods, too.

- Thoroughly reheat leftovers to 165°F or above. Use a cover to help get food hot in the center and keep it moist. Bring gravies to a rolling boil.

3. Keep cold foods cold

- Set the refrigerator between 35°F and 40°F, and the freezer at 10°F or lower. Check the temperature using a refrigerator or freezer thermometer.

- When you shop, put perishable foods, such as eggs, milk, poultry, meat, fish and seafood or the dishes that contain them, in the cart last.

- Buy food labeled "keep refrigerated" only if it is in the refrigerated case and is cold to the touch.

- Select frozen foods that are frozen solid without lots of ice crystals or frost on the package. These are signs that the food may have been thawed and then refrozen.

- Put packages that can leak, such as poultry, meat, fish or seafood, into plastic bags.

- Take perishable foods straight home, and refrigerate them immediately.

- If it will be more than 30 minutes before you get home, bring a cooler containing ice packs or ice to bring to put perishable foods in.

- Avoid rewrapping packaged foods, unless the wrap is torn, because it may increase bacterial growth.

- Divide large amounts into smaller amounts and store foods in shallow containers so they chill faster.

- When cleaning your refrigerator or freezer, pack perishable food in a cooler with freezer packs or filled with ice.

- Never thaw foods at room temperature. Thaw it only in the refrigerator or microwave following manufacturer's directions, and cook it immediately.

4. Don't cross-contaminate

- Don't chop fresh produce or any food that won't be fully cooked on a cutting board that was used for raw poultry, meat, fish or seafood without cleaning it first.

- Wash knives and utensils that were used with raw poultry, meat, fish or seafood with hot, soapy water.

- Don't put cooked food on an unwashed plate that was used for raw poultry, meat, fish or seafood.

Throw It Out!

- If a food looks or smells bad throw it away.

- Some foods may look and smell good but actually be harmful so if it is past the recommended use date on the package or stored longer than the time recommended on the Refrigerator and Freezer Storage Times chart (page 271), throw it away.

Electrical Power Outage

- Keep the refrigerator and freezer doors closed to protect food.

- Refrigerated foods are safe for 4 to 6 hours.

- If the power is out more than 6 hours, store the refrigerated food in a cooler packed with ice. It will keep up to 2 days if the cooler isn't opened often.

- Foods in a fully stocked freezer are safe up to 2 days, but if half full, for only 24 hours.

- If the power is off longer than 2 days, purchase dry ice to place in the freezer and refrigerator to help keep the food cold.

- Keep raw poultry, meat, fish or seafood separate from cooked and ready-to-eat foods in your grocery cart.

- Thaw foods in the refrigerator on a tray with sides large enough to catch all the juices.

- Place raw poultry, meat, fish and seafood on the bottom shelf of the refrigerator so it won't drip on other food.

- Wash sinks and sink mats with hot, soapy water if they've come in contact with raw poultry, meat, fish or seafood.

Keep Foods Safe

Keeping food safe is important when learning to cook and storing foods properly, both before and after cooking, is key to help preventing food-borne illnesses.

Canned Foods:

- Don't buy or used food in cans that are leaking, bulging or dented.

- Jars of food should not have cracks or loose or bulging lids.

Uncooked Eggs:

- Store eggs in the carton on a shelf in the refrigerator for as long as the date on the carton indicates. Don't store eggs in a compartment in the refrigerator door because it isn't cold enough.

- "Do-ahead" recipes that contain raw eggs should be refrigerated only 24 hours or less before cooking.

- Even though it may be tempting, don't eat cookie dough or cake batter containing raw eggs.

Packing Picnics

- Chill picnic food before packing in freezer-pack or ice-filled cooler.

- Use one cooler for food and one for beverages because beverage coolers are opened more frequently.

- Tightly wrap raw poultry, meat, fish and seafood to keep them from dripping onto other foods, or pack them in a separate cooler.

- Bring along a bottle of instant hand sanitizer, antibacterial moistened towelettes or a bottle filled with soapy water for washing.

- Raw eggs should not be used in recipes that will not be cooked or baked. Use pasteurized eggs or egg substitutes.

Fruits and Vegetables:

- Before eating, wash with cold running water.

- Use a vegetable or small scrub brush if necessary.

Ground Meats:

- Don't eat or taste raw ground meat—it's simply not safe.

- Ground meat dishes such as burgers and meat loaf should be completely cooked until a meat thermometer inserted in the center of the thickest part reaches 160°F.

Luncheon Meats and Hot Dogs:

- Keep refrigerated and use within 2 weeks.

- If the liquid in a package of hot dogs is cloudy, throw it out.

- Hot dogs are fully cooked but reheat them until they're steaming hot all the way through.

Marinades:

- Place food to be marinated in a heavy plastic food-storage bag or nonmetal dish.

- Always refrigerate food when marinating and don't leave at room temperature.

- Toss out leftover marinade that has come in contact with raw poultry, meat, fish or seafood. Or, heat it to a rolling boil and boil at least 1 minute, stirring constantly, before serving.

Chicken:

- Choose wrapped packages without tears, holes or leaks. The package should be cold and feel firm.

- Check for fresh odor. If it smells spoiled, don't buy it.

- Check the sell-by date and plan to use within 2 days of the date.

- If it is more than 30 minutes before you arrive home, keep chicken cold in a cooler with ice packs and refrigerate as soon as you get home.

- Chicken wrapped in butcher paper should be repackaged tightly in plastic wrap or a plastic freezer bag. Chicken packaged in clear plastic wrap on a plastic or Styrofoam tray doesn't need to be repackaged.

- Store chicken in the meat compartment or coldest part of the refrigerator, or freeze as soon as possible.

- If chicken is frozen, thaw it in the refrigerator and use within 1 or 2 days.

- Be sure fully cooked rotisserie or fast food chicken is hot when you purchase it. Use it within 2 hours or cut into several pieces and refrigerate in a covered container. Eat within 3 to 4 days, either cold or reheat to 165°F (hot and steaming). It is safe to freeze ready-prepared chicken and use within 4 months.

Turkey:

- Select a wrapped turkey without tears, holes or leaks.

- Make sure the turkey is cold and feels firm.

- Avoid turkeys that have been stacked too high in the meat case because they may not have been kept cold enough.

- Refrigerate a fresh turkey or freeze a frozen turkey as soon as you get home from shopping.

- Store a fresh turkey in the coldest part of the refrigerator and place it in a shallow pan with sides so the juices don't drip on other foods and cause contamination.

- Thaw a frozen turkey in the refrigerator by placing it (in its original wrap) in a shallow pan with sides. Allow approximately 24 hours per 4 to 5 pounds of turkey. A thawed turkey can remain in the refrigerator 1 to 2 days.

- Stuff a turkey or chicken just before cooking to prevent any bacteria from contaminating the stuffing. Never prestuff and put in the refrigerator or freezer to roast later.

- The stuffing cooked in the turkey or a casserole dish should reach 165°F.

Room Temperature Storage

Many foods are labeled with a "sell by" or "use by" or expiration date. This is helpful information you should check before purchasing to make sure the food is fresh. Food stored at room temperature should be kept in a cool, dry place to prolong freshness. Avoid areas over the stove or microwave, near the dishwasher or above the refrigerator because they tend to be warm. Here are some guidelines for storing food at room temperature.

Room Temperature Storage

FOODS	LENGTH OF TIME	STORAGE TIPS
BREADS AND ROLLS	5 to 7 days	Store in tightly closed original package; refrigerate in hot humid weather
CANNED FOODS	1 year	Date the cans; use oldest first
CEREALS		
Ready-to-cook	4 to 6 months	
Ready-to-eat	Check package label	Refold inner lining after opening to keep crisp
CHOCOLATE SYRUP	Use within 2 years*	Refrigerate after opening
CRACKERS	8 months	After opening, close tightly
FLOUR		
All-purpose	15 months	Store in airtight container; may be refrigerated or frozen. Bring to room temperature before using.
Whole wheat	6 to 8 months	Same as all-purpose flour
HONEY	1 year	
JAMS AND JELLIES	1 year*	Refrigerate after opening
OLIVES, canned or bottled	Use within 1 year*	Refrigerate after opening
PASTA, dried	1 year	Store in original package or in airtight glass or plastic container
PEANUT BUTTER		
Unopened	Use within 9 months*	
Opened	2 to 3 months	
RICE		
Brown or wild	1 year	Use seasoned mixes within 6 months
White		
SALAD DRESSING, bottled	Check date on bottle	Refrigerate after opening
SUGAR		
Brown or powered	4 months	
White (granulated)	2 years	Store airtight
SYRUPS	1 year	Store in cool, dark place
VEGETABLE OIL		
Unopened	Use within 6 months*	
Open	1 to 3 months	Store in cool, dark place

This is total storage time, including the time after it has been opened

Refrigerator and Freezer Storage

Food storage is important not only to keep food safe to eat but also to keep it at optimal quality. Remember "FIFO"—first in, first out—is the best policy so food that is stored the longest is used first.

Refrigerator Storage

- Refrigerator temperatures should be between 35°F and 40°F. When you add large amounts of warm or room-temperature foods, adjust the temperature to a colder setting. Readjust to the normal setting after about 8 hours.

- Cover food or close the original containers tightly to prevent the food from drying out or transferring odors from one food to another.

- Keep foods in the refrigerator until just before you're ready to use them.

Freezer Storage

- Freezer temperatures should be 0°F or lower.

- Look for freezer paper, resealable food-storage plastic bags or plastic containers recommended for the freezer. If you use regular containers, be sure they have tight-fitting lids or wrap tightly in heavy-duty foil.

- Label and date all packages and containers.

- To prevent freezer burn, remove as much air from packages as possible.

- Store purchased frozen foods in their original packages.

- Always thaw frozen meats, poultry and seafood in the refrigerator—never at room temperature. Allow about 5 hours per pound of frozen food. Or thaw food in your microwave following the manufacturer's directions, then cook immediately.

Refrigerator and Freezer Storage Times

These are recommended times to store food in your refrigerator or freezer. Be sure to wrap, seal and label properly to maintain flavor and quality

FOOD	REFRIGERATOR (34°F–40°F)	FREEZER (0°F OR BELOW)
BAKED PRODUCTS		
Breads, coffee cakes, muffins, scones, quick breads and yeast breads	5 to 7 days	2 to 3 months
Cheesecake, baked	3 to 5 days	4 to 5 months
Cookies, baked	Only if stated in recipe	Unfrosted: 12 months
		Frosted: 3 months
PIES		
baked pumpkin pies, unbaked or baked fruit pies and baked pecan pies	Baked pumpkin pies, 3 to 5 days. Store fresh fruit or baked fruit pies and baked pecan pies loosely covered at room temperature no longer than 3 days	Unbaked fruit pies: 2 to 3 months
		Baked fruit pies: 3 to 4 months
PIE SHELLS		Unbaked: 2 months
		Baked: 4 months
DAIRY PRODUCTS		
Cheese		
Cottage and ricotta	1 to 10 days	Not recommended
Cream	Up to 2 weeks	2 months
Hard	3 to 4 weeks	6 to 8 weeks
Butter	2 weeks	4 months
Margarine	1 month	2 months

continued on next page

FOOD	REFRIGERATOR (34°F–40°F)	FREEZER (0°F OR BELOW)
EGGS		
Raw, Whole in shell	3 weeks	Not recommended
Cooked		
Whole in shell	1 week	Not recommended
Yolk, whites	1 week	Not recommended
MEATS		
Uncooked		
Chops	3 to 5 days	4 to 6 months
Ground	1 to 2 days	3 to 4 months
Roasts and steaks	3 to 5 days	6 to 12 months
Cooked	3 to 4 days	2 to 3 months
Processed, Cold cuts	Opened: 3 to 5 days	Not recommended
	Unopened: 2 weeks	Not recommended
Cured bacon	5 to 7 days	1 months
Ham		
Canned, unopened	6 to 9 months	Not recommended
Whole or half, fully cooked	5 to 7 days	1 to 2 months
Sliced, fully cooked	3 to 4 days	1 to 2 months
Hot dogs	Opened: 1 week	1 to 2 months
	Unopened: 2 weeks	1 to 2 months
MILK PRODUCTS		
Buttermilk	1 week	Not recommended
Cream, half-and-half and whipping	5 days	Not recommended
Cream, whipped	1 or 2 days	3 months
Milk: whole, 2%, 1% and fat-free (skim)	5 days	1 month
Sour cream	1 week	Not recommended
Yogurt	3 weeks	1 month
POULTRY		
Uncooked		
Whole	1 to 2 days	12 months
Pieces	1 to 2 days	9 months
Ground	1 to 2 days	3 to 4 months
Cooked	3 to 4 days	4 months
FISH AND SHELLFISH		
Fin fish		
Uncooked full-flavor fish (salmon, trout, tuna)	1 to 2 days	3 to 6 months
Uncooked mild-flavor fish (cod, halibut, tilapia, snapper)	1 to 2 days	3 to 6 months
Cooked and breaded fish		2 to 3 months
Shellfish		
Uncooked	1 to 2 days	3 to 4 months
Cooked	3 to 4 days	1 to 2 months

Emergency Substitutions

Using the ingredients recommended in a recipe is best. But if you have to substitute, try the following:

INSTEAD OF	AMOUNT	USE
BAKING POWDER	1 teaspoon	½ teaspoon cream of tartar plus ¼ teaspoon baking soda
BALSAMIC VINEGAR	1 tablespoon	1 tablespoon sherry or cider vinegar
BREAD CRUMBS, dry	¼ cup	¼ cup finely crushed cracker crumbs, corn flakes or quick-cooking or old-fashioned oats
BROTH, chicken, beef or vegetable	1 cup	1 teaspoon chicken, beef or vegetable bouillon granules (or 1 cube) dissolved in 1 cup boiling water
BROWN SUGAR, packed	1 cup	1 cup granulated sugar plus 2 tablespoons molasses or dark corn syrup
BUTTERMILK OR SOUR MILK	1 cup	1 tablespoon lemon juice or white vinegar plus enough milk to make 1 cup; let stand 5 minutes before using. Or 1 cup plain yogurt.
CHOCOLATE		
Semisweet baking	1 ounce	3 tablespoons semisweet chocolate chips or 1 ounce unsweetened baking chocolate plus 1 tablespoon sugar or 1 tablespoon baking cocoa plus 2 teaspoons sugar and 2 teaspoons shortening
Semisweet chips	1 cup	6 ounces semisweet baking chocolate, chopped
Unsweetened baking	1 ounce	3 tablespoons baking cocoa plus 1 tablespoon melted shortening or margarine
CORN SYRUP		
Light	1 cup	1 cup sugar plus ¼ cup water
Dark	1 cup	1 cup light corn syrup; ¾ cup light corn syrup plus ¼ cup molasses; or 1 cup maple-flavored syrup
CORNSTARCH	1 tablespoon	2 tablespoons all-purpose flour or 4 teaspoons quick-cooking tapioca
EGG, 1 whole	1 large	2 egg whites; ¼ cup fat-free cholesterol-free egg product; 2 egg yolks (for custards or puddings); or 2 egg yolks plus 1 tablespoon water (for cookies or bars)
FLOUR		
All-purpose	1 cup	1 cup plus 2 tablespoons cake flour
Cake	1 cup	1 cup minus 2 tablespoons all-purpose flour
Self-rising	1 cup	1 cup all-purpose flour plus 1½ teaspoons baking powder and ½ teaspoon salt
GARLIC, finely chopped	1 medium clove	⅛ teaspoon garlic powder or ¼ teaspoon instant minced garlic
GINGERROOT, grated or finely chopped	1 teaspoon	¾ teaspoon ground ginger
HERBS, chopped fresh	1 tablespoon	¾ to 1 teaspoon dried herbs
HONEY	1 cup	1¼ cups sugar plus ¼ cup water or apple juice
LEMON JUICE, fresh	1 tablespoon	1 tablespoon bottled lemon juice or white vinegar
LEMON PEEL, grated	1 teaspoon	1 teaspoon dried lemon peel
MILK, regular or low-fat	1 cup	½ cup evaporated milk plus ½ cup water; or nonfat dry milk prepared as directed on package
MUSHROOMS, fresh	1 cup cooked sliced	1 can (4 ounces) mushroom pieces and stems, drained
MUSTARD, yellow	1 tablespoon	½ teaspoon ground mustard plus 2 teaspoons cider or white vinegar
POULTRY SEASONING	1 teaspoon	¾ teaspoon ground sage plus ¼ teaspoon ground thyme
PUMPKIN OR APPLE PIE SPICE	1 teaspoon	Mix ½ teaspoon ground cinnamon, ¼ teaspoon ground ginger, ⅛ teaspoon ground allspice and ⅛ teaspoon ground nutmeg.
RAISINS	½ cup	½ cup currants, dried cherries, dried cranberries, chopped dates or chopped dried plums
RED PEPPER SAUCE	3 or 4 drops	⅛ teaspoon ground red pepper (cayenne)
TOMATO PASTE	½ cup	1 cup tomato sauce cooked uncovered until reduced to ½ cup
TOMATO SAUCE	2 cups	¾ cup tomato paste plus 1 cup water
TOMATOES, canned	1 cup	About 1⅓ cups cut-up fresh tomatoes, simmered 10 minutes
YOGURT, plain unsweetened	1 cup	1 cup sour cream

Yields and Equivalents

FOOD	IF YOUR RECIPE STATES	YOU WILL NEED APPROXIMATELY
APPLES	1 cup sliced or chopped	1 medium (6 ounces)
	1 pound	3 medium
ASPARAGUS	16 to 20 stalks	1 pound
BACON	½ cup crumbled	8 slices, crisply cooked
BANANAS	1 cup sliced	1 medium or 2 small
	1 cup mashed	2 medium
BEANS, dried	5 to 6 cups cooked	1 pound dried (2¼ cups)
BEANS, green or wax	3 cups 1-inch pieces	1 pound
BROCCOLI	2 cups flowerets, 1-inch pieces or chopped	7 ounces
BUTTER OR MARGARINE	2 cups	4 sticks (1 pound)
	½ cup	1 stick (¼ pound)
CABBAGE		
Chinese (napa)	1 medium head	1¼ pounds
Green or Red	1 medium head	1½ pounds
Slaw (packaged)	4 cups shredded	1 pound
	7 cups	1 pound
CARROTS	1 cup shredded	1½ medium
	1 cup ¼-inch slices	2 medium
CAULIFLOWER	3 cups flowerets	1 pound
CELERY	1 cup thinly sliced or chopped	2 medium stalks
CHEESE		
Hard, shredded or crumbled	1 cup	4 ounces
Cottage	2 cups	16 ounces
Cream	1 cup	8 ounces
CORN, sweet	1 cup kernels	2 medium ears
CRANBERRIES		
Fresh	4 cups	1 pound
Dried	1 cup	4 ounces
CREAM		
Sour	1 cup	8 ounces
Whipping (heavy)	1 cup (2 cups whipped)	½ pint
CRUMBS, finely crushed		
Chocolate wafer	1½ cups	27 cookies
Graham cracker	1½ cups	21 squares
Saltine cracker	1 cup	29 squares
Vanilla wafer	1½ cups	38 cookies
CUCUMBERS	1 cup chopped	¾ medium
EGGPLANT	1 medium	1½ pounds
	2 cups ½-inch pieces	12 ounces
EGGS, large		
Whole	1 cup	4 large eggs
	1 egg	¼ cup fat-free cholesterol-free egg product
Yolks	1 cup	8 or 9 large eggs
FLOUR	3½ cups	1 pound
GARLIC	½ teaspoon finely chopped	1 medium clove

FOOD	IF YOUR RECIPE STATES	YOU WILL NEED APPROXIMATELY
LEMONS OR LIMES	1½ to 3 teaspoons grated peel	1 medium
	2 to 3 tablespoons juice	1 medium
LETTUCE, Iceberg or romaine	1 medium head	1½ pounds
	2 cups shredded	5 ounces
	6 cups bite-size pieces	1 pound
MEAT, cooked (beef, pork and poultry)	1 cup chopped or bite-size pieces	About 6 ounces
MELONS, Cantaloupe or honeydew	1 medium	3 pounds
	2 cups 1-inch chunks	1 pound
MUSHROOMS, Fresh	6 cups sliced	1 pound
	2½ cups chopped	8 ounces
NUTS (without shells)		
Chopped	1 cup	4 ounces
Whole or halves	3 to 4 cups	1 pound
ONIONS		
Green, with tops	2 tablespoons sliced	1 medium
	¼ cup sliced	2 to 3 medium
Yellow or white	½ cup chopped	1 medium
ORANGES	1 to 2 tablespoons grated peel	1 medium
	⅓ to ½ cup juice	1 medium
PASTA, macaroni, egg noodles or spaghetti	4 cups cooked	6 to 8 ounces uncooked (dried)
PEACHES OR PEARS	2 cups sliced	3 medium (1 pound)
PEAS, green	1 cup shelled	1 pound in pods
PEPPERS, bell	½ cup chopped	1 small
	1 cup chopped	1 medium
PINEAPPLES, fresh	4 cups cubed	1 medium
POTATOES		
Red, white, sweet or yams	1 medium	5 to 6 ounces
Red or white	1 cup ½-inch pieces	1 medium
Small red	10 to 12 small	1½ pounds
PUMPKIN	1 cup mashed cooked	1 pound uncooked or 1 cup canned pumpkin
RICE, regular long grain	3 cups cooked	1 cup uncooked
SHORTENING	2⅓ cups	1 pound
SPINACH	4 cups leaves	6 ounces
	2 cups shredded	2½ ounces
SQUASH	2 cups ¼-inch slices, chopped or shredded	1 medium
Summer: Crookneck (yellow) or zucchini		
Winter: Acorn, buttercup, butternut or spaghetti	1 medium	1½ to 2½ pounds
STRAWBERRIES	4 cups sliced	1 quart
SUGAR	2¼ cups packed	1 pound
Brown		
Granulated	2¼ cups	1 pound
Powdered	4 cups	1 pound
TOMATOES	1 cup chopped	1 large

Helpful Nutrition and Cooking Information

Nutrition Guidelines

We provide nutrition information for each recipe that includes calories, fat, cholesterol, sodium, carbohydrate, fiber and protein. Individual food choices can be based on this information.

RECOMMENDED INTAKE FOR A DAILY DIET OF 2,000 CALORIES AS SET BY THE FOOD AND DRUG ADMINISTRATION

Total Fat	Less than 65g
Saturated Fat	Less than 20g
Cholesterol	Less than 300mg
Sodium	Less than 2,400mg
Total Carbohydrate	300g
Dietary Fiber	25g

Criteria Used for Calculating Nutrition Information

- The first ingredient was used wherever a choice is given (such as ⅓ cup sour cream or plain yogurt).

- The first ingredient amount was used wherever a range is given (such as 3- to 3½-pound cut-up broiler-fryer chicken).

- The first serving number was used wherever a range is given (such as 4 to 6 servings).

- "If desired" ingredients and recipe variations were not included (such as sprinkle with brown sugar, if desired).

- Only the amount of a marinade or frying oil that is estimated to be absorbed by the food during preparation or cooking was calculated.

Ingredients Used in Recipe Testing and Nutrition Calculations

- Ingredients used for testing represent those that the majority of consumers use in their homes: large eggs, 2 percent milk, 80 percent lean ground beef, canned ready-to-use chicken broth and vegetable oil spread containing not less than 65 percent fat.

- Fat-free, low-fat or low-sodium products were not used, unless otherwise indicated.

- Solid vegetable shortening (not butter, margarine, nonstick cooking sprays or vegetable oil spread as they can cause sticking problems) was used to grease pans, unless otherwise indicated.

Equipment Used in Recipe Testing

We use equipment for testing that the majority of consumers use in their homes. If a specific piece of equipment (such as a wire whisk) is necessary for recipe success, it is listed in the recipe.

- Cookware and bakeware without nonstick coatings were used, unless otherwise indicated.

- No dark-colored, black or insulated bakeware was used.

- When a pan is specified in a recipe, a metal pan was used; a baking dish or pie plate means ovenproof glass was used.

- An electric hand mixer was used for mixing only when mixer speeds are specified in the recipe directions. When a mixer speed is not given, a spoon or fork was used.

Metric Conversion Guide

VOLUME

U.S. Units	Canadian Metric	Australian Metric
¼ teaspoon	1 mL	1 ml
½ teaspoon	2 mL	2 ml
1 teaspoon	5 mL	5 ml
1 tablespoon	15 mL	20 ml
¼ cup	50 mL	60 ml
⅓ cup	75 mL	80 ml
½ cup	125 mL	125 ml
⅔ cup	150 mL	170 ml
¾ cup	175 mL	190 ml
1 cup	250 mL	250 ml
1 quart	1 liter	1 liter
1½ quarts	1.5 liters	1.5 liters
2 quarts	2 liters	2 liters
2½ quarts	2.5 liters	2.5 liters
3 quarts	3 liters	3 liters
4 quarts	4 liters	4 liters

WEIGHT

U.S. Units	Canadian Metric	Australian Metric
1 ounce	30 grams	30 grams
2 ounces	55 grams	60 grams
3 ounces	85 grams	90 grams
4 ounces (¼ pound)	115 grams	125 grams
8 ounces (½ pound)	225 grams	225 grams
16 ounces (1 pound)	455 grams	500 grams
1 pound	455 grams	½ kilogram

MEASUREMENTS

Inches	Centimeters
1	2.5
2	5.0
3	7.5
4	10.0
5	12.5
6	15.0
7	17.5
8	20.5
9	23.0
10	25.5
11	28.0
12	30.5
13	33.0

TEMPERATURES

Fahrenheit	Celsius
32°	0°
212°	100°
250°	120°
275°	140°
300°	150°
325°	160°
350°	180°
375°	190°
400°	200°
425°	220°
450°	230°
475°	240°
500°	260°

NOTE: The recipes in this cookbook have not been developed or tested using metric measures. When converting recipes to metric, some variations in quality may be noted.

How-Tos

Index

Page numbers in *italics* indicate photo.

Complete your cookbook library with
these *Betty Crocker* titles

Betty Crocker Baking for Today

Betty Crocker's Best Bread Machine Cookbook

Betty Crocker's Best Chicken Cookbook

Betty Crocker Christmas Cookbook

Betty Crocker's Best of Baking

Betty Crocker's Best of Healthy and Hearty Cooking

Betty Crocker's Best-Loved Recipes

Betty Crocker's Bisquick® Cookbook

Betty Crocker Bisquick® II Cookbook

Betty Crocker Bisquick® Impossibly Easy Pies

Betty Crocker Celebrate!

Betty Crocker's Complete Thanksgiving Cookbook

Betty Crocker's Cook Book for Boys and Girls

Betty Crocker's Cook It Quick

Betty Crocker Cookbook, 10th Edition— *The* BIG RED *Cookbook*®

Betty Crocker Cookbook, Bridal Edition

Betty Crocker Cookbook, Heart Health Edition

Betty Crocker's Cookie Book

Betty Crocker's Cooky Book, Facsimile Edition

Betty Crocker Decorating Cakes and Cupcakes

Betty Crocker's Diabetes Cookbook

Betty Crocker Dinner Made Easy with Rotisserie Chicken

Betty Crocker Easy Everyday Vegetarian

Betty Crocker Easy Family Dinners

Betty Crocker's Easy Slow Cooker Dinners

Betty Crocker's Eat and Lose Weight

Betty Crocker's Entertaining Basics

Betty Crocker's Flavors of Home

Betty Crocker 4-Ingredient Dinners

Betty Crocker Grilling Made Easy

Betty Crocker Healthy Heart Cookbook

Betty Crocker's Healthy New Choices

Betty Crocker's Indian Home Cooking

Betty Crocker's Italian Cooking

Betty Crocker Just the Two of Us Cookbook

Betty Crocker Kids Cook!

Betty Crocker's Kitchen Library

Betty Crocker's Living with Cancer Cookbook

Betty Crocker Low-Carb Lifestyle Cookbook

Betty Crocker's Low-Fat, Low-Cholesterol Cooking Today

Betty Crocker More Slow Cooker Recipes

Betty Crocker's New Chinese Cookbook

Betty Crocker One-Dish Meals

Betty Crocker's A Passion for Pasta

Betty Crocker's Picture Cook Book, Facsimile Edition

Betty Crocker Quick & Easy Cookbook

Betty Crocker's Slow Cooker Cookbook

Betty Crocker Ultimate Bisquick® Cookbook

Betty Crocker's Ultimate Cake Mix Cookbook

Betty Crocker Whole Grains Cookbook

Betty Crocker Why It Works

Betty Crocker Win at Weight Loss Cookbook